ez101 study keys

Psychology

Second Edition

Don Baucum, Ph.D.

DEDICATION

This book is dedicated to my former wife Karen and my son Van, who are my two most significant others.

The publisher acknowledges gratefully the following for permission to adopt material: D. Baucum, Ph.D. BARRON'S COLLEGE REVIEW SERIES. Barron's Educational Series, Inc., Hauppauge, N.Y., 1999. Material from pages 40, 44, 46, 62, 70, 115, 170, 171.

All inquiries should be addressed to:
Barron's Educational Series, Inc.
250 Wireless Boulevard
Hauppauge, New York 11788

Library of Congress Catalog Card No. 2005052177

ISBN-13: 978-0-7641-3421-0
ISBN-10: 0-7641-3421-3

Library of Congress Cataloging-in-Publication Data
Baucum, Don.
    Psychology / Don Baucum.—2nd ed.
        p. cm. — (Barron's EZ-101 study keys)
    Includes index.
    ISBN-13: 978-0-7641-3421-0
    ISBN-10: 0-7641-3421-3
    1. Psychology—Textbooks. I. Title. II. Barron's EZ 101 study keys.
BF121.B34 2006
150—dc22   2005052177

PRINTED IN THE UNITED STATES OF AMERICA
9 8 7 6 5 4 3 2 1

CONTENTS

FOREWORD

Welcome to *EZ-101 Psychology*, your condensed tour of the most popular and important topics in the subject. Whether you're doing coursework, reviewing, or simply reading about psychology out of curiousity, *EZ-101* is for you. It's streamlined and accurate, and it's intended to be highly readable. So kick back, relax, and delve in.

Keys and Themes emphasize customary topics and ways of organizing a survey of psychology, which means that *EZ-101* can be read in conjunction with any psychology textbook. It's assumed that you might not be reading *EZ-101* from beginning to end, however, since psychology textbooks do differ somewhat. With that in mind, topics are extensively cross-referenced and indexed to help you jump back and forth, and there's a glossary for quick reference. Also note that sources for further reading can be obtained by consulting any comprehensive psychology text.

Comments and suggestions are encouraged. Address regular mail to the author via Barron's or e-mail to dgbaucum@uab.edu via the Internet.

Don Baucum, Ph.D.
January 2006

Theme 1 PSYCHOLOGY
THEN AND NOW

*M*odern psychology is a broad discipline with many subdisciplines, each of which has its own rich history and each of which might define psychology in its own distinctive way. But, setting aside differences between the subdisciplines in what they study and at times how they go about it, there's still a lot of common ground. And there are many milestones in the history of psychological theory and research that are commonly agreed upon.

Theme 1 explores where psychology came from and where it is today.

INDIVIDUAL KEYS IN THIS THEME

1	Defining psychology
2	Psychology before the 20th century
3	Psychoanalysis: The first force in modern psychology
4	Behaviorism: The second force
5	Humanistic psychology: The third force
6	Other approaches and where psychology is today

Key 1 Defining psychology

OVERVIEW *Modern psychology is defined as the scientific study of behavior and mental processes.*

The term **psychology** has its roots in the Greek terms *psyche*, indicating life or self, and *logos,* indicating reasoning and logic. Consistent with the origins of its name, psychology is potentially concerned with studying and understanding the behavior of any living organisms that qualify as animals. But the emphasis is on humans. And though psychological research methods often involve groups of subjects or participants, the overall goal is to understand the individual.

- **A subject** is any living organism that is the focus of study and research, from small and simple creatures such as flatworms, up to chimpanzees—our closest relatives.
- **Participant** is the preferred term for humans in psychological research. (To avoid repetitiveness, this text uses *subject,* except for cases that specifically involve human research.)
- **Research on groups** most often looks at processes that help explain the behavior of the individual in the sense of what behavior is typical and what causes that behavior in the first place.

Scientific study has many requirements, most of which relate to providing knowledge that is reliable and factual. Like any true science, psychology strives to be objective, empirical, and systematic as it observes and collects data, and it proceeds by testing hypotheses and generating theories.

- **Objective** means that observations are not affected by any hopes or preferences or other possible biases on the part of the researcher.
- **Empirical** is closely related to objective, meaning that the same observations can readily be made by anyone and therefore can be taken as fact. Note that researchers at times use sophisticated laboratory equipment that not just anyone could manage, but the observations are still empirical.
- **Systematic** has to do with how observations are collected and also what observations are collected. In other words, researchers must have a plan and then execute the plan in an orderly way if the research is to be meaningful and useful.

- **Hypotheses** are educated guesses and predictions about what will happen under specific conditions and circumstances. Although psychological research is sometimes exploratory and open-ended, it is more often oriented toward testing specific hypotheses.
- **Theories** are statements that organize and summarize research and information. In turn, theories often generate the hypotheses that are tested by research. And theories are never "true" or "false"; they are simply accurate or inaccurate with regard to what is under consideration. In other words, theories can never be *proved*, though they can and should be *supported* by research.

Behavior is a broad term that has different meanings in psychology depending upon the context. In the definition of psychology, behavior refers to absolutely anything the subject or participant does, whether it's overt or covert.

- **Overt behavior** is that which can be observed and measured empirically, whether it's external (environmental) or internal (physiological-biological).
- **Covert behavior** is that which cannot be observed directly and empirically—as yet. Thinking and remembering are examples: Psychologists can empirically observe various kinds of brain activity, but can't yet empirically observe what a person is actually thinking or remembering.
- **Behaviorism**, in contrast, is a term often used in reference to the idea that *only overt behavior* can be studied scientifically (Key 4). Modern psychologists do not tend to take such an extreme view, as indicated in the definition. And yet, modern psychology is often characterized as a "behavioral" science.

Mental processes, then, are **covert** behavior, and the standard definition of psychology specifies mental processes mainly for emphasis on what psychology is today. Also note that **cognition** is a popular term for thinking, remembering, perceiving, problem solving, and many other mental processes that can only be studied indirectly and *inferred* from overt behavior—so far.

Key 2 Psychology before the 20th century

OVERVIEW *Modern scientific psychology traces some of its origins back to the logic and ideas of the ancient Greeks, skipping forward from there to the philosopher-scientists near the end of the Renaissance. The following are concepts and major thinkers often cited.*

Associationism began with Plato and especially Aristotle, who proposed that we learn and understand by forming mental associations between events we observe.
- **The principle of temporal contiguity**, for example, is that we tend to associate two events and think of them as related to each other if they occur more or less at the same time. Such principles are still considered important in understanding learning and memory.

In the 17th century, Rene **Descartes** wrote extensively on the issue of "mind" and "body," proposing that the two are somehow separate entities that interact to determine who we are and what we know. Today, psychologists still differ in their views of mind and body, though many assume that mental processes must somehow correspond to underlying neurological functioning. Descartes was also an early advocate of the view that came to be known as nativism.
- **A nativist view** emphasizes **nature** in the form of genetics and heredity in accounting for who we are and what we know. To say that intellectual skills, personality characteristics, and morality are mostly innate and built-in is to take an extreme nativist position.

Also in the 17th century, Thomas **Hobbes** and then John **Locke** argued instead that who we are and what we know comes entirely through our basic senses, with emphasis on the learning of associations between the events we observe. In Locke's view, each person is a "tabula rasa" at birth, to be shaped and molded by experience. This became known as the extreme empiricist position.
- **Tabula rasa** means "blank slate," implying that nothing psychological is innate or built-in. And, as it happened, Locke also believed that we are amoral and inherently "bad" unless society teaches us to be "good."

- **An empiricist view** emphasizes **nurture** in the form of environment and experiences. To say that intellectual skills, personality characteristics, and morality are mostly learned is to take an extreme empiricist position.
- **Empiricism** in a different sense, however, is the basis for all modern science. Empirical science requires that you have observations and facts to back up what you say, as discussed in detail in Key 7.

In the 18th century, Jean Jacques **Rousseau** retaliated with an extreme nativist position on morality, proposing that we are inherently good unless society corrupts us into being bad. Both the empiricist and the nativist views of where "morality" comes from are still alive today, though modern psychologists don't tend to endorse either in the extreme.

In the 19th century, the influence of Charles **Darwin** and the theory of natural selection as an explanation for evolution eventually gave rise to the functionalism proposed by William **James**, a major founder of psychology.
- **Functionalism** stressed the idea that who we are and what we know is strongly influenced by adaptation to the environment, a view still popular in psychology.

Meanwhile, Wilhelm **Wundt** founded the first experimental psychology laboratory in 1879, using a research method called introspection and using an overall approach that came to be known as structuralism.
- **Introspection** means looking inside oneself and trying to describe what's going on. In a sense, this general approach is still used throughout psychology, especially in clinical psychology, with regard to insight and understanding oneself.
- **Structuralism**, later named by E. B. **Titchener**, was the view that human conscious experience (and therefore much of the psychological world) could best be understood by breaking it down into component parts. Thus, trained observers introspected and reported what they experienced, and the structuralists tried to formulate general theories based on their participants' reports.

Key 3 Psychoanalysis: The first force in modern psychology

OVERVIEW *Historians designate three major "forces" that shaped modern psychology, the first of which was Freud's psychoanalysis.*

Psychoanalysis (Key 57) grew out of the clinical work of Sigmund **Freud** that began just before the beginning of the 20th century, and has had many advocates and students since. Freudian (classical) psychoanalytic theory assumes that all motivation comes from within the person, as a result of "instinctual" desires that are basically hedonistic. In complex ways, personality then results from how we perceive and deal with our instinctual desires—especially sex—plus our interactions with parents and others during infancy and early childhood. Later psychodynamic theorists who diverged from Freud's "classical" psychoanalysis are discussed in Keys 29 and 59.

- **Hedonism** here means seeking pleasure and avoiding pain, with little concern about anything else—such as other people's feelings.
- **Psychodynamic** theorists and practitioners place much more emphasis on conscious processes than on the unconscious, instinctual processes Freud proposed.
- Carl **Jung** was an early student of Freud who broke away from classic psychoanalytic theory and instead emphasized the "collective unconscious," which he thought we all share, as the primary source of motivation and personality.
- Alfred **Adler** was another early student of Freud who rebelled and stressed "social interest" and striving to improve oneself and one's society. He also coined the term *inferiority complex* for people who see themselves as inferior to others across the board.
- Erik **Erikson** was an early student who initially went along with most of Freud's theorizing and expanded it into a theory of lifelong personality development. However, in the end Erikson's theory bore little resemblance to Freud's.
- Karen **Horney** was a later psychodynamic theorist who developed a much more contemporary explanation of male-female differences in personality than that proposed by Freud. She stressed that any consistent male-female personality differences were cultural, not biological as Freud had thought.

Key 4 Behaviorism: The second force

OVERVIEW *The early behaviorists rejected what they saw as the deep and unobservable mysteries of psychoanalysis (and also structuralism). The impact of the behaviorists exists throughout modern psychology, though with emphasis on conditioning and learning as discussed in Theme 8.*

Psychology was dominated from the turn of the century into the 1950s or so by what is often called "strict" or "S-R" behaviorism. This approach emphasized scientific study taken to the extreme that *only empirical data* and *overt behavior* were acceptable. Who and what we are with regard to motivation and personality, for example, was viewed in terms of the consequences of our behavior—usually as a result of reinforcement and punishment, though still with the assumption that we are basically hedonistic.

- **The S-R behaviorists** formulated their research on "stimulus-response" relationships, where a **stimulus** is any sensory event the subject is capable of detecting and a **response** is any behavior the subject is capable of performing. Stimuli and responses are overt and empirically observable, and therefore acceptable to the S-R behaviorists. In turn, the S-R behaviors argued that *all* behavior could be explained and understood that way. The S-R behaviorists also tended to study learning and behavior using laboratory animals, within the view that the basic "laws" of behavior apply equally to lower animals and to humans. The behaviorist approach is discussed in detail in Theme 8.
- E. L. **Thorndike** was an early behaviorist and educator best known for the law of effect (Key 43), which is in essence that living organisms tend to repeat behavior that leads to reward and not to repeat behavior that leads to punishment.
- Ivan **Pavlov** was the originator of classical conditioning (Key 41), in which responses are understood in terms of associations between stimuli.
- J. B. **Watson** was a researcher and general spokesperson for S-R behaviorism, perhaps best known for his arguments that the human infant is a tabula rasa, in keeping with Locke's view.
- B. F. **Skinner**, somewhat later than the rest, but with perhaps the greatest influence of all, refined and extended S-R behaviorism into what became known as operant conditioning (Key 42), which is based entirely on observable behavior and its consequences.

Key 5 Humanistic psychology: The third force

OVERVIEW *In the 1950s, a third force emerged and came to be known as humanistic psychology. With its emphasis on self and distinctly human motives, humanistic psychology was a reaction against both psychoanalysis and S-R behaviorism.*

The founders of **humanistic psychology** (Key 60) objected to the basic hedonism of psychoanalysis and behaviorism alike, arguing that too much emphasis had been placed on the "animal" side of human nature. The humanists proposed that we have uniquely human, positive motives that include sharing, belonging, helping others, and especially achieving one's own unique potential, with the effect that personality must be understood in such terms. Relatedly, personality is best understood from a phenomenological perspective.

- **The phenomenological perspective** stresses trying to see things from the individual's own unique point of view.
- Carl **Rogers** was one of the founders of humanistic psychology, with his emphasis on the person-centered approach, which he had earlier called the client-centered approach. Rogers argued that we should understand the individual as being motivated toward getting in touch with self and achieving a sense of fulfillment in life, noting that each individual is unique and therefore can only be understood from her or his own unique point of view.
- Abraham **Maslow** was another founder, best known for his hierarchy of needs: biological and hedonistic needs are at the bottom to be satisfied first; above that are characteristically human needs such as belongingness, esteem, and especially self-actualization. Self-actualization essentially means achieving one's own unique potential as a human being.

Key 6 Other approaches and where psychology is today

OVERVIEW *Modern psychology can be understood in part as a result of the three dominant forces discussed previously, but other ways of looking at things were developing at the same time and have had major impact. Today, psychology is distinctly cognitive and increasingly biological.*

Gestalt psychology was concerned primarily with perception, problem-solving, and other cognitive processes—at a time when the S-R behaviorists were in control and rejected the study of cognitive processes as wholly unscientific. Gestalt psychologists are discussed in Keys 21 and 46.
- **Gestalt** means, basically, that the whole is more than the sum of the parts. Thus, Gestalt psychology was in part a reaction against the structuralists and their attempts to break consciousness down into separate components.

Perhaps ironically, **early cognitive psychology** as such also traces in part to the work of the behaviorists, notably those who encountered serious obstacles to the explanation of behavior in strict, S-R terms. For example:
- Clark **Hull** and colleagues dedicated themselves to S-R explanations of behavior and devised extensive formulas to predict behavior both under specific and general circumstances. However, the formulations became so elaborate and so far removed from what was directly observable that in the end—most agree—it was covert behavior that was actually being studied.
- Much of the work of Edward **Tolman** (Key 46), during the heyday of S-R behaviorism, was designed to refute it. Tolman argued, for example, that animals in mazes (one way of studying animal learning) use **cognitive maps** to find their way around. Thus, in effect, the animals *think* rather than simply perform mechanical responses to the stimuli present.

Hence, down the line occurred what has become known as **the cognitive revolution**—especially from the 1960s on. In large part, this revolution grew out of a widespread realization throughout psychology that humans (*and* other animals) could not be understood adequately in strictly behavioristic terms. But the development of information-processing theory and computer science also helped a lot by providing a starting point for the scientific study of that which can't be directly observed as yet. Many thousands of research efforts later—with respect to the first three forces—the cognitive revolution has affected all areas of psychology, from the study of learning and memory to the study of abnormal behavior and treatment.

- **Information-processing theory** as applied to humans treats behaviors such as thinking and remembering as sequential, beginning with input and then proceeding through various kinds of processing to output in the form of memory storage or overt behavior. By studying characteristics of the input and the output, the mental processing that took place in between can be inferred scientifically.
- **Computer science** has helped by providing the capability of creating "models" for human mental processes, through which theories can be tested in great detail. That doesn't mean, of course, that computers and humans "think" the same ways (Key 47).

Otherwise, modern psychology is also strongly influenced by ongoing advances in the **biological** and **medical** sciences. As more sophisticated measurement techniques and better ways of understanding physiological processes develop in those disciplines, psychology comes closer to understanding relationships between mind and body.

- **Behavioral neuroscience** and **cognitive neuroscience** use brain imaging techniques (Key 17) to study relationships between behavior and processes in the brain. The latter includes an emphasis on what constitutes "mind."
- **Behavioral medicine** studies and applies the methods and approaches of psychology to the diagnosis and treatment of physical illnesses (Key 72).

And nowadays, psychologists still have professional preferences about how to look at things and what methods to use in studying behavior and perhaps controlling and changing it. But modern psychologists tend to be eclectic and therefore disinclined to look at things only one way.

- **Eclectic** means taking the best from differing and sometimes conflicting theories and approaches, as the situation warrants. In particular, being eclectic means recognizing that the global theories and explanations such as those of the first three forces in psychology may be helpful in understanding the behavior of one individual but not necessarily that of everyone, or perhaps in one situation but not in another.

Theme 2 RESEARCH METHODS
IN PSYCHOLOGY

*I*n studying behavior and developing theories, psychologists use an array of research methods—some that are common to most scientific research and others that are more specific to psychology and the social sciences.

Psychologists prefer **experiments** where possible, because experiments provide the clearest information about what causes what. The experimental method is much the same for all scientific disciplines and existed well before modern psychology came along. On the other hand, psychologists often use **correlation** and nonexperimental methods when experiments are not an option. Correlation is a more recent approach arising from research that was psychological (and biological) in nature.

Theme 2 covers experimental and nonexperimental methods in psychology, plus practical and ethical considerations important to all psychological research.

INDIVIDUAL KEYS IN THIS THEME	
7	Experimental methods in psychology
8	Methodological considerations in experiments
9	Nonexperimental methods in psychology
10	Correlation
11	Psychological research and the real world
12	Ethical considerations in psychological research

Key 7 Experimental methods in psychology

OVERVIEW *In an experiment, the researcher does something to the subjects and expects their behavior to be affected by it. What the researcher does is called the experimental treatment, and how the researcher does it determines whether the experiment is a good one.*

Experimental research designs can involve several groups of subjects who experience different combinations of experimental treatments to see how their behavior will differ. That's the most common type of experiment in psychology today, though a useful experiment can be as simple as having only two groups experience variations of one treatment. Otherwise, some group designs involve a series of experimental treatments on the same subjects, with measures of their behavior at each point. There are also "single-subject" designs, typical of operant conditioning and behavior modification, in which one subject receives a series of treatments. For any experiment, however, the logic is the same: If the researcher can *cause* the subjects' behavior to differ or change meaningfully, the researcher demonstrates that the experimental treatment has an *effect*.

- **Understanding cause-and-effect relationships** is essential to most scientific knowledge. On the road to knowledge about the physical world, a researcher fires a beam at the nucleus of an atom to assess the particles that are dislodged. On the road to knowledge about the psychological world, a researcher presents a series of words to a participant to assess the effects on verbal memory. Regardless of what is being studied, over the course of perhaps many precise and systematically differing experiments, the scientist gradually acquires an understanding of how things work. And, eventually, the scientist may be in a position to make a major contribution to the body of scientific knowledge and perhaps create things or change things for the better.

The basics of a group experiment: In a group design, at least two equivalent groups of subjects undergo procedures that are the same *except* for what the researcher is studying. If the groups then behave differently, what the researcher is studying must have caused it.

- The **experimental hypothesis** is what the researcher predicts will happen.

- The **independent variable** is what the researcher is studying and how the groups are treated differently.
- The **dependent variable** is the behavior the researcher measures to determine if the independent variable has an effect.
- The **experimental group** is the group that experiences what the researcher is studying.
- The **control group** exists essentially for purposes of comparison to the experimental group.

KEY EXAMPLE

A researcher has a hypothesis that watching graphic violence in movies decreases people's emotional responsiveness to violence. That is, graphic violence becomes less upsetting, with implications that repeated exposure might even make people more likely to commit violence themselves. Emotional responsiveness alone, however, is the focus of the present experiment. Two equivalent groups of young adults are selected (volunteers from introductory psychology classes). On the first day of the experiment, one group undergoes a five-hour marathon of graphically violent horror movies. The other group watches five hours of horror movies with the most graphic blood-and-gore shots edited out (i.e., the network TV versions). On the second day, the participants come back and are hooked up to physiological recording equipment while they all watch a graphic documentary film on the by-products of drunken driving.

- The **experimental hypothesis** is that the participants who see the graphic violence on the first day will be less emotionally responsive to blood and gore on the second day.
- The **independent variable** is exposure to graphic violence—high for one group, low for the other.
- The **dependent variable** is emotional responsiveness, using physiological recording equipment.
- The **experimental group** gets sustained exposure to graphic violence, which is what the researcher is studying.
- The **control group** sees the same movies without the graphic violence, so the researcher can compare the experimental group to it.

Key 8 Methodological considerations in

experiments

OVERVIEW *If an experiment is to be meaningful and valid, the researcher must pay careful attention to detail and take many precautions throughout.*

Operational definitions "translate" what the researcher is studying into what the researcher actually does. In the graphic-violence experiment in Key 7, for example, the researcher is interested in the very general issue of graphic violence and its effects on emotionality. But it isn't even remotely conceivable to assess all forms of violence with all kinds of people in all kinds of situations. So the researcher goes with experimental "operations" that make the research possible. The **independent variable**, exposure to graphic violence, is operationally defined as a specific series of movies, with or without major doses of blood and gore. The **dependent variable**, emotional responsiveness, is operationally defined as a group of measures such as heart rate, blood pressure, breathing rate, and perspiration—the same measures used on "lie-detector" tests, which tend to change as emotional states change (Key 34). And the participants are specific people, not entire populations (see subjects and sampling in Key 11).

Equivalence of procedures: Except for what the researcher is studying, the subjects ideally are treated the same in all respects throughout the experiment. In the example experiment, each group spends the same amount of time watching movies of the same type, in the same type of room, and so on. Each group is treated the same in all respects on the second day as well, with regard to the procedures involving the equipment and any observers who are present. If not—if there is some difference between the groups in procedures *other* than the independent variable—the experiment might not work. Or if it does work, it might be confounded.

- **Confounding** occurs when something other than the independent variable could be responsible for differences in the groups' behavior, with the effect that the researcher can't tell what caused what.

Equivalence of groups: No two or more groups of subjects can ever be exactly the same, but they should be as alike as possible in all potentially relevant respects. If they aren't, the researcher again risks confounding. Even in the relatively simple graphic-violence experiment, the groups should have about the same average age, the same proportion of males and females, and anything else that might matter. Random assignment to groups is one way researchers help achieve equivalence.

- **Random assignment to groups** can involve simply drawing names from a box or more formally using a table of random numbers to determine which subject goes into which group. Random assignment doesn't guarantee that the groups will be equivalent, but it greatly increases the chances that they will.

Statistical analysis: When the results are in, the researcher then applies what can be elaborate statistical tests to determine if the observed differences between groups are likely to be real. If, for example, the graphic-violence group behaves as expected and displays less emotional responsiveness, it is still necessary to rule out the possibility that it happened entirely by chance. Essentially, the experimental group must be *enough* less responsive than the control group to support a scientific conclusion that the experiment caused it. Thus, typically, the researcher would compare the "average" levels of emotional responsiveness between the groups, also taking into account individual differences within each group (some subjects would be more responsive, some less, as a result of individual differences that have nothing to do with the experiment). If the group difference is then **statistically significant**, meaning unlikely to have happened merely by chance, the researcher concludes that the independent variable caused the difference.

Validity: In the context of experiments and similar research efforts, *validity* involves quality and generalizability. **Internal validity** refers to how well the study was conducted with regard to the procedures discussed in this Key. In an experiment, high internal validity means that conclusive statements about cause-and-effect relationships can be made. Low internal validity means that they cannot be, often because of confounding. **External validity** refers to the extent to which the results can be extended beyond the particulars of the study, say, from the laboratory to the real world. The results of an experiment with high external validity can be, the results of one with low external validity cannot be. (A different meaning of validity is discussed in Key 53.)

Key 9 Nonexperimental methods
in psychology

OVERVIEW *Nonexperimental methods are those in which the researcher observes or measures but does not deliberately alter the subjects' behavior. These methods can be of considerable value in research, though they cannot provide conclusive information about cause and effect.*

Case studies and biographies: Sometimes dubbed the "clinical" method, case studies and the like are entirely descriptive and consist of gathering as much relevant information as possible about one individual at a time. Prior to clinical treatment, for example, clients and often their families too are interviewed in depth with regard to the client's current functioning, relevant social history, and so on (Key 62). Such information is used to determine an appropriate treatment approach and any diagnosis that applies, but can also be incorporated into theory and research on mental disorders and overall personality.
- **The strength** of this approach is the richness and thoroughness of detail about an individual that is possible through in-depth interviews.
- **A basic weakness** is that it isn't possible to know for sure if past experiences in a person's life are actually relevant to current functioning. For example, one individual who was physically and psychologically abused as a child might still be emotionally scarred, whereas another individual might have overcome such abuse to the extent that it has little to do with current functioning and problems.

Surveys typically involve self-report questionnaires that can be distributed efficiently to many people at the same time, with the goal of providing information about virtually any aspect of attitudes and behavior. Large-scale surveys of human sexuality are examples, as are political polls and product-marketing surveys.
- **The major strength** of surveys is their scope; surveys can even be nationwide.
- **The major weakness** of surveys is the same as with case histories: It is not possible to determine what causes what.
- **Additional weaknesses** involve the potential for **bias** in various ways. One source of bias is that not all of the people contacted for a survey will respond, and the people who don't respond might share an important opinion or attitude that gets overlooked—

there's no good way to know. Another weakness revolves around whether respondents tell the truth on surveys. With regard to sexual behavior, for example, respondents might report what they think is socially correct instead of what they actually do, and again there's no good way for the researcher to know.

Quasi-experiments: In a true experiment, the researcher assigns subjects to groups, sets up the experimental conditions, and exerts a great degree of control over what happens. In a quasi-experiment, the researcher instead takes subjects and conditions as they naturally occur, with little if any control over what happens. Thus, strictly speaking, the researcher cannot make conclusive statements about what causes what. On the surface, however, quasi-experiments often look like true experiments and use the same statistical analysis. Developmental psychologists (and others) sometimes use quasi-experiments:

- **A longitudinal design** follows a group of participants across a period of time, such as from early childhood to adolescence. Their behavior and functioning are assessed at various points from beginning to end, with the goal of assessing change.
- **A cross-sectional design** also assesses change, though instead by comparing groups of participants of different ages. Thus, different children in early childhood, middle childhood, and beginning adolescence might be compared at one point in time.

KEY EXAMPLE

Various research projects have assessed the benefits of early childhood intervention (such as Head Start) by identifying children who receive the intervention and children who don't and then comparing their intellectual and social development in years to come (see also Key 56).

- **This is a quasi-experiment** if the researchers play no part in assigning the children to intervention versus nonintervention groups, as is usually the case. Thus, the researchers cannot be sure the groups are initially equivalent in all relevant respects and later cannot be sure what causes any benefits displayed by the intervention group. Yet, if the children in each group are similar on psychological tests before intervention, and if the intervention group later displays substantially better intellectual and social development, valuable evidence in favor of early childhood intervention is obtained.
- **This is a longitudinal design** because both groups of children are assessed over a period of years. No cross-sections are involved.

Key 10 Correlation

OVERVIEW *Correlation assesses the correspondence between two or more psychological measures across a group of subjects or "cases."*

Correlation as a method means collecting data potentially through any of the psychological research methods and then looking at correspondence without regard to cause and effect. That is, researchers would perhaps prefer to assess cause and effect in any research they conduct, but that's not possible through correlational analysis.

Correlation as a technique underlies much statistical analysis relevant to differing areas of psychology, examples being the procedures used to refine and validate psychological tests, to determine characteristics of people with mental disorders, and to evaluate genetic heritability of psychological traits from parents to children.

A coefficient of correlation is a mathematical index of the correspondence between measures. Correlation takes various forms and names, depending upon the measures being compared and especially the kinds of data, but the most commonly used index is Pearson's *r*.

- **Pearson's *r*** originated in the work of Karl Pearson and colleagues around the beginning of the 20th century and was the starting point in developing the various other correlation coefficients.
- **A correlation coefficient can vary from 0 to +1.00 or from 0 to –1.00**. A correlation of 0 means that no correspondence exists. Correlations near 0 are considered weak, correlations in the range of about .20 to .60 are considered moderate, and correlations beyond .60 are considered strong—independent of whether they're positive or negative.
- **Positive correlation** means that the two measures vary in the same direction across subjects, say from low to high. Thus, if some participants consistently score low on both measures and others score high on both, the correlation will be positive. For example, measures of intelligence and measures of academic achievement tend to be positively correlated: Those who score higher on intelligence tests tend to make higher grades, and vice versa.
- **Negative correlation** means that the two measures vary in the opposite direction. Here, some participants score high on one measure and low on the other, whereas some score low on one measure and high on the other. For example, measures of intelligence and measures of "reaction time" tend to be negatively cor-

related: Those who score higher on intelligence tests tend to react faster (and therefore have lower reaction times) to stimuli, and vice versa.

KEY EXAMPLE (positive correlation)

A researcher is interested in assessing the relationship between "parental discipline" and child delinquency across a group of families, meaning cases. Suppose the researcher uses a scale for parental discipline on which parents score high if they intimidate and threaten their children regularly, if they often use harsh physical punishment without explanations, and if they generally advocate the view that children are inherently bad and must be corrected severely for even the slightest misbehavior. Parents who do not approach discipline those ways score lower. Child delinquency, in turn, is defined and measured in terms of violations of social rules and laws, truancy, and generally antisocial behavior toward others, so that markedly delinquent children get the higher scores. With the variables so defined, the correlation tends to be strong and positive: Families high on that kind of parental discipline tend to include children high on delinquency; parents low on that kind of discipline do not.

KEY EXAMPLE (negative correlation)

Again across a group of families, and with the same definition of child delinquency, suppose instead that the researcher uses a scale for parental discipline that emphasizes the brighter side of parental involvement with their children. This time, high scores go to those parents who set and enforce reasonable limits for their child, who use appropriate punishments and explain why certain behaviors are right and others wrong, and who generally take an active and constructive interest in their children's lives. Here, the correlation tends to be strong and negative: Families high on that kind of parental discipline tend to have well-adjusted children who score low on delinquency, and vice versa.

What correlation does and does not mean: Correlation indicates the extent to which two measures correspond, plus whether the correspondence is positive or negative. Correlation *by itself* does not indicate what causes what.

- **In the brief examples noted earlier**, a positive correlation between intelligence test scores and school grades could mean that students' grades depend upon their intelligence, or that students' intelligence depends upon their study habits and grades, or simply that intelligence tests and academic tests measure much the same skills, or something else entirely. There's no way to know without more information. Similarly, a negative correlation between intelligence test scores and reaction time could be because of a relationship in either direction, or something in common between tests of intelligence and tests of reaction time, or something else entirely.
- **In the example of positive correlation**, it's perhaps easy to suppose that harsh discipline hardens and alienates children and "causes" them to become delinquent. However, it's just as easy to suppose that children might become delinquent for other reasons and drive their parents to the point of using harsh discipline. Yet another possibility is that some third factor is responsible for both: Perhaps some of the families live in neighborhoods with maladaptive norms that encourage both harsh parental discipline and child delinquency, and other families do not.
- **In the example of negative correlation**, it could be that constructive discipline produces well-adjusted, nondelinquent children. Or it could be that well-adjusted children cause their parents to take a more constructive and even-handed approach. Or again, other factors such as neighborhoods and social norms could be responsible.
- **Correlation can provide valuable clues** about cause and effect, however. And, importantly, correlation is sometimes the only method available in psychological research on humans. It would not be ethically possible or desirable, for example, to conduct experiments in which some parents are encouraged to use harsh discipline so that the long-range effects on their children could be studied.

Key 11 Psychological research
and the real world

OVERVIEW *In conducting research, psychologists in particular are often faced with decisions about whether to conduct research in the laboratory or in the field, and, in turn, must consider whether their research generalizes to the populations and phenomena being studied.*

Laboratory versus field research: Research in carefully controlled laboratory settings can be more efficient, more precise, and otherwise better in terms of methodology, but research in field settings can sometimes produce results that are more applicable and generalizable to behavior in the real world. Just as a rat does not necessarily behave the same in a lab as it does in its natural environment, people do not necessarily behave the same in the lab as in the everyday world— especially if people know they're participating in a research effort. Thus, psychologists study what they can in laboratory settings but regularly venture out into field settings too.

- **Laboratory experimentation** is essential in studying basic processes such as perception, learning and memory, emotionality, and many others that require precise measurement and control of stimuli and conditions. And researchers can duplicate many real-world settings and behaviors reasonably well in the lab.
- **Laboratory observation** without experimentation is also at times employed to achieve better measurement and control, an example being laboratory research on the human physiology and psychology of sex.
- **Field experimentation** is preferable in research on situations and behaviors that cannot be duplicated well in the lab. An example is research on "bystander intervention," in which researchers study what characteristics of a person in distress determine whether passers-by will stop and help (Key 82). Here, the intensity and urgency of the situation might be hard to duplicate, so the researchers have at times yielded control over factors such as noise, crowding, and especially selection of the passers-by (the participants) in favor of conducting the research under conditions that can elicit a full range of bystander behavior.
- **Field observation**, also called **naturalistic observation**, is sometimes the primary research effort in itself. Describing and cataloging

animal behavior in the wild is an example. At other times, describing and cataloging behavior through field observation is preliminary to laboratory research. Observing children's behavior as it naturally occurs on a school or neighborhood playground would be an example, say, if the researcher later reconstructed a play setting in the lab to study behaviors such as aggression or cooperation.

Subjects and sampling: A related consideration in whether or not psychological research generalizes to the real world concerns the subjects and the procedures used to select them. Critics have argued, for example, that psychology is a science built on rats, monkeys, and introductory psychology students. That isn't the case, of course, but at the same time it *is* very important to consider the subjects and how they were selected when evaluating any research effort in psychology.

- **Experimentation with animals** has a long history in psychology, within a continuing view that *some* basic processes underlying behavior are similar for all animals, including humans. If so, research utilizing rats and pigeons—and especially primates—can be generalized to humans. And some psychological (and biological/medical) research cannot ethically be conducted using human participants. Otherwise, however, in keeping with the "cognitive revolution" in psychology, it is recognized nowadays that some processes and behaviors are unique to humans and therefore can only be studied using human participants.

- **Experimentation with college students** also has a long history, because students in introductory psychology courses are a convenient participant pool for psychological researchers, many of whom work in college and university settings. In general, if the processes and behaviors being studied are thought to be the same for all humans, then college students are as good a sample as any. Psychologists fully recognize, however, that human populations such as children versus adolescents versus adults, such as people of different ethnic and socioeconomic backgrounds, and so on, can differ in ways that might be important to research. Participants tend to be selected accordingly.

- **Survey research**, in contrast, must always address whether the samples are representative of the overall populations being studied. Here, various forms of **random sampling** are typically employed: In a random sample, every member of a population has an equal likelihood of being selected, which in turn provides the best chance that the sample will reflect the characteristics of the population. For example, in a poll of voters before election day, a random sample has the best chance of giving an accurate idea of how the election will turn out.

Replication: Scientific research typically involves a series of related experiments rather than a single experiment. In modern psychology, researchers tend to develop "lines of research" on important questions about behavior, and in addition there are often different researchers working on the same questions independently and using different subjects and settings. Replication requires that predictable and consistent results be obtained wherever the behavior in question is studied. Importantly, researchers tend to avoid making broad statements about how their theories apply to situations and behavior in general until the theories have been broadly tested.

- **Considering the group experiment from Key 7,** it would not be appropriate to make broad statements about graphic violence and emotional responsiveness on the basis of a single experiment—regardless of how much less emotionally responsive the experimental group turned out to be. General statements would require replicating the experiment with different types of participants, different types of violence, different measures of emotionality, and so on.

Key 12 Ethical considerations in psychological research

OVERVIEW *In any psychological research, animal or human, ethical considerations are of prime importance to everyone concerned.*

The American Psychological Association (APA) is a large professional organization of psychologists. The APA serves many functions, one of its major functions being to help ensure that those who call themselves psychologists maintain high ethical standards. The ethical issues addressed by the APA apply throughout research and practice in psychology, including social issues such as gender equality and racial/ethnic equality, clinical issues such as psychological testing and therapist-client interactions, and research issues such as the treatment of experimental subjects and participants, which is the focus here.

Ethical guidelines for animal research have been formalized in keeping with a general societal recognition of animal rights. Psychologists must, for example, provide acceptable housing and day-to-day care and otherwise avoid causing research animals unnecessary harm. And, in turn, most of the actual research conducted with animals doesn't in any way involve hurting them. Some does, though, and when it does, psychologists who must harm animals as part of their research pay careful attention to:

- **Minimizing any discomfort or pain the animals are subjected to**. A researcher using electric shock, for example, would use the minimum levels of shock necessary to the research question being addressed.
- **Sacrificing animals in a humane way, if sacrifice is required**. Researchers who conduct animal research on drug effects, for example, sometimes sacrifice the animals to study the effects on brain tissue.
- **Making sure that the research is valuable in the first place**. Even the most basic research should have identifiable and worthwhile goals, especially where discomfort and pain to animals is involved.

Ethical guidelines for research with humans are extensive, having been developed and refined over the years in part as a result of a few controversial experiments in psychology that were conducted in times past but that probably couldn't be conducted today. And the guidelines continue to be updated regularly in light of new considerations. Where human participants are involved—and especially children—modern psychologists must go to great lengths to ensure that no physical or psychological harm can result from experimental procedures. And if it does anyway, inadvertently, the researcher is responsible for following up and remedying the situation as much as possible. Plus, as another safeguard, psychologists must submit their research proposals in advance to review boards for evaluation and suggestions regarding potential harm to participants. Review boards are comprised of peers and other professionals, and if the review board says no, the research doesn't happen. Specific ethical considerations include:

- **Minimizing any discomfort or pain the participants are subjected to,** as in animal research, plus more generally placing the participants at **minimal risk** and avoiding any lasting effects—physically and psychologically. In the example of a group experiment in Key 8, the graphically violent movies would be like those shown in theaters nationwide and would not be expected to have any lasting effects even if they were temporarily upsetting to some participants. Note that if the movies weren't at all upsetting, the experiment would be pointless.

- **Obtaining and maintaining informed consent.** People who participate in psychological research must do so voluntarily, having been told in advance about anything that might influence their decision to participate. Where the participants are children, informed consent is obtained from parents or legal guardians. And any participant must be allowed to withdraw at any time during the research, for any reason and without penalty. In the graphic-violence experiment, participants would receive an advance briefing at least to the effect that they would be watching horror movies that could be upsetting. And, importantly, participants would be allowed to stop participating at any time they wished, without losing any "bonus points" or other incentives they might have been offered for participating. Informed consent applies *throughout* an experiment, not just beforehand, and there's no requirement that the participants justify or otherwise explain why they wish to withdraw.

- **Debriefing:** "Deception" is often involved in psychological research with humans, necessarily to prevent participants from perhaps behaving differently than they normally would (Key 9). Participants cannot be deceived as to anything that would influence their decision to participate, in keeping with informed consent, but they're often deceived as to the true nature and purposes of the experiment. Especially in such cases, participants must be debriefed afterward, with an explanation of what the research was about and also with the opportunity to discuss anything that may have made them uncomfortable. In the graphic-violence experiment, participants would be told the details afterward and given the opportunity to discuss any aspects of the experiment they wished— including their own behavior and how they felt about it. They would also have access to the overall results, when available.

- **Confidentiality:** Although psychologists typically publish and otherwise share their findings with other researchers, which is what science is all about, psychologists cannot disclose any information about participants that might allow participants to be identified. In a published clinical case history, for example, no details would be released that might in any way indicate who the client was, even though the client's dynamics and problems would probably be discussed at length. Similarly, with experiments, as well as with surveys, no details about the individual participants could be given that might in any way allow them to be identified, even though their behavior or responses would be discussed extensively. To divulge identifying information is grounds for a lawsuit.

Theme 3 PHYSIOLOGICAL PSYCHOLOGY AND THE BIOLOGY OF BEHAVIOR

*I*n *science*, all behavior is ultimately measurable. In a science of the behavior of living organisms, all behavior is assumed to be caused by something that is physical and therefore potentially observable, whether the cause is within the organism or outside of it.

In turn, all behavior that can be studied scientifically is a result of genetics or environment (usually in interaction). In other words, all behavior stems from what is built-in or from what is experienced along the way, from the moment of conception.

Although psychologists know a great deal about the external, environmental causes of behavior, psychologists still have a long way to go in developing a thorough and detailed understanding of how the internal worlds of living organisms work—especially with regard to links between the overt (such as neuron electrochemical processes in the brain) and the covert (such as mental processes).

Theme 3 summarizes what *is* known, with emphasis on what's helpful in understanding discussions in other Themes.

INDIVIDUAL KEYS IN THIS THEME

Key 13 Neurons and the nervous system

OVERVIEW *Neurons are the basic units of the nervous system, and they function electrochemically.*

Neurons are specialized cells that transmit and process information. In the peripheral nervous system, neurons mostly transmit, meaning that they relay information from one area of the nervous system to another. In the central nervous system (CNS), neurons both transmit and process information. Neural information processing, it is assumed, somehow gives rise to covert mental processing such as in thinking and reasoning and remembering and using language.

- **The peripheral nervous system** consists of all the **sensory (afferent) neurons** and **motor (efferent) neurons** that relay information to and from the CNS. Sensory neurons carry information inward to the CNS from receptor neurons in sensory areas throughout the body, allowing the CNS to monitor the external world as well as internal bodily functions. Motor neurons carry information outward from the CNS to effector neurons in muscles and glands, allowing the CNS to act on the external world as well as control internal bodily functions. **Nerves** are bundles of sensory and motor neurons.

- **The central nervous system** consists of all the neurons in the brain and spinal cord, with emphasis on the brain and its **interneurons**. There are many billions of tiny interneurons in the brain—estimates vary widely. Something about the complex electrochemical processes that occur in and between those billions of neurons, along with something about the incredibly complex ways in which those neurons interconnect, gives rise to mental processes. It is known from research with nonhuman animals, for example, that learning produces enlargement of CNS neurons and also increases the complexity of the interconnections between them.

Electrochemical activity in neurons: Neurons pass along information across synapses (see Figure 3-1). An interneuron's cycle begins when biochemical neurotransmitters from other neurons cross synapses to receptor molecules in the neuron's dendrites and excite it. The neuron fires "all or none," meaning that it either fires completely or it doesn't fire at all. Then the electrical impulse travels down the neuron's axon to its synaptic terminals, where neurotransmitters are released and the cycle starts all over again, in perhaps a couple of milliseconds.

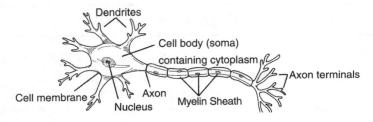

Figure 3-1. An idealized neuron, with features that most neurons have in common. [Figure is from Baucum, D. (1999), Barron's *College Review Series: Psychology,* p. 40.]

- **Synapses** are junctions across gaps; neurons do not actually touch at the synapses. And a major complexity in trying to comprehend how the brain works is that a neuron can have hundreds of "incoming" synapses with other neurons (at its dendrites) and likewise many "outgoing" synapses with other neurons (at its synaptic terminals).
- **Neurotransmitters** are biochemicals that are released at the synapses. Another complexity in how the brain works is that some of the dozens of neurotransmitters that have been identified are excitatory, meaning that they tend to make the next neuron fire, whereas other neurotransmitters are inhibitory, meaning that they tend to prevent the next neuron from firing. And to further complicate things, some neurotransmitters can be excitatory to one neuron and inhibitory to another, depending upon the neuron's receptor molecules. But in general, whether a neuron fires depends upon how much excitation and inhibition are present at its dendrites at a given point in time.
- **The axon** of a neuron is its "trunk," connecting the main body of the cell and the dendrites at one end to the synaptic terminals at the other. In a resting or "waiting" state, the cell membrane of the axon is polarized, meaning that it's electrically positive on the outside and negative on the inside. When the neuron fires, **depolarization** occurs and the electrical potential reverses. The neural impulse then ripples down the axon to the synaptic terminals and releases neurotransmitters to the next neurons in line. Some axons also have a **myelin sheath**, a whitish coating that insulates them from adjacent neurons and increases the speed of transmissions.

Key 14 The peripheral nervous system

OVERVIEW *In terms of functions, the peripheral nervous system is subdivided into the somatic nervous system and the autonomic nervous system. In turn, the autonomic nervous system is further subdivided into the sympathetic and parasympathetic nervous systems.*

The somatic nervous system consists of those sensory and motor neurons that ultimately allow the CNS to communicate with the external world. For example, the sensory neurons of the somatic nervous system include those that relay visual and auditory information, which originates in specialized sensory receptor neurons in the eyes and ears (Keys 20 and 22). And the motor neurons of the somatic nervous system include those that relay information to specialized motor effector neurons that activate skeletal muscles and produce movement.

- **Sensory receptor neurons** "transduce" energy, which means that they convert it into neural impulses. Sensory receptors in the eyes transduce light, sensory receptors in the ears transduce sound, and so on for the other senses.
- **Motor effector neurons** also transduce energy, converting neural impulses into what becomes movement and behavior.

The autonomic nervous system consists of those sensory and motor neurons that connect the CNS with internal bodily functions such as respiration, digestion, and regulation of heart rate and blood pressure—in other words, the "smooth" muscles and the glands. Autonomic is similar to "automatic," in that the autonomic nervous system is self-regulating and does not necessarily require conscious attention. Breathing, heart rate, and digestion are basic homeostatic mechanisms that occur quite normally even during sleep.

- **Homeostasis** is the general tendency of the body to keep itself within functional limits and thus stay alive. A homeostatic process—whether autonomic or conscious and deliberate—is one that uses feedback and control mechanisms to maintain itself. Breathing is homeostatic, in that respiration rate changes in part because of feedback on the amount of oxygen in the bloodstream. Hunger is homeostatic, in that eating depends in part on the level of sugars in the bloodstream; when the level drops, the organism seeks food. (These and other homeostatic mechanisms in motivation and emotion are discussed in Theme 6.)

Within the autonomic nervous system, the sympathetic nervous system serves to arouse the organism, particularly in emergencies (such as "fight or flight"). The parasympathetic nervous system is mostly antagonistic and calms the organism, plus maintains normal bodily processes that occur while the organism is in a resting state. The opposing functions of the sympathetic and parasympathetic nervous systems can also be thought of as homeostatic.

- **The sympathetic nervous system**, in response to emergency, gets busy and increases heart rate and respiration, at the same time shutting down digestion and other processes that aren't immediately necessary. The sympathetic nervous system also stimulates the release of hormones by the endocrine (glandular) system, with the effect of temporarily increasing physical strength and reducing pain—an example hormone is **beta endorphin**, which functions like endorphin neurotransmitters. Thus, the person is temporarily better prepared to withstand and cope with assault and battery, and more generally, with **stress** (Key 35).

- **The parasympathetic nervous system** tends to return the organism to a normal state when the emergency is over—one bodily function at a time. Heart rate and respiration decrease, digestion resumes, and so on. Note, however, that sexual behavior is somewhat of an exception to how the autonomic nervous system usually works: Sexual arousal is parasympathetic, occurring first, and sexual orgasm is later sympathetic.

Key 15 The central nervous system (CNS)

OVERVIEW *The central nervous system consists of the spinal cord and the brain, with emphasis on the latter. The brain contains numerous identifiable structures and divisions, though how brain structures relate to mental functions is far from clear.*

The spinal cord contains sensory and motor neurons that carry information to and from the CNS, plus interneurons like those in the brain. In some cases, sensory and motor neurons connect directly in the spinal cord. Relatively simple reflexes such as the patellar (knee-jerk) reflex involve direct sensory-motor connections. More complex reflexes such as jerking a hand back from something painful involve interneurons that connect sensory and motor neurons, plus other interneurons that transmit the painful experience to the brain.

- **Reflexes** are more-or-less automatic reactions that are built-in or "prewired," i.e., that do not result from learning and experience. Reflexes can be modified, however, by learning and experience. And some purely voluntary behaviors can become so well learned and habitual that they look like reflexes.

The human brain, in contrast to the spinal cord and the rest of the nervous system, is the center of information processing and especially behavior that's subject to voluntary control—behavior that's characteristically human, whether the behavior is primarily genetic and structural in origin or primarily learned through experience. The brain, in other words, is where mind has to be. That may seem obvious, but it wasn't always thought to be so. Over the centuries, different structures in the body have been proposed as the "location" of mind (or soul), one example being the heart, and before that, the liver.

Areas of the brain are suggested by shape, by differences in the type of neural tissue, and—to an extent—by the processes they're known to be involved in. However, it's important to remember the "principle of mass action," which states that most behaviors and certainly all complex behaviors involve the entire brain, not just a certain area or structure. In other words, an area or structure may be a primary "center" for a certain process or behavior, like a subprocessing station, but the rest of the brain tends to be involved too. The brain tends to function as a whole.

Viewed from an evolutionary perspective, the human brain consists of the hindbrain, the midbrain, and the forebrain. The hindbrain and the midbrain combined constitute the brain stem, all of which sits at the top of the spinal cord. The much larger human forebrain in turn sits on top of the brain stem structures and partially encloses them, filling out all the rest of the skull cavity.

- **The hindbrain** is the most primitive area, primarily involved in regulating basic bodily functions such as heart rate and breathing, coughing, and sneezing. Also, the hindbrain includes the **cerebellum** or "little brain," which is a processing center for reflexes involved in balance and gross motor coordination.
- **The midbrain** is next in an evolutionary sense and is involved to an extent in vision and audition, including control of eye movements and transmission of visual information from higher brain centers to the cerebellum. The midbrain also includes portions of the **reticular formation** (originating in the hindbrain), which is involved with sleep and arousal and sustained attention. In humans, axons in the reticular formation do not become fully myelinated until adolescence, which is a partial explanation of children's shorter attention span.
- **The forebrain** is the most recent evolutionary structure and includes the thalamus, hypothalamus, limbic system, and cerebrum.

Viewed from the center outward, the brain consists of the central core, the limbic system, and the cerebrum. In this way of looking at things, the central core includes the brain stem structures (hindbrain and midbrain) as discussed above, plus the thalamus and hypothalamus. The limbic system is a set of structures that partially surround the central core, and the cerebrum surrounds the limbic system (see Figure 3-2).

- **The thalamus** begins essentially where the brain stem and the reticular formation end, and is also involved in sleep and arousal. One area of the thalamus also acts as a relay station between sensory receptors (such as visual and auditory) and the cerebrum.
- **The hypothalamus**, much smaller than the thalamus and located just below it, has long been a structure of particular interest to psychologists. The hypothalamus is a major processing area with regard to hunger, thirst, sex, and emotionality, plus stress reactions and other functions executed by the autonomic nervous system. The hypothalamus thus plays an important role in homeostasis.
- **The limbic system** is tightly interconnected with the hypothalamus, and includes structures that are apparently regulatory with regard to basic behaviors such as eating and drinking and sex. The limbic system is also involved in the display or inhibition of aggression. And limbic system structures such as the **hippocam-**

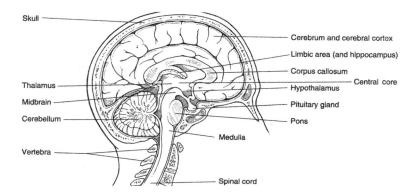

Figure 3-2. The human brain in cross section. [Figure is from Baucum, D. (1999), Barron's *College Review Series: Psychology*, p. 44.]

pus play a role in higher functions such as memory processes, especially the ability to remember relatively recent events.
- **The cerebrum** is by far the most extensively developed brain structure in humans. It consists of two visibly distinct layers, the outer layer being called the cerebral cortex. The cerebrum contains two-thirds or more of all the neurons in the nervous system, and has its own set of subdivisions and classifications. It is also by far the most extensively studied area of the CNS, because it is clearly the primary location of mental and cognitive processes in nonhuman animals as well as in humans. What is known and what is not known about the functions of the cerebrum—with emphasis upon the cerebral cortex—is summarized in the next Key.

Key 16 The cerebral cortex

OVERVIEW *The cerebral cortex, which is the outer layer or "bark" of the cerebrum, is our final destination in surveying the nervous system.*

The cerebral cortex is the grayish outer layer of the cerebrum and consists of the cell bodies of interneurons and also unmyelinated axons. It is extensively convoluted (wrinkled and folded), which yields a primary distinction between the human brain and that of other animals: There are animals that have larger brains, even when the brain is considered proportionally to overall body weight, but the human brain is by far the most extensively convoluted. Thus, the surface area of the brain is proportionally greatest in humans, whatever the reason.
- **The inner layer of the cerebrum**, in contrast, contains the whitish, myelinated axons of interneurons, also **glial cells** that provide support and nourishment plus a variety of other functions.

The cerebral cortex is divided into two more-or-less symmetrical **hemispheres** (left and right), connected centrally by a wide band of neurons called the **corpus callosum** [see Figure 3-3]. In turn, each hemisphere is divided into four **lobes**. Viewed from the right side and taken clockwise from the brain-stem area, these are the **temporal,**

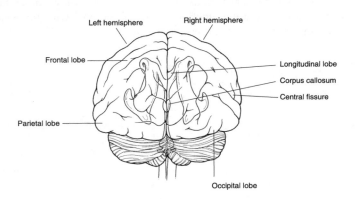

Figure 3-3. The human brain viewed from above. [Figure is from Baucum, D. (1999), Barron's *College Review Series: Psychology,* p. 46.]

occipital, **parietal**, and **frontal** lobes. Surface **fissures** or "valleys" mostly separate and therefore demarcate the lobes. And over the years, functions of the hemispheres and lobes from this perspective have been extensively mapped, meaning that researchers have studied what the areas connect to and what functions they are involved in. Again, however, the principle of mass action applies in all cases.

- **In each hemisphere**, the **motor cortex** runs along the rear of the frontal lobe, and the **somatosensory cortex** runs along the front of the parietal lobe. The motor cortex is involved in all bodily movements, gross and fine, with much more area devoted to fine motor control. The somatosensory cortex is involved in all bodily sensation, with more area devoted to sensation in the fine motor areas of the body. Each of these cortexes mostly connects to the opposite side of the body, so that the left hemisphere monitors and controls the right side of the body, and vice versa. In contrast, the **auditory cortex** (an area in the upper temporal lobe) and the **visual cortex** (most of the occipital lobe) each receive information from both sides of the body—i.e., both ears and both eyes. In vision, for example, what is seen in the right "visual field" (the left half of each eye) goes to the left hemisphere, and vice versa, through branching called the **optic chiasma** (Key 20). Finally, everything else in the hemispheres is referred to as **association areas**. These are not directly involved with sensory and motor functions, and are therefore assumed to be involved in our higher mental processes. The largest areas of the temporal lobe, the parietal lobe, and especially the frontal lobe are apparently devoted to such processes. Note, however, that knowing where an activity primarily occurs still leaves a great deal to be learned about how it works.

- **Some association areas are specialized according to hemisphere**. For a majority of people, for example, the areas involved in speech production are in the left hemisphere along the lateral fissure that divides the frontal and temporal lobes. Most other language functions are also in the left hemisphere. Other mental functions that appear to be primarily left hemisphere include the kinds of thinking involved in logic and math. Right-hemisphere functions include pattern-oriented thinking such as in art and music, plus perhaps creativity, because there is evidence that these areas are busiest when participants are engaging in such activities. Such functions have not yet been as thoroughly researched as speech localization, however. And the idea that personality is determined in part by being a "left-brain" or a "right-brain" person is even less well researched than that.

Key 17 Altering and monitoring CNS functioning

OVERVIEW *Some of what is discussed in this Key is involved in how researchers study brain functioning. Other procedures have more to do with detection and treatment of brain disorders.*

Altering brain functioning: In a real sense, any stimulus or situation the organism experiences affects brain functioning. Discussed here, however, are procedures that directly affect brain functioning through physical and chemical means.

- **Psychoactive substances** (drugs; Keys 39, 40, and 72) are by far the most extensively used means of directly affecting CNS functioning—though the systematic use of drugs to control and alleviate mental disorders did not become widespread until about the 1950s. Alcohol and drugs have their main effects at the level of neural synapses and neurotransmitters in the CNS and especially the brain. Some drugs stimulate neurotransmitter production, others interfere with it. Some drugs cause more of a certain neurotransmitter to be present by interfering with its "reabsorption." And some drugs, such as painkillers, directly substitute for natural neurotransmitters at the receptor molecules. An example of the latter involves **endorphins**, the body's natural painkillers that are released in response to emergency and stress, and that also tend to produce good feelings and euphoria. Opiate and synthetic painkillers fit the same receptor molecules and produce similar effects, though often more drastically. In turn, by varying the chemical makeup of painkillers, subtle differences in the effects on the CNS and overall behavior occur—and can be observed and studied. Aside from adding to knowledge about how neurotransmitters work, such procedures have produced the many different painkillers available today, some of which are not nearly as euphoric and addictive as painkillers once were. Similar research procedures also continue to be used in developing better drugs to treat mental disorders.
- **Lesions to the CNS** (cuts, whether small or large) can occur accidentally or as the result of surgical or experimental procedures. Today's understanding of the left-hemisphere speech areas, for example, began with the work of Paul **Broca** and later Carl

Wernicke in the 19th century: Speech difficulties in patients were traced to accidental lesions in the brain areas noted. Another example involves extensive research on the functions of the hypothalamus, here using experimental lesions in rats. One type of lesion produces rats that are hyperphagic and won't stop eating; another type produces rats that are hypophagic and won't eat at all. Still other lesions affect drinking and sexual activity. As a third example, human patients with severe epilepsy sometimes have the corpus callosum severed, with the effect that the left and right hemispheres of the brain cannot directly communicate. If stimuli and information are then presented only to one hemisphere at a time, the relative ease with which that information is processed provides clues about what that hemisphere does best.

- **Electrical brain stimulation** is sometimes used for diagnostics and sometimes for research in mapping what different areas of the cortex do. Using patients that must undergo neurosurgery anyway, small and harmless electrical currents are administered to specific areas of the cortex to assess what happens. If a muscle twitches, a motor area has been stimulated. If the patient reports a sensation or a memory, then the area must have something to do with that.

Monitoring CNS functioning: Older techniques and technology for monitoring brain functioning tend to provide information about brain structures or brain activity in general areas. Newer approaches and especially newer equipment are providing much more detailed information about brain activity.

- **The electroencephalograph (EEG)** is one of the older approaches to studying overall or global brain activity, especially with regard to wakefulness and sleep and other variations in states of consciousness (Theme 7). An EEG consists of small electrodes that are attached harmlessly to the subject's skull and that lead to recording equipment that produces a graph across time. Such measurement yields an ongoing composite of what the brain is doing electrically. If many neurons are firing at the same time, for example, a peak is produced on the graph. If neurons are firing without much synchronization, the graph looks much more irregular and noisy. Consistently identifiable graphs emerge (Key 37).

- **Quantitative electroencephalography (QEEG)** is a much more refined approach that uses many more electrodes. Their location is standardized by fitting them into a cap that covers the participant's head. Tiny fluctuations in brain electrical activity—called *event-related potentials (ERPs)*—are subjected to computer processing to assess what specific areas of the brain are involved in activities such as perceiving, thinking, and remembering. There is a slight time delay, however, which complicates the task of sorting out what the brain is doing in response to what.

- **Magnetic resonance imaging** (**MRI**), also called **nuclear magnetic resonance** (**NMR**), produces information like that of the CAT scan except with much better resolution and detail. MRI is based on properties of tissue at the atomic or "nuclear" level; the imaging is accomplished by collecting minute magnetic field changes that occur when the tissue is subjected to harmless radio waves. Again, however, the images are structural and do not assess ongoing brain activity.

- **Functional magnetic resonance imaging** (**fMRI**), a much newer technique, also assesses and localizes minute magnetic changes during brain activity, here by monitoring the natural metabolism of oxygen when clusters of neurons are active in perceiving and thinking and the like. Thus, in contrast to MRI, fMRI measures ongoing brain activity. Compared to QEEG, there is a somewhat longer time delay, so QEEG is often used in conjunction with fMRI for calibration.

- **Positron emission tomography** (PET) is based on the energy expenditure of cells when they metabolize blood sugars, i.e., when they're active. Blood sugars tagged with harmless radioactive isotopes are injected into the subject's blood stream, and as the neurons in the brain use them, the radioactive "positrons" that are emitted show up in areas of brain that are active. The PET equipment then processes and displays the activity in real time, as it is occurring. PET scans thus far continue to be used for mapping the brain, and there is also preliminary evidence that the brain activity patterns of normal people versus those with major mental disorders differ in ways that can be identified by PET scanning. People in active stages of schizophrenia, for example (Key 69), display markedly and consistently different PET scans as compared to normal people. There is also preliminary evidence that males and females often differ in PET activity with regard to language functions and the extent to which they are localized by hemispheres. In either case, however, PET scans as yet provide no information about what *causes* what.

Key 18 Genetics and heredity

OVERVIEW *Genetic inheritance is potentially important in understanding any behavior. This Key outlines the basics of how genetic processes work, with emphasis on what applies to complex human behavior and what does not.*

Genes are the basic building blocks of heredity and were inferred long before it was possible to examine their biochemical makeup (they were named by Gregor **Mendel** in the 19th century). As it turns out, genes are segments of deoxyribonucleic acid (DNA), molecules that exist in the nuclei of cells and that are encoded with all the biochemical information necessary to reproduce themselves, to diversify cells into the many different types found in the body, and eventually to produce an adult organism.

Chromosomes are relatively long, threadlike clusters of genes; each is comprised of perhaps a thousand or more genes. And chromosomes are paired, in the sense that for each chromosome there is a corresponding chromosome set up to perform the same work. Thus, genes are paired as well, and in many cases compete to determine the characteristics actually displayed by the individual organism. In the nuclei of normal human cells, except in the gametes, there are 23 pairs of chromosomes for a total of 46.

- **Genes are equivalently paired except** for the 23rd chromosome pair in human males. The 23rd pair determines sex, and is "XY" in males, designated that way because the Y chromosome is smaller and contains fewer genes than the X. In females, the 23rd pair is "XX," with an equivalent number of genes on each chromosome.
- **Gametes** are reproductive cells (sperm and ova), which contain only 23 chromosomes—one member of each pair—therefore setting the stage for conception. The child thus gets half from the mother and half from the father, back to a total of 46.

Genotype is the biochemical makeup of an individual's genes, determined primarily by inheritance from the individual's parents. **Phenotype** is the characteristic or trait the individual displays. Simple characteristics such as eye color are determined by a single pair of genes according to which gene is dominant and which gene is recessive. Some genes, however, such as those for blood type, combine rather than compete (Type AB blood occurs when the individual has both Type A and Type B genes). And complex psychological traits such as intelligence and personality are **polygenic**, meaning that they are determined by a great many genes in interaction. Or so it is assumed, because the actual gene combinations for intelligence and other complex traits have yet to be specified.

- **Simple dominance and recessiveness** patterns occur between pairs of genes, meaning that the genes compete to do the same work. These are called **alleles**. There is a different allele for each human eye color, for example, and some alleles are dominant over others. Compared to the allele for brown eyes, which tends to be dominant, the allele for blue eyes is recessive. If "**B**" represents brown and "**b**" is blue, then an individual who is **BB, Bb,** or **bB** will display the phenotype brown eyes. Only an individual who is **bb** will have blue eyes.

- **Inheritance of simple traits**, in turn, can be predicted on a probability basis. Suppose both the father and the mother are **heterozygous** for brown and blue; that is, each parent has the genotype **Bb** or **bB**, a "mix," and each therefore each has the phenotype brown. By chance, the child could then be **BB, Bb, bB,** or **bb**, depending upon which gene the child gets from each parent. Because only one combination will produce blue eyes (**bb**), there's a one-fourth or 25% chance the child will have blue eyes. On the other hand, suppose one parent is **homozygous** for brown (**BB**). No matter what the other parent's genetic makeup is, there's no way the child can have blue eyes (barring mutation).

- **Phenotype begins with genotype**, but can also depend upon environment and experience—especially where complex psychological traits are concerned. Intelligence, for example, is sometimes assumed to begin with a polygenic "predisposition" that's entirely built-in. However, the individual's eventual intelligence depends greatly upon the environment along the way, with emphasis on early experience in the home and especially education and related experiences later. Thus, genes would determine a broad range within which a normal child's intelligence will fall, but environment would determine all the rest (Key 56).

- **To complicate things further**, there are **modifier genes** that sometimes alter the effects of other genes—even the simpler ones, such as those for eye color. And, more generally, the parents' gametes do not divide or recombine along the same lines that existed when each parent was conceived. In other words, an ovum or a sperm cell is a *random* half of the original genetic material of the parent, with the effect that each ovum and each sperm cell is unique. In addition to that, **mutation** sometimes occurs during the production of gametes and during conception, with the effect that some genetic material gets changed in unpredictable ways. Most mutations aren't viable, but some are. All things considered, it is estimated that a single pair of human parents could produce many *trillions* of different children, i.e., children who would each be unique genetically. But human children do still tend to resemble their parents both in physical and psychological ways, in part because of genetics.

Genetic anomalies and disorders can markedly affect both physical and psychological traits. Genetically based disorders can occur as a result of simple dominance and recessiveness, can be sex-linked (involving the XY mismatch on the 23rd chromosome pair in males), can result from having too few or too many chromosomes, and can be a result of mutation—or any of those in combination. There are many such disorders, some severe and some not. The following are examples often cited.

- **Phenylketonuria (PKU)** is a disorder involving a lack of the ability to digest a specific amino acid, which then builds up in the body and progressively destroys the central nervous system, with severe mental and physical impairment and death if not treated early. PKU is a recessive disorder, meaning that the child displays it only if both parents contribute the recessive PKU gene.

- **Down syndrome** is typically caused by the presence of an extra chromosome on the 21st pair. Another name for the disorder is thus Trisomy-21. People with Down syndrome tend to have somewhat Asian facial features (hence the archaic term "mongolism"). They also tend to be mentally retarded, though usually not severely. Why the extra chromosome occurs is not known, although the disorder is more likely when middle-aged and older parents conceive.

- **Some types of color blindness** are **sex-linked** recessive disorders, involving the 23rd chromosome pair. Red-green color blindness, for example, is more likely in males because the Y chromosome doesn't contain a gene that could suppress the recessive one if it's present on the X chromosome. By contrast, a female (XX) doesn't express the disorder unless the recessive gene is present on *both* chromosomes. **Male pattern baldness** is another example, as is the severe disorder **hemophilia**.

Theme 4 SENSATION AND
PERCEPTION

*S*ensation is the process by which we gain information about the external world—as well as the internal world of our bodies. Sensation means detecting the various forms of energy appropriate to our sensory apparatus and transducing (converting) that energy into neural impulses.

Perception refers to higher processing of sensory information as it reaches the central nervous system. Perceptual processes include filtering, interpreting, organizing, recognizing, and understanding sensory stimulation, whether consciously or otherwise. Perception, in other words, is cognitive; it includes use of prior learning and knowledge as we "make sense" of the world around us.

Theme 4 covers the basics of sensation and perception, with emphasis on vision and audition, which are primary senses in humans and which therefore have been the most extensively studied. Also covered are smell, taste, and the skin senses, plus bodily kinesthesis and equilibrium.

INDIVIDUAL KEYS IN THIS THEME

Key 19 Measuring and describing sensations

OVERVIEW *Sensations occur when specific kinds of energy stimulate our sensory apparatus. Psychophysics is the study of relationships between stimulation and sensation, as is the more recent signal detection theory.*

Sensory thresholds are limits within which stimulation can produce sensations. Classic research focused on determining minimum levels of stimulation necessary to produce sensations, in the form of absolute thresholds and difference thresholds. Note in passing, however, that there are also "upper" thresholds for stimulation beyond which tissue damage occurs, which is a good thing to bear in mind the next time you decide to watch a solar eclipse or sit close to the stage at a rock-and-roll concert.

- **Absolute thresholds** have been assessed by the psychophysical "method of constant stimuli." Here, for example, tones of varying amplitude close to the suspected threshold might be presented randomly to the subject, with the subject responding "yes" or "no" as to hearing each tone. The absolute or minimum threshold, then, by convention among psychophysicists, is the amplitude the subject correctly detects 50% of the time. Research on absolute thresholds has been applied to all the basic senses, to determine "average" or "typical" levels of stimulation necessary to produce sensations, noting that individuals can vary considerably in their sensory capabilities.

- **Difference thresholds** have to do with how much a stimulus must change before the subject can tell it has changed. Here, using visual stimulation as an example, the researcher might repeatedly present slightly differing intensities of lights, in pairs, with the subject responding "yes" or "no" as to whether they are different. Then the **just noticeable difference** (JND) is the difference correctly identified 50% of the time, again by convention. Research on difference thresholds has also been applied to all the basic senses, yielding average or typical values. Also note **Weber's law**, derived from work by Ernst Weber in the 19th century, which describes how JNDs vary as a function of the intensity of the stimulus. Generally, the more intense the stimulus, the greater a difference will have to be before that difference will be detected reliably. Weber's law, however, turns out to be only a rough approximation.

- **Sensory thresholds are also determined by** stimulus properties other than amplitude or intensity. Reds and purples, for example, at the extremes of the visible light spectrum, have higher absolute thresholds than the more central spectrum colors such as yellows and greens. And low or high frequency sound waves, such as basses and trebles, have higher thresholds than midrange sounds.

Sensory adaptation refers to a decrease in sensitivity (and therefore increase in threshold) that occurs as sensory receptors are repeatedly exposed to the same stimuli. Repetitive sights, sounds, smells, tastes, and so on become less noticeable with sustained exposure, in part because of adaptation at the level of the sensory receptors. Attention also plays a role, of course, in "tuning out" sensory information that's uninteresting or irrelevant.

- **Attention** doesn't actually block sensations at the receptor level; it determines what information gets dropped and what information is passed along for further processing. Attention is thus a cognitive process.

Signal detection theory takes into account a wider range of variables that determine whether stimulus information is accurately sensed. "Background noise" refers to conflicting or competing stimulation that can prevent a stimulus from being detected even when it's well above threshold. Busy radar screen displays provide an example: If there are many objects flashing on the screen, an object of interest can go undetected even though it's clearly there. Similar effects occur in audition and the other senses. And other factors such as fatigue, motivation, and mental set can also affect whether a stimulus is accurately detected. In sum, as many researchers have pointed out, much more than simple thresholds are involved in determining what gets sensed and what does not.

Key 20 Vision

OVERVIEW *Vision is the most highly developed and complex sense in humans, and the structures and functions of the eyes have been thoroughly researched.*

Light and color: Electromagnetic energy is measured in wavelengths, where a specific band of wavelengths within the visible energy spectrum produces what we call light and color. Understanding the experience of color also requires understanding brightness, saturation, and hue, in conjunction with color mixing.

- **Wavelength** is literally that, measured in nanometers (nm), meaning billionths of a meter.
- **The visible spectrum** is a band of wavelengths from about 400 to 750 nm, wavelengths just between the ultraviolets and infrareds we normally can't see.
- **Brightness** refers to the intensity or amount of the light present.
- **Hue**, the main determinant of color, depends mostly on the wavelength(s) of the light present.
- **Saturation** refers to the purity of the light, i.e., the mix of wavelengths present.
- **Color mixing**, with respect to what we see, can be **additive** or **subtractive**. Additive color mixing applies to direct light, which is what happens in our eyes and also on a color television screen. A TV picture tube contains three electron guns that fire tiny beams of light and produce red, blue, and green on the screen, which can be mixed to produce any other color as well. White results from mixing all three. In contrast, subtractive mixing is what happens with pigments and paints, where we only see the light that's reflected from an object. If red, blue, and green pigments are mixed, most of the color spectrum is absorbed and not reflected, so all we see is dark brown or black.

The eye functions somewhat like a TV camera: Light from an image enters through a transparent, protective outer surface, passes through an aperture that limits the amount of light entering, and then goes through a lens that focuses the image and projects it onto a receptive surface. There, the light is transduced and transmitted, with the transmissions being continuously updated as the entering light changes. Correspondingly, in the human eye, the protective outer surface is the cornea, the aperture is the pupil (controlled by the iris), the lens is the lens, and the receptive area comprising most of the rear hemisphere of the eye is the retina (see Figure 4-1).

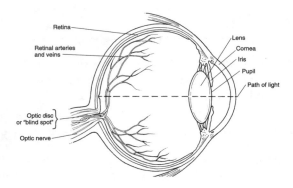

Figure 4-1. A cross section of the human eye. [Figure is from Baucum, D. (1999), Barron's *College Review Series: Psychology,* p. 62.]

- **The cornea**, in addition to protecting the interior of the eye, helps focus incoming light.
- **The iris** contracts and expands reflexively to control the amount of light entering through the **pupil**.
- **The lens** accommodates (changes its thickness) to further focus the image, at the same time reversing and inverting the projected image.
- **The retina** is where the image is projected and where visual sensation as such begins.

The retina is comprised of layers of neurons, the deepest being the **rods** and **cones**, which are the actual receptors—photochemical activity in the rods and cones generates neural impulses that produce vision. Their names derive from their shapes as seen under a powerful microscope. With complexity similar to that of the CNS, the rods and cones synapse with bipolar "relay" cells that in turn synapse with the ganglion cells of the optic nerve, which then proceeds out the rear of the eye eventually to the occipital lobe. There are also "horizontal" interneurons that synapse between rods and cones, providing a sort of cross-linking. Similar interneuron cross-linking occurs between ganglion cells. Otherwise, note that the **fovea** is an area near the center of the retina where images maximally project and where cones are the most densely packed. The "blind spot" is a nearby area where the ganglion cells converge into the optic nerve and the retina is insensitive to light.

- **There are 100 million or more rods**, distributed evenly throughout the retina except for the fovea. Rods are sensitive to light intensity (brightness), and are primarily responsible for black-and-white vision. At night, for example, rods are predominant and we see only in black-and-white and shades of gray. **Dark adaptation** occurs as rods undergo internal chemical changes that make them more sensitive to light and improve our night vision, noting that complete dark adaptation takes about 30 minutes.

- **There are 6 million or so cones**, packed densely in the fovea and found only sparsely throughout the rest of the retina. Compared to rods, cones have a much higher threshold for light, but cones can differentiate wavelengths and are therefore responsible for color vision. Different cones are more sensitive to different wavelengths, and three kinds of cones have been identified. Cones are also responsible for our ability to see fine detail. In good lighting, we automatically tend to position our eyes so that the image of an object of interest falls directly on the cone-packed fovea for the best clarity. In darkness, images are fuzzier because the cones are mostly inactive, although clarity improves a bit if we deliberately look slightly to the side of an object so the image doesn't fall directly on the fovea.

- **There are only about 1 million ganglion cells** to accommodate all the rods and cones (through bipolar cells), which indicates that considerable summation of neural impulses takes place at the ganglion synapses. Also note that there many instances in which a single cone synapses with a single ganglion cell, which may be related to the greater visual acuity the cones provide.

Visual mapping in the brain is divided between the left and right occipital lobes (and some other areas of the cortex) because of the optic chiasma.

- **The optic chiasma** is a point where each of the optic nerves merge and partially cross, with the effect that visual sensations from the right visual field (meaning the left half of each retina) are sent to the left occipital lobe. Vice versa for the left visual field, which projects into the right occipital lobe.

Visual impairment can occur at various stages. In **astigmatism**, the cornea is irregularly shaped and cannot adequately focus images. In **presbyopia**, associated with aging, the lenses stiffen and cannot accommodate well to distance. In **myopia** (nearsightedness), the eyeball is too long and the focal point of an image is ahead of the retina; in **hyperopia** (farsightedness) the eyeball is too short and the focal point is behind the retina. All of the above are correctable with one or another type of eyeglasses or contact lenses. Also note **cataracts**, in which the lens of the eye becomes clouded and fails to pass sufficient light, correctable by surgery; and **glaucoma**, an increase in fluid pressure within the eye that alters focus and can eventually destroy the retina unless corrected by medication.

Key 21 Visual perception

OVERVIEW *Visual perception involves cognitive processes that serve two basic functions: Identifying "what" objects are and localizing "where" objects are in the world around us.*

An understanding of visual perceptual processes begins with the work of the **Gestalt psychologists** in the early 20th century. Within their view that the whole is more than the sum of the parts, their research focused on how we organize the elements of visual sensation into percepts that often go beyond what we actually see. Principles or "rules" we use in forming percepts include figure-ground, closure, proximity, similarity, and continuity.

- **Percepts** are individual instances of perception.
- **Figure-ground** means that we see most objects as figures against some kind of background, i.e., as being distinct from the background. And some figure-ground relationships are "reversible," indicating the effects of expectations (mental set) on perception. A classic example that appears in most textbooks is a white vase on a black background, which can be seen either as a vase or as the outline of two faces in profile looking at each other against a white background.
- **Closure** is our perceptual tendency to see figures as complete even when portions are missing. For example, a cartoon character is perceived as a complete figure even if some of its line details are omitted.
- **Proximity** has to do with how we group objects perceptually. For example, if coins of one denomination are spaced evenly in a row, we tend to see one group of coins. But if the same coins are spaced so that the first two are close together, then separated from the next two, and so on, we tend to see several pairs of coins instead.
- **Similarity** also relates to perceptual grouping. If the coins are of different denominations and are grouped accordingly, we tend to see pennies, nickels, dimes, and so on, rather than one big group of coins.
- **Continuity or "good continuation"** can be illustrated by spacing coins of different denominations evenly in a row. The even arrangement inclines us to see the row as a whole, not the coins as different.

Research on how we perceive **depth and distance** is somewhat more recent. Normally, we use binocular cues and monocular cues simultaneously in localizing objects in the world around us.

- **Binocular cues** are based on information from both eyes. **Convergence** involves information about the muscular positioning of the eyes, wherein the brain distinguishes objects as near or far according to how much the eyes converge. **Retinal disparity** refers to the slightly different views of an object on each retina; the greater the difference, the closer the object is.

- **Monocular cues** mean that a person with only one functional eye can still perceive depth and distance. They also explain, for example, how we can observe a two-dimensional cartoon drawing and perceive depth and distance within it. Common monocular clues are: **Relative size**, by which—other things equal—a larger object is perceived as closer, a smaller object as farther away. With **interposition** or **superposition**, an object seems closer if it partially blocks the view of another object. With **height in field**, an object higher in a two-dimensional plane is seen as farther away. With **linear perspective**, two logically parallel lines converge at a point on the horizon, indicating distance. With **texture gradients**, a logically consistent pattern or texture becomes finer at a distance. And with **shading** or **shadowing**, an object gains depth if it's appropriately shaded around the edges or on the sides.

Perceiving motion, if the motion is real, basically involves progressive changes in images on the retina as an object moves across our visual field (plus, typically, changes in the positioning of the eyes). But we can also perceive motion where there is none, motion that's only "apparent." For example, displays such as theater, hotel, and casino marquees convey an optical illusion of motion by turning lights on and off in a carefully timed sequence that mimics the changes in images on the retina produced by an actual moving object.

Perceptual constancies are highly adaptive and essential to everyday functioning. We view objects under different lighting conditions, from different perspectives, and so on, in each case experiencing markedly different retinal images. Yet we see them as the same and unchanging, based primarily on our accumulated knowledge about what changes and what doesn't in the real world. Examples are brightness constancy, color constancy, shape constancy, and size constancy.

- **Brightness and color constancy** mean that even when the amount of illumination on an object changes, we do not perceive the object as changing in brightness or color. A white piece of paper is a white piece of paper regardless of the lighting present, and a red bicycle is a red bicycle in daylight or at dusk.

- **Shape constancy** can be illustrated by viewing a desk from differing angles. Even though the retinal images are quite different, we perceive the desk as rectangular regardless, because that's what we expect to see.
- **Size constancy** occurs when we move closer to or farther away from a familiar object. Close to a desk, for example, the retinal images are large; farther away, the retinal images are small. Yet the desk perceptually remains the same size.

Theories of color vision date to the 19th century and are still accepted today, with continuing refinements. Thomas Young and later Hermann von **Helmholtz** developed the Young-Helmholtz or trichromatic theory, which was eventually followed by Ewald **Herring's** opponent-color theory.

- **Trichromatic theory** notes that there are three different kinds of cones, each maximally sensitive to specific colors (blue, green/yellow, and red), which has been borne out by modern research. The experience of color, then, depends on different rates and combinations of the firing of these receptors, with the brain somehow interpreting the patterns of firing. All colors are possible because the color mixing is additive, as noted earlier. And color blindness is explained as a deficiency in the functioning of one or more kinds of cones.
- **Opponent-color theory** incorporates trichromatic theory at the receptor level, but goes on to propose that there are two systems— somewhere from the bipolar cells on—that operate in opponent fashion in determining the neural information that is passed along to the brain. There is a red-green system and a blue-yellow system, each of which assesses differences in the firing of the three kinds of cones and sends that information along to the brain. The theory is supported in part by higher neural systems that seem to respond in an opponent manner, and color blindness could involve a deficiency in the higher systems rather than in the cones.

Key 22 Hearing and auditory perception

OVERVIEW *Audition is second only to vision in its complexity, and the structures and functions of the ears have also been thoroughly researched.*

Sound waves are produced when objects move, vibrate, strike other objects, and so on. Molecules in the air are displaced, and the resulting cyclical air pressure changes are sound waves—described in terms of frequency, and measured in Hertz (Hz). Frequency is the primary determinant of pitch. In turn, the amplitude of the sound wave primarily determines loudness, measured in decibels (db).

- **Frequency** in Hertz means cycles per second, where one cycle consists of one expansion and compression of the air. Humans generally hear sounds in the range of 20 to 20,000 Hz, although individuals vary in sensitivity both at the extremes and at points within the range.

- **Amplitude** in decibels is a measure based on the psychophysical threshold for hearing, where 0 db is the absolute threshold for a frequency of 1000 Hz. From there, decibel increases correspond to geometric increases in sound pressure, so that, for example, a 20-db tone is 100 times stronger than a 1-db tone, and a 30-db tone is 1,000 times stronger than a 1-db tone. Also remember that the absolute thresholds for sounds vary considerably as a function of frequency, with the lowest bass sounds and the highest treble sounds having the highest thresholds. Thus, in music, bass and treble instruments must generate more air pressure if they are to blend with midrange sounds such as vocals.

In the human ear (see Figure 4-2), sound waves enter the **outer ear** (pinna) and are "funneled" through the **auditory canal** to the **eardrum** (tympanic membrane). Vibrations of the eardrum are picked up by the ossicles of the **middle ear**, which amplify and relay the vibrations to a membrane called the **oval window**. The oval window relays the vibrations to the fluid-filled **inner ear**, the cochlea, where transduction takes place. From there, the auditory nerve carries the impulses out to various locations in the brain, though mostly to the auditory projection areas in the temporal lobes.

- **The ossicles** are the **hammer** (malleus), **anvil** (incus), and **stirrup** (stapes), named for their shapes. The hammer picks up vibrations from the eardrum and transmits them mechanically to the anvil, which in turn transmits them to the stirrup.

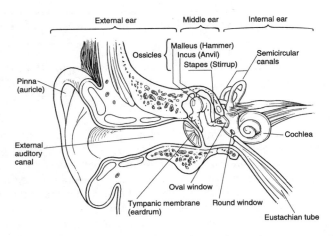

Figure 4-2. The human auditory apparatus. [Figure is from Baucum, D. (1999), Barron's *College Review Series: Psychology,* p. 70.]

- **The cochlea** is a coiled tube that consists of (1) the **vestibular canal**, which relays vibrations from the oval window and is also involved in bodily balance and equilibrium; (2) the **tympanic canal**, which balances sound wave pressures by vibrating the **round window** just below the oval window; (3) **the basilar membrane**, which ripples in response to vibrations; and (4) **the organ of Corti** on the basilar membrane, which contains thousands of tiny hairs that bend and sway and perform the transduction, generating impulses in the 30,000 or so neurons of the auditory nerve upon which they synapse.

Auditory impairment can result from damage or deterioration at any stage from the eardrum to the auditory nerve. **Conduction deafness** results from punctured eardrums or from fusion or other damage to the ossicles, with the effect that sounds do not reach the oval window with sufficient amplitude. Both can be repaired surgically, to an extent. **Sensory-neural loss,** as a result of aging or exposure to very loud sounds, can cause the basilar membrane to deteriorate or be damaged. Damage can also occur to the hairs of the organ of Corti. Hearing aids are the common solution, though in extreme cases a cochlear implant may be required. Damage to the auditory nerve, however, caused by disease, physical trauma, or birth defects, can result in complete deafness that can't be corrected.

Theories of audition explain reasonably well how the ear discriminates loudness, but have difficulty explaining how the ear discriminates pitch. Loudness appears to be straightforward: The more receptor hairs on the organ of Corti that are stimulated, the louder the sound. There are two differing theories of pitch, however: "place" theory and "frequency" theory, each of which explains some aspects of the process but not others.

- **Place theory** dates to **Helmholtz** in the 19th century and proposes that different areas of the basilar membrane are sensitive to different pitches. Surgical research by Georg von **Bekesy** in the 1940s bore this out to a major extent, at least for high-frequency and midrange sounds: Highs cause the area of the basilar membrane nearest the oval window to ripple the most, midranges an area farther along. However, differentially sensitive areas have not been observed for low-frequency sounds. And place theory also doesn't fare well in explaining the extremely fine sound discriminations we're normally capable of.

- **Frequency theory** dates to Ernest **Rutherford** in the 19th century. In this view, also supported by subsequent research, the frequency at which hairs of the organ of Corti send neural impulses to the brain matches the frequency of the sound. This works well for low-frequency sounds, but neurons cannot fire faster than about 1,000 times per second and therefore can't directly match midrange and higher sound frequencies. To address that problem, E. G. **Wever** in the 1940s proposed the **volley principle**, which is basically that neurons work together in sequential loops to achieve higher rates—by firing as a group. This explanation still doesn't work well for extremely high-frequency sounds, however, and so the eventual resolution of how we discriminate the 20 to 20,000 Hz range may involve a synthesis of place and frequency theory.

Localization of sounds, like loudness discrimination, appears to be straightforward. Any sound that isn't exactly in front of or behind the head affects the ears differently in two ways that the brain can use to determine the sound's location. One is **intensity**: A sound off to the left, for example, will be somewhat louder in the left ear. The other is **timing**: A sound off to the left will reach the left ear slightly (but perceptibly) sooner, noting that sound waves travel relatively slowly, especially in the lower frequencies. And if a sound is directly in front or behind and therefore confusing, we automatically turn our heads slightly to determine where the sound is coming from.

Key 23 Sensation and perception in the other senses

OVERVIEW *Smell, taste, and the skin senses, plus kines-thesis and equilibrium, have been less thoroughly researched but are nonetheless important to daily functioning and adaptation.*

The sense of smell (olfaction) is a chemical sense and is less developed in humans than in many other animals. But it is still very sensitive. Only a tiny fraction of the airborne molecules given off by something with an odor are necessary to stimulate the olfactory receptors located high in each nasal cavity, in an area known as the **olfactory epithelium**. From there, the neural impulses generated are sent directly to the **olfactory bulbs** and on to the central core of the brain. No widely accepted theory exists as to how the necessary water- or fat-soluble molecules are transduced into neural impulses, except to note that the millions of smell receptors seem to respond differen-tially to the "shape" of molecules that impinge upon them. Similarly, various attempts to catalog the many different smells we can perceive have not been very successful.

The sense of taste (gustation) is also a chemical sense, the necessary stimuli being substances that are soluble in saliva. The receptors for taste are sensory neurons located in the 10,000 or so taste buds mostly in the surface of the tongue. As with smell, neural impulses from these receptors are sent primarily to the central core.
- **Taste buds**, however they work, are organized so that different areas of the tongue are maximally sensitive to four basic tastes: "Sweet" is detected mostly on the tip of the tongue, "salty" on each side of the tip, "sour" farther back on the sides, and "bitter" across the rear.

The experience of "flavor" involves a complex interplay between smell and taste that's also not well understood. Both senses are nec-essary, however, for us to perceive the many different flavors we're capable of. And both senses tend to decline as we age, which explains why older people sometimes complain of lack of tastiness in foods and may use more salt and spices to compensate.

The skin senses include receptors for pressure (touch), temperature, and pain, most of which lie just below the outer surface of the skin. These receptors vary in physical shape and structure, and are maximally sensitive to different types of stimulation, but overall experiences of touch, temperature, and pain involve complex combinations of these receptors rather than simple one-to-one correspondence. Neural impulses from skin receptors are sent more or less directly to the cerebral cortex, noting that the most sensitive areas of the body are correspondingly mapped the most extensively in the cerebral cortex (Key 16).

- **Touch sensors** respond to mechanical pressure and distension of the skin, whether major or minute.
- **Temperature sensors** subdivide into those that respond to "cold" and those that respond to "warm."
- **Pain sensors** also subdivide into several types, but the experience of pain can occur when any skin receptors are stressed to the point of damage. And individuals vary widely with regard to thresholds for pain as well as the ability to tolerate pain, indicating that the experience of pain is under higher cortical control (meaning cognitive control) to a major extent.

Kinesthesis involves receptors throughout the body, mostly in the muscles, tendons, and joints, that provide information to the CNS about what the body is doing—especially with regard to motion of specific parts of the body. Kinesthesis, for example, allows us to move our arms and legs without having to look to see what they're doing.

Equilibrium (balance) is a vestibular sense, providing information to the CNS about the body's position and orientation and overall motion. Receptors for equilibrium are within and around the semicircular canals of the inner ear.

- **The semicircular canals** are fluid-filled chambers that connect just above the oval window and cochlea, and movement of the fluids stimulates cilia that in turn connect to sensory neurons.

Theme 5 DEVELOPMENTAL PSYCHOLOGY

Developmental psychology is primarily concerned with *change*. Developmental psychologists study how heredity and environment interact to produce change from conception on, literally throughout the human life span. And though theorists and researchers tend to focus on specific aspects of physical, cognitive, and personality development, the overall goal of developmental psychology is to understand the "whole" person. That makes developmental psychology an extremely broad discipline.

Theme 5 begins with an overview of life span developmental psychology and then emphasizes infancy and childhood, where developmental psychologists have done the most work. Bear in mind, however, that many topics important to understanding human development appear in other Themes instead, in keeping with traditional ways of organizing subject matter of such breadth. Such topics are noted along the way.

INDIVIDUAL KEYS IN THIS THEME

Key 24 Life span developmental psychology

OVERVIEW *Human development throughout the life span is a fairly orderly process, even though individuals vary widely in the ages at which they progress through stages and reach developmental milestones, and even though the stages and milestones are often not easy to specify and pinpoint.*

Milestones are markers for talking about where a person is developmentally. Birth is an obvious milestone that begins, say, with labor and ends when the umbilical cord is separated. But the many subtler milestones developmental psychologists and parents alike talk about, such as "first words," "first steps," and down the line, "puberty," aren't always so clear-cut. Thus, thinking in terms of milestones is always approximate.

That leads to a discussion of **stages**, which can be generally defined as when specific aspects of development—both physical and psychological—are prominent, and during which specific kinds of experiences tend to occur. Theorists such as Piaget and Erikson (discussed later in this Theme), and also Freud (Key 57) delineate such stages.
  - **Conceptually**, stages can be useful in describing development, in the sense that they give us a way of summarizing what a person is *likely* to be thinking and experiencing at a given point in time.
  - **In practical terms**, however, it's good to bear in mind that development is usually not as neat as the theories imply. In child cognitive development, for example, children are often in two (or more) stages at the same time with regard to how they think and reason. In other words, stages are not "discrete," which means that children generally don't pass smoothly and suddenly from one stage to the next. Instead, they often move back and forth and straddle stages.

A related issue has to do with critical and sensitive periods during development, especially with regard to acquiring skills. The idea of important periods in child development is a long-standing issue in educational psychology, but also derives in part from the work of the ethologists.
  - **Critical periods**, by definition, apply to skills and behaviors that must be acquired during a certain period or they won't be acquired

at all. **Visual perception** is one of many possible examples: Based on experiments with animals (and historically, research on children born with cataracts that could not be removed until adolescence or adulthood), it appears that even fairly simple perceptual skills such as distinguishing circles from squares depend critically upon experience during early life. **Learning a second language** is another example: People who do not acquire a second language prior to adolescence can still become thoroughly fluent, but they will probably never sound like a native speaker of that language. A third and extremely important example is **intelligence**: Children who are severely intellectually deprived during the early months and years of life are unlikely ever to catch up, even when they participate in quality accelerated learning programs (Key 56).

- **Sensitive periods** apply to skills and behaviors that can be acquired most efficiently during a certain age range, but which can also be acquired later. **Motor skills** generally fall in this category. For example, children who are deprived of the opportunity to practice skills leading up to walking during the first year may later require some time to catch up, but they do catch up and walk normally. And there may be aspects of personality that involve sensitive periods, in that they are more easily acquired (or changed) at one time than at another. Morality is a likely candidate.
- **Ethology** is the study of biological determinants of behavior in the natural environment (Key 45). Relevant here is the phenomenon of **imprinting**, which illustrates the existence of critical periods for animals such as geese. There is a critical period during a gosling's first day of life when it becomes bonded to its mother (or some other moving object, as in ethological experiments). The gosling does not imprint before or after that brief period, and once imprinted, the bond is permanent. Note, however, that *human* attachment is not nearly so simple, depending instead on complex interactions between child and caregivers throughout infancy and beyond.

Stages, then, are approximations that refer to the kinds of physical and psychological development taking place. **Periods**, in contrast, refer more to typical age ranges used in describing development. Also note that developmental periods in part relate to the society and culture the child grows up in, as in the overview of the human life span that follows.

A human life potentially begins at **conception**, when sperm and ovum unite. The next nine months or so comprise the **prenatal period**, which is sometimes broken down into trimesters but more often into the **zygotic**, **embryonic**, and **fetal stages** (Key 26).

- **The three trimesters** are periods, not stages.

The period of infancy begins at birth and consists of the next 12 to 24 months, depending upon whom you read. Newborn infants are also called *neonates*.
- **The term "infant"** derives from French for "incapable of language," which is not exactly the case (Key 51).
- **The neonatal period** refers roughly to the first two or three weeks after birth.

Toddlerhood is next after infancy, from when the child starts walking up to about 24 months. Toddlers toddle mainly because they're top-heavy, in keeping with both the cephalocaudal and proximodistal growth trends. There is also a general-to-specific growth trend.
- **The cephalocaudal growth trend** (meaning "head" to "tail") actually begins soon after conception: The upper part of the body develops earlier.
- **The proximodistal growth trend** (meaning "close" to "distant") also begins early: The inner part of the body, such as the trunk, develops earlier than the arms and legs.
- **The general-to-specific growth trend** is that, for example, gross motor control develops before fine motor control. An infant can reach out and touch an object before being able to grasp it, and in turn grasp it before being able to manipulate it.

The preschool period, in American society, refers to the age range from about 24 months to 6 years, at which point the child enters elementary school.
- Whether a child in kindergarten is still a "preschooler" is debatable; take your pick.

Middle childhood covers the age range from about six years to puberty. Cultures vary widely, however, in the extent to which children in this age range are treated as children versus being given adult responsibilities. In American society, which is relatively "child-centered" now, many children historically dropped out of school and went to work in this age range—prior to the advent of child labor laws.

Adolescence is marked by attaining puberty, on average by about age 12 to 13 years for girls and by age 14 to 15 years for boys—though in each case with wide variability as to when the adolescent growth spurt and then sexual maturation begin and are completed.
- **The adolescent growth spurt** begins first, triggered by hormone changes, and rapid growth typically lasts about three years.
- **Sexual maturation** lags somewhat and is complete after about two years.

Definitions of **young adulthood** and **adulthood** vary, beginning perhaps with graduating high school or reaching the legal voting age of 18 in American society, then continuing to anywhere from age 30 to age 45, depending upon whom you read.

- **Adulthood** in some societies begins as early as puberty. And in many societies, adulthood is defined more in keeping with where the person is in terms of self-sufficiency, marriage, and the like rather than in terms of age.

Middle adulthood is roughly 40 to 65, again with no clear consensus except that the period perhaps ends with traditional retirement, at least in American society.

Older or later adulthood, for lack of a better term, is then logically from 65 or so on. The preferred term is probably **older adult**, noting that terms like "old folks" and "the elderly" and "seniors" tend to be associated with frailty or dementia stereotypes that by no means apply to all people in this age range. Many older adults retain their capabilities and vitality on into their "advanced" years.

Key 25 Heredity and environment in interaction

OVERVIEW *The heredity-environment issue has various names and still generates controversy, though theorists nowadays tend to look at heredity and environment in interaction.*

Nature versus nurture is another way of talking about heredity and environment, and the issue has been with us a long time (Key 2). Locke proposed that we are born tabulae rasae, or blank slates, indicating that who we are and what we know is all a result of nurture. J. B. **Watson** later agreed, and went on to make statements to the effect that, given complete control of a child's environment, he could turn that child into just about any kind of person he wished—for better or for worse. On the other side, **Rousseau**, back in the 18th century, strongly favored nature—as have many others since, though typically with regard to specific aspects of development and typically not with Rousseau's intensity. Most of early language development, for example, is now widely accepted as being based on inborn biological mechanisms (Key 51). But controversies do continue. With regard to intelligence, some still argue that as much as 80% of what determines our intellectual potential is genetically based and in turn related to race—conclusions most psychologists intensely reject (Key 56).

Maturation versus learning is yet another way of putting things. Biological maturation, for example, is based on heredity—assuming adequate nutrition and ruling out untreated diseases along the way. From conception on, all normal human children undergo physical development and changes that eventually result in an adult organism, and the process is governed by genetic codes. By contrast, learning is based on the myriad experiences children have along the way, beginning at birth and perhaps even before that. And, as with nature and nurture, there are still those who argue that one or the other is more important to various aspects of development.

Nowadays, however, the trend is to study how heredity and environment *interact* to determine development, rather than focus on "how much" of each is involved. For example, early motor development that leads up to being able to walk obviously depends on maturation of the necessary musculature and such—as a result of nature. But walking also depends on the opportunity to firm up those muscles and practice balance and coordination—in other words, nurture. Thus, nature and nurture are both essential to learning to walk, and when viewed this way, the question of how much each contributes seems much less important.

Psychological characteristics also are determined by heredity and environment in interaction, and the primary questions involve how that interplay works—especially with regard to what can be done to enhance development in areas such as intelligence and personality. It may be the case, for example, that heredity determines a range within which an individual's intellectual abilities will fall, but that range is normally broad and the individual's abilities are profoundly affected by environment. And it clearly is the case that infants are born with differing temperaments, but an individual's eventual personality is likewise determined by interactions between that individual and significant others all along the way.

- **Temperament** refers to general characteristics such as cuddliness, irritability, responsiveness to others, and activity level, all of which can dynamically affect personality.
- **Significant others** include parents, peers, teachers, and anyone else who is important in a person's life.

Key 26 Prenatal development

OVERVIEW *Development from conception to birth occurs in identifiable stages, leading up to the appearance of a newborn infant who already possesses many adaptive skills and behaviors.*

Conception occurs when a sperm cell penetrates the ovum, typically in the upper fallopian tube near the ovary. Each gamete's 23 chromosomes unite, producing the normal human complement of 46, and thereby creating a **zygote**. The zygote then begins its journey to the mother's uterus, growing all the way through cell division. This **zygotic** or **germinal** stage lasts from one to two weeks.
- **The fallopian tubes** are passageways from each ovary to the uterus, and ovaries tend to alternate in releasing ova. If an ovum is not fertilized, it continues down to the uterus and is discharged during menstruation.

Implantation in the uterus marks the beginning of the **embryonic stage**.
- In **implantation**, the tiny **zygote** "burrows" into the blood vessels of the uterine wall and attaches itself. Only about one out of four zygotes implants successfully. Some don't implant at all, others implant improperly and later "spontaneously" abort.
- **Very soon after implantation**, what is now called the **embryo** begins to secrete a hormone that cancels the mother's menstrual cycles and triggers the other changes in her body associated with pregnancy. This hormone is the basis for early home pregnancy tests.

During the embryonic stage, the outer cells differentiate into the amniotic sac, the umbilical cord, and the placenta. The inner cells differentiate into the embryo proper, and recognizable internal organs and external body features begin to appear. By the end of the eight weeks of the embryonic stage, the developing child is about an inch long and is recognizable as being humanoid.
- **The amniotic sac** fills with fluid to cushion and protect the embryo.
- **The umbilical cord** soon begins to nourish the embryo from the mother's blood stream.
- **The placenta** is a semipermeable membrane that "filters" the flow through the umbilical cord, acting as a partial barrier. Incoming oxygen and nutrients and outgoing carbon dioxide and wastes pass through the placenta. Blood cells are too large and cannot.

Teratogens, such as drugs and other chemicals, and viruses, can pass the placental barrier and harm the developing child at any time during the remainder of the prenatal period, but they are by far the most dangerous during the embryonic stage. Major abnormalities of body parts and especially the central nervous system can occur, *perhaps before the mother even knows she is pregnant.*

- **Rubella** (German measles) is a relatively minor virus in adults, but it can cause blindness, deafness, and mental retardation in the developing child.
- **AIDS**, though also viral, apparently does not get transmitted to the developing child during the embryonic stage; instead, it is thought to be transmitted by exposure to the mother's blood and other fluids during childbirth. Sexually transmitted diseases such as **syphilis** and **gonorrhea** work the same way.
- **Alcohol** can pass the placental barrier, causing **fetal alcohol syndrome**, which can include gross physical malformations and mental retardation. Other drugs such as **narcotics, cocaine, tranquilizers**, and just about anything else psychoactive can also cause permanent physical and psychological damage to the child.

The fetal stage is designated somewhat arbitrarily as beginning at the two-month point of pregnancy, comprising the remaining seven months of the prenatal period. The **fetus** continues to develop and differentiate, attains viability, and eventually reaches the typical six to eight pounds newborn infants weigh. Selected notes follow.

- **Sexual characteristics** are discernible early in the fetal stage, and the fetus already has immature ova or sperm.
- Techniques such as **ultrasound** and **amniocentesis**, to assess normality of the child, are possible from about the fourth month of pregnancy on. Ultrasound involves a harmless scanning of the fetus for physical features. Amniocentesis involves extracting discarded fetal cells from the amniotic sac, making genetic assessment possible. Many genetic disorders (Key 18) are detectable through this procedure and others that yield fetal cells.
- The **age of viability**, meaning the age at which the child has a good chance of surviving outside the womb, is reached around the 24th week of pregnancy. That's why the maximum time limit for voluntary abortion is set there or earlier.
- **Premature babies** are at risk and can require special life support, but do not necessarily experience long-term difficulties in physical or psychological development.

Key 27 Development during infancy and early childhood

OVERVIEW *Newborn infants don't know much, but they possess an array of capabilities that set the stage for the rapid learning that takes place during the first several years of life.*

Neonates display many reflexes, some of which are immediately important to survival. Others—the "primitive" reflexes—are thought to have been important at some distant time in our evolutionary history. Checking for survival and primitive reflexes, in conjunction with other observations, provides information about whether the infant is neurologically normal—at birth, and also down the line.

- **Survival reflexes** include **breathing, sucking,** and **swallowing,** plus **rooting,** in which the neonate turns its head in the direction of a touch on the cheek. Such reflexes soon come under voluntary control.

- **Primitive reflexes** tend to disappear over the first year, and their disappearance is an indication of normalcy. The **Moro reflex** is triggered by a loud noise or sudden change in body position: The neonate quickly extends the arms sideways and brings them back in, as if trying to grab onto something. The **Babinski reflex,** whatever its evolutionary importance was, involves spreading and then curling the toes when the bottom of the foot is stimulated.

Sensory-perceptual capabilities of newborns are quite extensive, contrary to what was once thought. A common technique for studying such capabilities is the **habituation method:** For example, a tone of a given frequency is presented until the infant gets bored with it and "habituates"; then, if the tone is changed slightly and the infant appears interested again, it's clear that the infant can discriminate the difference between the tones. As another example, to assess infant "preferences," researchers use a special nipple connected to lab equipment that measures rate of sucking and also causes things to happen. The infant might get to see one stimulus when sucking at a low rate, another stimulus when sucking at a high rate. Variations on such techniques indicate the following capabilities:

- Neonates can distinguish **human voices** from other sounds, and tend to prefer them.

- Neonates can distinguish **higher-pitched female voices** from lower-pitched male voices, and tend to prefer them. Newborns can also quickly learn to tell the difference between mother's voice and that of another woman, and they prefer mother.
- Neonates prefer looking at **human faces** rather than other objects, apparently because of features such as curvature, contrast, and movement. Newborns look mostly at the edges and outlines of faces, however, and don't look much at interior features until they are about two months old. That, plus the limited visual acuity neonates display, means the infant probably won't be able to recognize people's faces until about two months of age.
- **Smell and taste** discrimination are also present at or very soon after birth. For example, given exposure (as in breast-feeding), neonates can readily distinguish mother's milk from that of another woman.

From there, research and theory tend to focus on one or another specific area of development. Early **motor development** is discussed later in this Key. **Cognitive development** and **social/personality** development are discussed in the next two Keys, and **language development** is discussed in Key 51.

The subject of **developmental norms**, however, applies to all areas of development and should be considered at this point. Much research in the early days of developmental psychology focused on "norms," with the goal of providing scales by which infant and early childhood progress could be assessed. Such norms were developed in great detail and involved highly specific behaviors, based on averages taken from large numbers of children. And the norms were widely published in popular media, at times misleading parents into believing that their children were abnormal.

- **Simple examples of developmental norms** are, as most people know, that children *on average* utter their first meaningful words and also take their first unsupported steps at about 12 months of age. Finer analyses indicate an orderly sequence of vocalizations leading up to those first words, and similarly, an orderly sequence of motor behaviors leading up to those first faltering steps.
- **The problem**, however, is the "on average" part: *Perfectly normal children vary widely in the ages at which they display specific skills and behaviors.* In other words, your child is not necessarily at all abnormal if your child doesn't talk much until long after the 12-month "milestone" has been passed. (Actually, you might consider yourself fortunate for such a reprieve; in the author's experience, once they start talking, they never shut up.) Neither is your child necessarily precocious, for that matter, if your child starts talking before that.

Motor development begins in the crib with gross movements of the body and limbs, and eventually, finer movements of the hands and fingers as the infant attempts to reach for and grasp objects, move around, vocalize, and so on (as a result of the interaction of the cephalocaudal, proximodistal, and general-to-specific growth trends as discussed in Key 28). For example, with regard to motor development leading up to walking (and assuming the opportunity to practice), the following sequence of behaviors is orderly and typical:

- By age four months or so (as always, with wide variation in the timing), **the infant begins to prop up and support the body** from time to time.
- By about six months (or a good bit more), the infant can **sit without support** and also can pull up and **stand while holding onto objects** such as furniture.
- In the range from seven to twelve months, the infant **crawls** (belly on floor), then **creeps** (belly not touching floor). **Scooting** comes next, which means creeping in haste.
- Toward the end of that range, the infant **stands without support** and, soon after, **walks without support**.
- And now the infant is a **toddler**, walking at first, and then running and capable of getting at potentially anything in the home that looks interesting.

Key 28 Piaget's theory of cognitive development

OVERVIEW *Many theorists and researchers have been involved in describing how children acquire and refine their thinking and reasoning, but Piaget's theory is by far the richest.*

Jean **Piaget** was a Swiss psychologist who began by presenting his three young children with situations to observe and problems to solve. He was interested more in their "wrong" observations and answers than in their "correct" ones, believing that their errors gave him more insight into their thinking. From there, he built an elaborate and complex **cognitive-developmental** theory around the basic idea that children—in stages—think in ways quite different from the ways adults think. As the years went by, his work and writings attracted adherents worldwide, eventually fostering institutes for studying and working with children, and in turn leading to teaching techniques based on his theory. Cognitive-developmental theory has also been extended, for example, to areas such as moral reasoning and the development of a sense of self.

- **Development of moral reasoning** is an area studied initially by Piaget but then pursued in greater detail by Lawrence **Kohlberg** and others. On the basis of responses to "moral dilemmas" presented in the form of stories, Kohlberg distinguished stages of the development of moral reasoning that appear to be universal across cultures—for least for males. There are six such stages, grouped into three levels: **preconventional**, **conventional**, and **postconventional morality**. Across the stages, two related trends emerge. (1) Morality starts out based on *concrete* consequences of behavior, such as rewards and punishments—that which is rewarded is "good," that which is punished is "bad." In progressively higher stages, however, what is good becomes considerably more *abstract* and generalized, without nearly so much regard to consequences. (2) Morality is initially based on *external* considerations, again such as rewards and punishments. In higher stages, however, it becomes progressively more *internal* in the sense that the person now evaluates good and bad according to ethical principles. And, notably, not everyone reaches the higher stages. Also, as has been pointed out by Carol **Gilligan** and others, Kohlberg's theory was derived from research on males only and focuses on a "morality of justice." Instead, it is possible that traditional childrearing practices, which are based on females being more nurturant, give them a different sense of morality, one based on "caring."

- **Development of a sense of self** includes, among other things, acquiring a sense of **gender identity**. Kohlberg, again, found that children younger than about five years of age don't fully realize that gender is permanent and unchanging. **Gender constancy** is when they later do.

Basic assumptions in Piaget's theory of cognitive development (and related theories) are:

- **Children are active thinkers**, inherently motivated to learn and understand. Education based on Piaget's theory emphasizes presenting the child with appropriate situations and tasks, then letting the child figure things out.
- There are **qualitative differences** in the ways children perceive and understand the world around them—compared to how adults do. These are discussed below, in the context of Piaget's proposed stages.
- **Knowledge** is intricately organized in **schemas** (or **schemata**), which can be understood as units of understanding ranging from tiny and specific to broad and extremely elaborate. A schema is a **cognitive** structure (*not* a physical structure in the brain). For example, a general schema might include the important features of "car," by which we understand all kinds of cars and how they work and what they do. A more specific schema within that might be one for Porsche, enabling us to differentiate that brand from others. Still more specific schemas within "car" would include myriad bits of understanding about engines, gasoline, wheels, motion itself, and on and on, most of which had to be acquired prior to acquiring a general schema for car.
- All learning is a blend of **assimilation**, in which the person understands objects and events in accord with prior learning, and **accommodation**, in which objects and events produce new learning. That's how schemas are acquired and elaborated. In other words, respectively, we routinely try to understand what's going on in the present tense by thinking about what we've seen before, and when we can't, we develop new understanding. If we encounter a four-wheeled car that fits our existing schema, we assimilate it. But if we encounter a three-wheeled car for the first time, accommodation occurs and the schema is extended.

Highlights of Piaget's proposed stages of cognitive development are as follows, also noting that each stage is built upon what went before.

The sensorimotor stage lasts from birth to about two years. The infant interacts with the world at first using reflexes, then using simple voluntary behaviors such as reaching and touching objects, all the while forming schemata about how the world works: Things move, things fall, things fly away. As the stage progresses and the infant's motor capabilities become more extensive, more and more exploration and learning take place. "Object permanence" appears during the first year, as does a beginning understanding of self versus other people. And by the end of the stage, the child is beginning to develop "mental" schemas. Egocentrism, however, still dominates the child's thinking.

- **Object permanence** is an understanding that things still exist even though they're out of sight. Piaget performed many small experiments with his children in which an interesting object is removed from view, and placed the realization of object permanence at about eight months of age. Researchers since place it much earlier.

- **Mental schemas** allow the child to understand things by *thinking* about them, as opposed to actually having to *do* them.

- **Egocentrism** is the child's tendency to see things only from his or her own perspective—not the perspective of others. It's as if the child is the center of the universe.

The preoperational stage lasts from two to six or seven years. Thinking becomes more symbolic and more language-based, but the child's understanding of things remains very limited to appearances—the child lacks mental abilities involved in what Piaget called "conservation." Egocentrism begins to wane toward the end of the stage.

- **Conservation** marks the end of the preoperational stage and the beginning of the concrete operations stage, discussed next: A classic test is called the "liquid/beakers" problem, in which the child watches while a liquid is poured from a short, fat beaker into a tall, thin one. Children who lack conservation tend to say that the tall beaker has more liquid, even though none was added or taken away. One source of this error is attending only to one dimension, such as the height of the beaker. Another is that the children lack **reversibility** in their thinking, meaning they don't realize that the liquid could be poured back into the short beaker and therefore must be the same.

The concrete operations stage is from age six or seven to age 11 or 12, marked at its beginning by acquisition of conservation abilities. Thought and problem solving are still "concrete," however, in that the child can only think about things that are real and observable, or at least mentally imaginable as such—the child still lacks the ability to deal with abstractions. And the child doesn't use systematic deduction or organized plans of attack, instead tending to try to figure things out by rote or by simple trial and error.

The formal operations stage is from age 11 or 12 on, marked by the beginnings of truly abstract thinking. A classic experiment here involves having the child experiment and systematically figure out that the frequency at which a pendulum swings depends only on its length, not on the weight at its bottom or the height from which it's dropped. Formal operations also include capability for thinking about higher, purely abstract mathematical operations, and for that matter, thinking about thinking itself. Note that not all children (or adults) attain the formal operations stage.

Piaget's theory is not without its critics, especially with regard to the **age ranges** he proposed for the child's acquisition of specific skills and knowledge. Not only do children vary widely, it also appears that children begin the successive stages earlier than Piaget proposed. And, as discussed in Key 24, some question whether "stages" are meaningful in the first place. But the basic **order** in which children develop cognitive abilities, as well as the kinds of skills that must be acquired along the road to adult thinking, hold up reasonably well.

Key 29 Erikson's psychosocial theory

OVERVIEW *Erikson's life span theory is the most compre-hensive to date, and is consistent with research on the impor-tance of early attachment and other social interactions.*

Erik Erikson was a student and then colleague of Freud, and Erikson's life span theory of personality development grew out of Freud's psy-choanalytic theory (Key 57). In contrast with Freud, however, Erik-son emphasized specific kinds of **social** interactions and experiences as primary in personality development. Erikson also viewed humans as essentially rational, conscious creatures who actively try to figure things out and therefore contribute to their own developmental progress—much like Piaget said. Freud instead built his theory on unconscious impulses and conflicts from within, with a basic view that we are passively at their mercy, and Freud believed personality to be more or less permanently determined by middle childhood. Erikson instead saw personality continuing to change and develop throughout the life span in accord with change in the social world around us. Erikson did not contradict Freud on major points, but Erikson's emphases are so different that his **eight psychosocial stages** (Table 5-1) constitute a major theory in its own right.

In **Erikson's theory**, each "age" or stage involves a **life crisis** to be resolved one way or the other over an extended period of time— adaptively or maladaptively. And each stage is built upon what went before, with the effect that a maladaptive resolution at one stage interferes with others down the line. It's especially important, in other words, to get off to a good start.
  - **Basic trust versus mistrust** is the first crisis to be dealt with and occurs during infancy, i.e., **birth to one** year of age. Based mainly on the quality of caregiving the child experiences, because care-givers constitute most of an infant's social world, the child devel-ops a general sense of the world either as a safe, welcoming place or as a place fraught with danger and neglect. Research by Mary **Ainsworth** and colleagues is especially relevant here (see also Key 56). Infants who receive **responsive caregiving** during the first year or so of life, meaning that their caregivers always attend to their physical and psychological needs promptly and effectively, develop **secure attachment** and display behaviors quite consistent with the idea that they view the world as a safe place. Down the line, such children are also more likely to display the autonomy and

Table 5-1. Erikson's eight psychosocial stages.

Stage	Age Range (years)
Basic trust versus mistrust	birth to 1
Autonomy versus shame and doubt	1 to 3
Initiative versus guilt	3 to 6
Industry versus inferiority	6 to 12
Identity versus role confusion	12 to 20
Intimacy versus isolation	20 to 40
Generativity versus stagnation	40 to 65
Ego integrity versus despair	beyond 65

relative independence Erikson talks about next, and more likely to be curious and exploring. **Insecure attachment**, which results from starting "independence training" too early, is associated with infants who are afraid of or unresponsive to others and who later display much less curiosity and willingness to explore.

- **Autonomy versus shame and doubt** is next, from about **one to three** years of age. Now the life crisis centers on the child acquiring a beginning sense of independence and self-reliance, as in activities such as dressing, eating, and toileting. The caregivers are prominent in encouraging a good resolution, as are preschool teachers and others the child may be exposed to. Note that a child who wound up with a basic sense of mistrust during infancy might now have a much harder time venturing into self-reliance (just as an insecurely attached child might now be fearful and anxious in doing so).
- **Initiative versus guilt** occurs in the age range from **three to about six** years. The crisis now involves the child's need to start making choices and displaying initiative and achieving short-term goals, though at the same time not infringing on the rights of others and getting punished and experiencing guilt. A good prerequisite, of course, is a basic sense of autonomy from the previous stage. But now the child's expanding autonomy must be tempered to fit the child's social world of parents and teachers and siblings and friends.
- **Industry versus inferiority**, ages **6 to 12** years, takes initiative and the like to a higher plane. Now the child is much more

involved in the world of teachers and friends, and now the child has larger projects to complete and longer-term goals to attain. Children are also spending more time competing and comparing themselves to peers, especially in terms of skills and abilities. And those who resolve the crisis well, again with the help of the social world around them, develop a good sense of self and self-confidence. For those who don't, the result is a tendency to feel inferior and to back away from challenges.

- **Identity versus role confusion**, characteristic of adolescence and therefore the range from about **12 to 20** years of age, involves a shift to issues of "Who am I?" and "Where am I going?" and the like. Consistent with his own life, Erikson placed major emphasis on exploration of self and sudden transitions in attitudes that adolescents often experience as they try to integrate a single, coherent personality with tangible life goals. And he saw adolescence as an extremely stressful time for most, proposing substages such as **moratorium** during which adolescents get tired of trying to figure it all out and take a break. As it happens, however, most adolescents don't experience the chaotic and rebellious extremes Erikson proposed.

- **Intimacy versus isolation** follows, corresponding to young adulthood, from about **20 to 40** years of age. In addition to the forming of close friendships, the crisis now focuses on achievement of marital intimacy and companionship. The alternative to intimacy is a sense of estrangement and isolation from others in general.

- **Generativity versus stagnation** characterizes middle adulthood, say from **40 to 65**. Generativity applies both to achieving a productive work life and successfully rearing children and taking care of family, the alternative being a chronic lack of purpose and a sense of pointlessness in life.

- **Ego integrity versus despair** is the final stage, applicable to life **after 65**. During this period, older adults tend to reflect back on life and assess whether it was meaningful and worthwhile. Again, resolution of the crisis depends primarily upon what went before, such as having achieved a good sense of intimacy and then generativity. The alternative is to spend the last of one's years with a sense of despair and a sense of having missed something in life.

Theme 6 MOTIVATION AND EMOTION

*M*otivation is the "why" of behavior, whether from moment to moment, from day to day, or over much longer periods. Motives are reasons why behavior occurs, and issues involving motives are implicit in virtually any discussion of an organism's behavior. Motivation in one form or another therefore crops up in most Themes.

Emotion is a closely related topic. Like some motives, emotions include both physical and mental components—we both "feel" and "think," though not necessarily in that order. And motives and emotions often augment each other in directing and determining behavior.

Theme 6 covers basic, "built-in" motives related to maintaining normal bodily functioning, surviving, and reproducing, plus selected problems and disorders related to basic motives. Popular theories of emotion are covered similarly, including selected disorders not discussed elsewhere.

Key 30 Primary and secondary motives

OVERVIEW *Primary, basic motives are biological in origin and common to all normal members of a species. Secondary motives are instead learned.*

Primary motives involve biological needs in the ongoing maintenance and normal functioning of our bodies. We need air, we need to maintain viable body temperature, we need liquids, we need food, and, in a sense, we need sex. These and other basic needs give rise to motives.

- **Needs** are physiological states of depletion, momentary or otherwise. The body is low on oxygen, water, nutrients, or whatever.
- **Motives** are a more cognitive way of looking at things: A need for oxygen produces the behavior to obtain it, and the organism is also consciously aware and planning and otherwise acting deliberately to obtain a goal of getting more oxygen, and fast. Motives arising from primary needs also tend to involve negative emotional states such as being uncomfortable, or at the extreme, being in pain.

Primary motives tend to be **homeostatic** (Key 14), at various levels, whether conscious or not. For example, if the summer sun causes body temperature to increase above normal, our temperature sensors kick in, send information to the hypothalamus and CNS, and cause us to perspire without our conscious intent. But perspiration is limited in its ability to cool the body adequately, so the next step in the process might be consciously seeking shade or some other cool place. Thus, the term homeostatic applies to any level of activity that is involved in the organism's attempts to maintain normal limits.

- **Also note**, however, that when homeostatic mechanisms involve conscious activity, the organism may choose *not* to react. If you're determined to get a lot of sun, you might force yourself to stay out in the sun and perspire uncomfortably for hours without doing much about it. Another example is fasting: In the extreme, people can refuse to eat even to the point of death.

Sex is a special case: Though a primary motive in the sense that it is biologically built-in and tends to press for release and satisfaction, an individual's sexual activity is not directly related to needs—contrary to what some of your friends might say. But as the ethologists and others would point out, sex is clearly essential to the survival of societies and overall species, and can therefore be viewed as homeostatic in a much broader sense: If a society's conception rate drops off too drastically, the society can die out.

Secondary motives are those that are **learned**, either through association with primary motives or in more complex "social" ways. Wanting money is a standard example of the former. Aggression and achievement motivation are likely examples of the latter.

- **Money** does not directly satisfy any physiological needs—you won't get much fulfillment from eating it. But even very young children, for example, understand how money can be exchanged for candy and ice cream and a host of better foods that do satisfy needs. So money gets associated with such things. And the pursuit of money can even become an "autonomous" motive, meaning that people come to pursue wealth well beyond what's necessary to satisfy their physiological needs.

- **Aggression** is usually classified as a learned motive, or more accurately, a complex set of learned motives and behaviors. Though Freud argued that aggression is a primary human motive (Key 57), as have others, the prevailing view is that aggression is a function of social interactions and observational learning beginning in childhood (Key 81).

- **Achievement motivation (*n* Ach)**, the ongoing personality trait of wanting to achieve for its own sake and perhaps for the satisfactions that ensue, also appears to be learned—through encouragement by parents and teachers and through success experiences along the way.

Key 31 Hunger, obesity, and eating disorders

OVERVIEW *The experience of hunger involves basic physiological sensors, but what determines when and how much we eat is distinctly cognitive and emotional as well.*

The physiological basis of hunger involves three sensing mechanisms, each of which monitors nutrient intake and levels and passes information along to the CNS through the hypothalamus. (1) The satiety sensors monitor food and nutrient presence throughout the digestive system; (2) the glucostatic system monitors blood sugar levels essential to brain functioning; and (3) the lipostatic system monitors fats and amino acids stored in fat cells.

- **Satiety sensors** are located in the mouth, throat, stomach, and elsewhere in the digestive system, and are the first sensors to detect the presence of food when we eat. Feeling hungry can result, for example, from having an empty stomach. Because satiety sensors are first in line, they help explain why we stop eating as well. We feel "full" well before the food is digested and turned into nutrients the other sensing mechanisms monitor.
- **Glucose sensors** in the liver and other parts of the body, when detecting a low blood sugar level, quickly transmit information that triggers the release of any stored sugars and, beyond that, gives rise to the experience of hunger. Feeling sated in part involves a return to normal glucose levels.
- **Lipid sensors** function more slowly, monitoring levels of stored fats that can be metabolized by the body as needed. A popular theory here states that each person has an individual **set point** for the level of stored fats, and that the experience of hunger occurs (and continues) whenever the individual's level drops below that set point.

Evolutionary theory of overeating is a starting point in understanding why many people have difficulty keeping their weight down to preferred levels. In essence, prior to agriculture and the domestication of animals, our ancient hunter-gatherer-scavenger ancestors routinely experienced periods of feast and famine. And it would have been highly adaptive for their bodies to evolve in ways that would store as much energy as possible in times of plenty, later using that energy as slowly as possible in times of deprivation. Thus, the argument goes, we evolved mechanisms to limit weight loss but *not* to limit weight gain, consistent with the following observations:

- **Metabolic rate** slows down during conditions of deprivation and hunger, with the effect that energy stored in fat cells and other parts of body is conserved and used more slowly.
- **Body temperature** similarly tends go down during deprivation, also conserving bodily energy.
- **The order in which stored energy is used** is such that muscle cells and other parts of the body are raided before fat cells. That makes fat cells the hardest to deplete, and it also means that the deprived organism is more likely to feel lethargic and avoid exercise and other activity that would use unnecessary energy.
- And **periods of deprivation and hunger tend to be followed by periods of overeating**, as we naturally tend to replace and store bodily energy as quickly as possible.

Thus, it may be that humans have an inherent tendency to gain weight and keep it as long as possible. But whereas many people have extreme difficulty staying under normal weight limits, other people have no difficulty at all, and so an understanding of overeating and obesity doesn't stop there.

- **Obesity** can be defined statistically, based on how far above normal or average weight the individual is. Generally, however, an obese person is one who is so seriously overweight as to be at risk for heart problems and other physical disorders related to supporting and carrying around all that weight.

Possible factors in overeating and obesity include the following, none of which is encouraging for dieters. Note that for a given individual, any might apply—there is no single reason why people have difficulty keeping their weight down.

- **Having a high set point for weight**, which is at best difficult to change. An individual's set point could be related to genetic predisposition, since being overweight tends to run in families (though the specific genes have yet to be identified). It's also possible that chronic overfeeding during infancy produces a high set point, because excess food intake increases both the size and number of fat cells in the body. And the extra fat cells are there for life, barring liposuction.
- **Having a more efficient metabolism:** Perhaps ironically, some overweight people's bodies are simply better at converting food into energy and stored fats, which would likely be genetic. Some chronically overweight people, in other words, eat no more than people of normal weight.

- **Overresponsiveness to cues for eating:** Whatever the reason, some people are more sensitive than others to the sights and smells and tastes of food, making it more difficult for them to resist (or stop) eating.
- **Eating as a coping mechanism:** Some people have a strong tendency to eat whenever they're upset, stressed, bored, or otherwise in a negative emotional state, one possible cause being that their caregivers inadvertently taught them to do so during infancy and childhood.

Another world of problems associated with eating is illustrated by anorexia nervosa and bulimia nervosa, two disorders specified in the American Psychiatric Association's *Diagnostic and Statistical Manual of Mental Disorders, Fourth Edition–Text Revision* (DSM-IV-TR, Key 65). Both are severe disorders requiring treatment.

- **Anorexia nervosa** involves chronic and progressive weight loss to levels dangerously below normal limits, typically accompanied by intense fear of being "fat" and by distorted self-perceptions that allow the person to see bodily fat where there is none. More prevalent in females during adolescence and young adulthood, one pattern is that the person regularly fasts and refuses to eat. Another is that the person binge eats and then purges by vomiting or by abusing laxatives and enemas—with side effects as noted below. Causes are basically unknown, except to note that the disorder is much more common in societies where being attractive means being thin, suggesting that a misguided sense of self-image is involved. And anorexia nervosa can readily result in death.
- **Bulimia nervosa** also involves intense concerns over body image and being fat, but differs from anorexia in that bulimia does not tend to result in weight loss or death. Here, the person stays at or around normal weight but occasionally binges ravenously and secretively, with low self-esteem and a sense of loss of control. And because bulimia involves purging by vomiting and other means, the primary health hazards are side effects from stomach-acid damage to the throat, mouth, and teeth, plus chronic stress on the digestive tract.

Key 32   Sexual motives

OVERVIEW *In humans, sexual activity is determined as much by psychological factors as by physiology.*

In most species of mammals, the females have estrous cycles that determine sexual fertility and receptivity. The estrous cycle therefore dictates when sexual behavior leading to intercourse occurs—both for females and for males, because it takes two to tango. While receptive, however, the females tend to mate frequently and with little selectivity of partners, which is adaptive in maximizing the chances of conception. In turn, it also follows out of adaptive necessity that the males be minimally selective and interested in sex most of the time, so they're ready when the opportunity arises.

- In the **estrous cycle**, the hormone **estrogen** is secreted by the ovaries during and after ovulation, increasing the female's sexual interest and preparing her physically for copulation. The female is "in heat" when estrogen levels are highest. Pheromones (minute biochemicals) are also released into the air, stimulating sexual interest in nearby males.

Human females, by contrast, have menstrual cycles that determine fertility but are physically unrelated to receptivity, which means that sexual behavior leading to intercourse can take place at any time. For humans, then, the only adaptive requirement is that sexual intercourse must sometimes occur while the woman is ovulating. Thus, sex is much more a matter of mutual consent, although patterns of sexual arousal and climax do differ markedly between men and women.

- In the human **menstrual cycle**, estrogen levels also increase during and after ovulation, but research has found no clear relationship between female sexual arousal and estrogen levels. It is also not clear whether human females secrete pheromones that stimulate male sexual interest.
- **In human males**, the **androgen** hormones such as **testosterone** are secreted regularly by the testes from puberty on. Research has at times found that higher testosterone levels are associated with increased sexual interest (and aggression), but at other times not. And men who are castrated, meaning that their testes have been removed, often still retain sexual interest in the absence of testosterone.

- The **male arousal cycle** consistently involves an **excitement** phase, with penile erection, followed by a slowly increasing **plateau** and eventually fairly sudden **orgasm** and ejaculation. There is then a **refractory period** during which another round of arousal is not possible.
- The **human female arousal cycle** is much less predictable. After **excitement**, with lubrication and nipple erection, females experience sometimes slow, sometimes rapid **plateaus**, and then varying degrees and kinds of **orgasm**—from a sudden and intense single orgasm to a series of less intense multiple orgasms. And females do not tend to experience refractory periods.

Otherwise, human sexual behavior is determined by an array of factors such as individual and cultural beliefs, whether the partners find each other attractive and desirable, and, of course, whether they're physically and mentally in the mood. In a very real sense, the "brain" is the sexiest zone of the human body.

Homosexuality, gay and lesbian alike, means having primary sexual interest in members of one's own sex—which is *not* a mental disorder. Nor is homosexuality necessarily associated with adjustment problems, personal distress, or the like, except to the extent that heterosexual society at times makes life quite difficult for lesbians and gays who have "come out"—meaning those who openly acknowledge their sexual orientation. Another point is that relatively few people are exclusively homosexual; there is, in other words, a continuum of sexual orientation ranging from purely homosexual to purely heterosexual, with many people falling somewhere in between. And as for where homosexuality comes from, possible origins run the gamut from psychological to biological. For example, some gays and lesbians trace their sexual orientation to specific childhood events (often traumatic) involving members of the opposite sex. Others say they were attracted more to members of the same sex as far back as they can remember, as if they were simply born that way.
- **Gay** is the preferred term for homosexual men.
- **Lesbian** is the preferred term for homosexual women.

Key 33 Stimulation motives

OVERVIEW *A normal waking condition is to be looking, listening, exploring, manipulating, or otherwise processing stimulation, and there are optimal levels for stimulation.*

Over the years, theorists have proposed a variety of terms to capture a basic characteristic of humans and perhaps all living creatures: Whether we're overtly busy or sitting quietly and thinking, we're doing *something* at all times. Under conditions of sensory deprivation, for example, the human brain quickly ceases to function normally. Hence the terms **need for stimulation** and **need for arousal**, which are central to proposed motives such as "exploration," "manipulation," and "curiosity."

- **Sensory deprivation experiments** involve isolating a participant in a special chamber to eliminate outside sights and sounds, and perhaps in a special suit that minimizes sensations such as touch, kinesthesis, and so on. In such experiments, participants quickly show decrements in thinking and problem solving, and they may also vividly hallucinate—as if manufacturing sensory stimulation of their own.

Then, it would seem that there's an **optimal level of arousal** for an individual at a given time, depending in part on what that individual has been doing just prior. After intense mental activity, for example, such as studying for a test, you might be in the mood for a period of mental relaxation and daydreaming. But after the rest, you might become bored and start looking for something else stimulating to do.

In turn, the idea of optimal levels relates directly to **performance** on tasks—physical, mental, or both. In taking a test, for example, your best performance will occur if you're at an optimal level of arousal for that test. In other words, you do best if you're sufficiently "up" for the test, as opposed to feeling flat or basically not caring, but not too "up" so as to be anxious and have difficulty concentrating. And the classic **Yerkes-Dodson law** describes how the *difficulty* of the test interacts with optimal level of arousal. On an easy task, especially one that doesn't require much in the way of concentration or complex problem solving, performance gets better at higher levels of arousal (given that you aren't too aroused to function). On an extremely difficult task, such as one that requires intense concentration, performance is better at lower levels of arousal (given that you are at least awake).

Key 34 Theories of emotion

OVERVIEW *Popular theories of emotion agree that an emotion always includes both physical and mental components, but the theories differ as to the order of the events that take place.*

A good starting point in discussing the nature of emotion is Robert **Plutchik's evolutionary theory**, which assumes that our distant ancestors developed emotions as an adjunct to survival. "Fear," for example, is an aid to hiding, fleeing, or otherwise avoiding something too dangerous to mess around with. "Joy" is associated with satisfaction and pleasure, plus perhaps the relief of successfully dealing with something dangerous. In all, Plutchik proposed eight basic emotions: **Fear, anger, joy, surprise, sadness, disgust, acceptance**, and **anticipation**, which in turn might combine to produce all of the subtly differing emotions humans are capable of experiencing. Although other theorists might specify different basic emotions, it is generally accepted that humans universally have the same emotions—consistent with evolutionary theory.

- **Evidence for the universality of human emotions** comes from various sources, one being the research of Paul **Ekman** and colleagues on facial expressions associated with emotions. Generally, it has been found that peoples of different parts of the world can accurately identify each other's emotions on the basis of facial photographs, indicating that both the facial expressions and the emotions that underlie them are common to all peoples.

Emotional responses basically involve the operations of the **autonomic nervous system** (Key 14). The "feelings" aspect of an emotion is a result of changes in heart rate, blood pressure, respiration, perspiration, and so on, in conjunction with secretion of hormones such as adrenaline. But many quite different emotions have very similar patterns of physiological arousal and autonomic nervous system effects, so there is a cognitive or "thinking" component to emotions as well. How physiological arousal and cognition interrelate is where the sometimes conflicting theories of emotion come into play:

- The classic **James-Lange theory** states that we experience arousal first, then cognitively interpret that arousal, producing the emotional response. For example, if you see a stranger hurrying toward you late at night on a dark street, your body reacts first, then you become aware of how your body has reacted and size up the situation, and then you're afraid.

- The classic **Cannon-Bard theory** states instead that cognitive appraisal of the situation is first and that arousal closely follows in completing the emotional response. Here, you first realize that its a dangerous-looking stranger coming at you, then your body reacts, and you become afraid.

- The more recent **Schachter-Singer theory** emphasizes a sort of dual cognitive appraisal that happens simultaneously: We appraise and interpret both the situation and our bodily responses. Thus, you size up the stranger and what's happening to your body at the same time, giving rise to being afraid. Research by Schachter and Singer has also indicated that the "quality" of an emotional response is influenced markedly by the situation in which it is experienced. For example, your body would get essentially the same arousal from skydiving as it would from accidentally falling off a cliff and plunging to your destiny. But with a parachute, you feel fun and excitement, whereas without one you feel mortal terror.

- Also note Richard **Solomon's opponent-process theory** here, which describes how body and mind react as emotional states come and go. In essence, external stimulation that produces emotional change is followed by internal, homeostatic processes that tend to counteract that change. And with repeated stimulation, the opponent processes occur more quickly and also counteract the change more effectively. For example, the "high" produced by using psychoactive substances is countered internally. And with repeated usage, the person develops **tolerance** (Key 39) and must use more and more of the drug to achieve a given level of effect.

Polygraph "lie detector" tests, in passing, do not directly measure truths and lies. Instead, they monitor autonomic nervous system changes associated with emotionality, which in turn might (or might not) be associated with lying and such. Electrodes monitor minute physiological changes such as in heart rate, blood pressure, galvanic skin response (GSR, which varies with perspiration), and respiration, and the person doing the assessment watches for patterns of change in response to questions. However, aside from the random error to be expected in such an indirect process, the personality of the participant can often interfere with the results. A guilty person who happens to be an accomplished liar, for example, won't be as emotional while taking the test and won't necessarily respond differently while lying versus telling the truth. And an innocent but highly sensitive person attempting to tell the truth may respond differently to "loaded" questions out of fear of not being believed, thus appearing guilty.

Key 35 Stress and adjustment disorders

OVERVIEW *Chronic, sustained stress can take a serious toll physically and psychologically, with extreme effects on emotionality.*

Stress, defined generally as forces that impinge upon us and likewise our reactions to those forces, is a natural accompaniment of life. It permeates our daily existence at home, at work, and at play. And most people, most of the time, cope with stress reasonably well, by dealing with the forces that confront them and at times avoiding those forces in the first place. This Key, however, is about what happens when stress becomes excessive and unavoidable.

As defined above, however, the term *stress* is somewhat misleading, because it can apply equally to causes, effects, or both in interaction. For example, you can be "under a lot of stress," causing you to feel "stressed out" as a result. Thus, a clearer way of approaching the topic is to think of "stressors" as the causes and "stress reactions" as the effects on the person.

- **Stressors** are events and situations that impinge upon us physically and psychologically, and they can be external or internal. Potential external stressors are everywhere around us, physically and socially (involving interactions with others). The list is endless, including noise, crowding, freeway driving, natural disasters, work pressures, financial pressures, pressures from family and friends and neighbors, loss of loved ones, and on and on. Internal stressors can be physical, as in chronic health problems, or mental, as in recurrent fears and worries and conflicts and especially prolonged grieving. But whether external or internal, what constitutes a stressor is highly phenomenological and specific to the individual. Also note that stressors tend to be *additive*: Completely unrelated stressors that just happen to occur at the same time can combine to increase the overall level of stress a person experiences.

- **Stress reactions**, then, are our psychological and physiological responses to stressors. Common psychological reactions to excess stressors include irritability, anger, poor concentration and memory, insomnia, and in general, the symptoms of anxiety (Key 66) or depression (Key 68). Common physiological reactions to excessive stressors include tremors, ulcers, digestive disorders such as constipation or diarrhea, reduced resistance to diseases such as colds and flu, and in the extreme, coronary heart disease.

Hans **Selye's general adaptation syndrome** is a classic description of how we react to sustained and excessive stressors in three phases: alarm, resistance, and exhaustion.

- The **alarm phase** occurs when, say, we suddenly encounter a major stressor (or go over the line because of a flood of minor ones). The body mobilizes its resources and the sympathetic nervous system kicks in, increasing heart rate, shutting down digestion, releasing compensatory hormones such as epinephrine, and so on (Key 14).
- In the **resistance phase**, assuming that the stressor continues, the parasympathetic nervous system reacts to keep bodily functioning within viable limits, and the sympathetic reactions continue at a reduced but still excessive rate, gradually draining bodily energy and resources.
- Eventually, the body can reach the **exhaustion phase**, at first with tissue damage and symptoms such as ulcers and reduced resistance to disease, later with physical collapse and even death.

Adjustment disorders, as categorized in the DSM-IV-TR (Key 65), are reactions to *identifiable* major stressors. The causes, in other words, must be known. And the prognosis is generally good, given that the stressors pass or are otherwise successfully dealt with. Designated categories include adjustment disorder **with anxiety, with depressed mood**, and **with disturbance of conduct**. Disturbance of conduct includes antisocial behaviors, mostly in the form of fighting back or taking it out on others. Also note that the everyday expression "nervous breakdown" fits here, most closely resembling a diagnosable adjustment disorder.

Theme 7 STATES OF

CONSCIOUSNESS

*C*onsciousness refers to the inner, subjective, private world of thinking and feeling. Whether considered introspectively or in terms of information processing, consciousness more or less equates with "mind." Theorists propose, however, that there's not simply one consciousness but several, and in a different sense that consciousness varies along a continuum from being awake to being asleep and dreaming.

Hypnosis may produce a special, altered state of consciousness, though not all psychologists agree. It is clear, however, that psychoactive substances such as alcohol and drugs produce distinctly altered states.

Theme 7 explores states of consciousness, known and hypothetical, and then concludes with discussions of the use of drugs in seeking altered states.

Key 36 Levels of consciousness

OVERVIEW *However consciousness is defined, it is one of several possible levels of mental functioning and awareness.*

"Normal," waking consciousness is what you're thinking and feeling right now (assuming that this book didn't just put you to sleep). Normal consciousness varies, however, from being fully alert and mentally active to being minimally alert and perhaps daydreaming. Similarly, sometimes your thinking is concentrated and focused; at other times it's more diffuse and flowing, like a "stream" of consciousness. But regardless of such variations, conscious activity of some kind is taking place at all times while you're awake and also at least part of the time while you're asleep. You are, in other words, "aware" to a varying degree of what's going on both inside and outside of your body.

Just beyond the conscious is what's called the **subconscious**, which is a borderline region of mental activity. You aren't aware of what's going on in your subconscious, but you might become aware at any moment if something directs your attention to it.

- **Some bodily functions** such as respiration and digestion are likely examples involving subconscious mental activity: You typically aren't aware of breathing unless something makes you cough and gasp for breath, and you aren't aware of digesting food unless your stomach growls or you get a case of heartburn.
- **Psychomotor functions** such as walking can also be understood as subconscious activity, in that you don't consciously put one foot in front of the other as you proceed. And if you do consciously try to direct your feet and legs, your walking may become awkward and unsteady.
- **Well-learned habits and behaviors** are subconscious. Consider driving a car, especially out on an open freeway in little traffic. The conscious mind of an experienced driver can be a thousand miles away, and yet an array of sensing, perceiving, and controlling functions that keep the car on the road and moving are constantly taking place. Many well-practiced behaviors work that way, and also work *best* that way: Being adept at playing a guitar, for example, involves practice to the point that the basic finger and hand movements are subconscious and "automatic," thus freeing your conscious mind to focus on the music itself.
- A final example is the **cocktail party phenomenon**, which also illustrates **selective attention**: In a crowded room noisy with

conversations, such as at a party, you selectively attend mainly to what the person you're talking with is saying. But if your name is suddenly mentioned elsewhere in the room, you hear it, indicating that you were subconsciously aware of the other conversations too.

The **unconscious**, as originally proposed by Freud (Key 57), is a region of mental activity to which you normally do not have access. In Freud's view, the unconscious contains illicit desires, bad memories, and all manner of conflicts and other stuff that's too painful or threatening to think about consciously, but which nonetheless exerts pressure and affects your behavior without your being aware of it. Bad stuff in the unconscious can seep out in disguised form, however, as in dreams (Key 37) and "Freudian slips." Other, perhaps more scientific views of the unconscious assign mental activity involving the most basic bodily functions, which we normally have no need to be aware of.

- **Freudian slips** are said to reflect thoughts and desires we can't openly express, according to Freud. If you happen to be male and married but have a female colleague you secretly find attractive, you might slip one day and say to a friend, "She's the *breast* colleague I've ever worked with," having intended instead to say *best*. Most psychologists, however, would categorize so-called Freudian slips as coincidences, noting that we remember occasional slips of the tongue that are provocative or embarrassing and don't remember the many others that aren't. That's also called the **fallacy of the positive case**.

Key 37 Sleep, dreams, and sleep disorders

OVERVIEW *The basic functions of sleep and dreaming are not well understood, although stages of sleep and the occurrence of dreaming can be identified reasonably well.*

A typical "good night's sleep" is about eight hours, though people vary widely, some needing more than eight hours and some needing substantially less. People also vary in the times of day they sleep best, some preferring to go to sleep and arise early, others preferring to stay up at night and sleep late in the morning. Relatedly, our circadian rhythms differ. And disrupting our preferred schedules can produce feelings of being out of sync and also temporarily cause sleep difficulties.

- **Circadian rhythms** apply to metabolism and to activities such as eating and digesting food, engaging in work and exercise, and being awake or sleep, all of which our bodies seem to prefer at specific times of day—whatever the reason. In other words, we each have an individual "biological clock" that governs our daily lives and that can be difficult to change.
- **Jet lag**, which occurs when flying across several time zones, produces a temporary disruption of circadian rhythms.

Why we need to sleep at all is debatable. Some argue that we sleep to recuperate, physically or mentally or both. Others argue that we sleep because it was adaptive in an evolutionary sense and has remained a necessary function. Note that such theories are not necessarily incompatible.

- Some **recuperative theories** look at biochemical processes that differ during waking activity and during sleep, but the relationship between sleep and recuperation is not a simple one. Other theories focus on mental processes, one possibility being that sleep allows us time to "consolidate" the thoughts and experiences of the day—perhaps, in turn, through dreams, as discussed later in this Key.
- **Evolutionary theory** notes that it would have been highly adaptive for our distant ancestors to be quiet and still during the night, so as to hide from predators and avoid other dangers attributable to our limited night vision. Logically, such theories imply that our ancestors didn't snore.

Stages of sleep can be assessed by an EEG (electroencephalograph, Key 17), which monitors global electrical activity in the brain. Consistently identifiable sleep stages are as follows (see Figure 7-1), also noting that people typically cycle back and forth through the lighter and deeper stages as sleep progresses (see Figure 7-2):

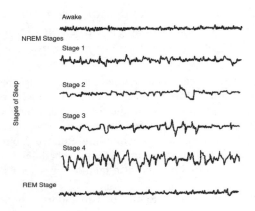

Figure 7-1. Sleep stages. [Figure is from Baucum, D. (1999), Barron's *College Review Series: Psychology,* p. 170.]

- **The initial transition to sleep** is similar to relaxed and drowsy wakefulness and is characterized by low-amplitude **alpha waves** of about 8 to 12 Hz (cycles per second). This sometimes includes a **hypnagogic state**, in which the person experiences stream-of-consciousness thoughts and images. It also tends to be a very pleasant and comfortable state.
- **Stage 1 sleep** yields **theta waves**, still low in amplitude but slower in frequency at about 6 to 8 Hz. The person is now only lightly asleep and still in transition, as heart rate slows and muscles relax further.
- In **Stage 2 sleep**, amplitude increases and frequency decreases to perhaps 4 to 6 Hz. **Sleep spindles**, brief bursts at about 12 to 16 Hz, begin to appear regularly.
- **Stage 3 sleep** is indicated by the regular appearance of **delta waves** at 1 to 4 Hz and markedly higher amplitude, as if overall brain activity is becoming more synchronized. The person is now completely asleep.
- **Stage 4 sleep** is the deepest, when delta waves constitute the majority of the EEG, and the person becomes most difficult to awaken. Cycles that include Stage 4 occur mostly during the initial hours of sleep, and later sleep is progressively less deep.
- **REM sleep** produces EEG patterns very similar to those observed when the person is alert and awake (much higher frequency and

lower amplitude), even though the person appears deeply asleep and is difficult to awaken. REM stands for the "rapid eye movements" that also occur, under closed eyelids. REM sleep is when most dreaming occurs. Stages 1 to 4, in contrast, are referred to as **NREM** sleep (non-REM). Few dreams occur during NREM sleep. Also, during REM sleep, the person is typically "paralyzed" with regard to voluntary movement. That's adaptive, perhaps, in preventing the person from trying to act out dreams in reality. During NREM sleep, however, the person can engage in voluntary behavior—as in parasomnias (sleep walking and sleep talking) discussed later in this Key.

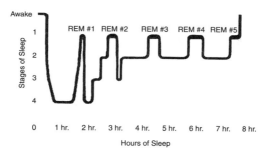

Figure 7-2. Typical sleep cycles. [Figure is from Baucum, D. (1999), Barron's *College Review Series: Psychology,* p. 171.]

Why we dream is even more debatable than why we sleep. Some theorists argue that dreams involve necessary organizing and consolidating of the day's experiences into permanent memories. Others argue that dreams involve the expression and perhaps resolution of ongoing conflicts in our thinking—conscious or otherwise. Yet another idea is that dreaming is involved in creativity, as when you "sleep on it" and wake up with a solution to a problem. Selected notes on dreams and dreaming are as follows:

- **Everyone dreams.** Many people, however, don't remember their dreams unless awakened while they're dreaming.
- **We apparently need to dream.** In experiments where participants' dreams are disrupted throughout the night (by awakening them whenever REM sleep occurs), the participants tend to show "REM rebound." REM sleep markedly increases the next night, as if the participants are making up for lost dreaming.
- **Some dreams are vivid, some more abstract.** Individuals consistently differ in the quality of dreams they have. Some people dream more often in color, others more often in "black-and-white"; some dream in images, others more in terms of feelings.

- **In Freud's view**, dreaming is a sort of outlet for pressures from the unconscious. What you actually dream is the **manifest content**, in disguise to make the material less unpleasant or painful. The real, underlying stuff is the **latent content**, and thus Freudian psychotherapy (Key 73) included trying to interpret what patients' dreams really meant. Note in passing, however, that although Freud thought there were a few "universal" dreams that meant the same thing for everyone, he regarded the meaning of most dreams as unique to the individual and the individual's problems. That's the prevailing view today: What a certain dream might mean for one person may be entirely different from what it might mean for another.

Sleep disorders as designated in the DSM-IV-TR (Key 65) can involve disruptions of sleep as well as sleep-related abnormal behaviors. "Primary" sleep disorders include dyssomnias and parasomnias. "Other" sleep disorders include those attributable to medical problems or to the use of psychoactive substances, noting that drugs can disrupt both sleep and dreaming and make you feel unrested regardless of how long you slept. Sleeping pills in particular tend to have that effect.

- **Dyssomnias** are those in which sleep is disrupted or otherwise abnormal. **Insomnia** is the most common, in which the person has difficulty falling asleep *or* staying asleep for a sufficient time, often because of excessive worries and life concerns. **Hypersomnia**, by contrast, involves excessive sleepiness or difficulty waking up and is less well understood. **Narcolepsy** is similar, except that falling asleep tends to be sudden and unpredictable and is thought to have a biological basis. Also included in this category is **sleep apnea**, which involves obstruction of the air passages and halted breath, often alternating with loud snoring and moments of wakefulness. In passing, sleep apneas during early infancy are one possible cause of sudden infant death syndrome (SIDS). Especially around age two months, when many reflexes are waning and higher cortical control is just starting to kick in, the infant might have an apnea and then simply fail to start breathing again. Special apnea monitors can alert caregivers in time to intervene.

- **Parasomnias** tend to accompany and sometimes disrupt sleep, though not the basic sleep cycle. Excessive **nightmares** and **sleep terrors** fall into this category, each of which can lead to panicky awakening. Nightmares are elaborate, frightening dreams that occur during REM sleep. Sleep terrors are episodes during NREM sleep that also cause intense arousal and fright, but essentially without dreaming. Also included here is **sleepwalking**, which occurs during NREM sleep and can involve anything from sitting up and looking around in bed to getting up and walking around and doing things.

Key 38 Hypnosis and hypnotic trances

OVERVIEW *Whether real or imagined, hypnosis produces a state of consciousness that seems different in many respects.*

Hypnosis is the process of inducing a hypnotic trance, which proponents argue produces a distinctly altered state of consciousness, as described below. People vary in hypnotic suggestibility, and it is a voluntary process: People generally cannot be hypnotized if they don't want to be. But given that the client is willing and that the hypnotist is competent, the outcome is a state in which the client exhibits behaviors and apparent mental status that differ from normal waking consciousness. And hypnotized clients are clearly not asleep: In a deep trance, clients can open their eyes and move around and perform otherwise normal behaviors.

- **Hypnotic trances** can be induced by various means. A classic technique is to use a metronome or to rhythmically move some other stimulus in front of the client's eyes, at the same time encouraging the client to relax and to focus on the stimulus and the hypnotist's voice. Moving stimuli are not actually necessary, however, and contemporary techniques are more likely to directly focus the client on relaxing, clearing away distracting thoughts, allowing consciousness to drift and flow, and so on. And clients can learn to enter a hypnotic trance very quickly, essentially hypnotizing themselves.
- **Hypnotic suggestibility** here refers to the extent to which a person can be hypnotized. As measured by standardized scales, people vary in the ease with which they can be hypnotized—if at all—as well as the depth of the trance they can achieve.

Others argue instead that the very willingness of the client completely accounts for the apparent state. That is, the client voluntarily and deliberately complies with the suggestions of the hypnotist, perhaps because of believing that hypnosis is real or perhaps simply from wanting to cooperate. In that case, a hypnotic trance would not truly be an altered state, but instead something of an act of self-deception. And attempts to find EEG support that a hypnotic trance is an altered state have mostly been unsuccessful.

- **On an EEG**, hypnotized participants display patterns that are difficult to distinguish from those of normal consciousness or perhaps a hypnagogic state with alpha waves (Key 37).

Whether truly in an altered state or not, however, hypnotized participants *act* as if they are, displaying behaviors and apparent mental status such as the following. Note that the phenomena overlap, that each depends upon the *depth* of the hypnotic trance, and that the first is essential to the rest:

- **Heightened suggestibility**, which here refers to an increase in the participant's ability to perceive, think, and do what the hypnotist suggests. Note, however, that even deeply hypnotized participants generally will not do things that are against their basic beliefs and ethics and the like.

- **Dissociation**, which to some theorists is the basis for hypnosis in the first place: The client's awareness becomes dissociated or "separated" from external reality. In a different sense, dissociation also refers to various psychotherapeutic uses of hypnosis. For example, a client's emotional distress might be dissociated from the thoughts and memories that produce it, thus enabling the client to talk about them in detail. As another example, a client with chronic physical ailments might dissociate the accompanying pain.

- **Vivid imagery**, to the point of hallucination. A participant might be persuaded, for example, that a stinkweed is a rose, after which the participant describes the stinkweed as pleasant and embraces it. Similarly, a participant might be led to believe that real objects don't exist, or that imagined objects do.

- **Enhanced memory:** Hypnotized people can often remember remote events in much greater detail. In **age regression**, for example, a person might mentally return to early childhood and describe events that normally aren't remembered at all, which can be useful in psychotherapy.

- **Posthypnotic suggestion:** Strong suggestions during the trance can remain in the cleint's mind after the trance is over. A client who is trying to quit smoking, for example, might retain a suggestion that whenever the urge occurs, he or she will instead relax and be disgusted by the prospect of lighting a cigarette. However, such posthypnotic suggestions tend to wear off with the simple passage of time and therefore are only temporarily helpful.

A cautionary note: Again, whether real or imagined, hypnosis often *seems* very real to the person who experiences it. It is therefore not something to be toyed with by people who are not trained to induce trances in other people and cope with what might happen. In other words, as the expression goes, do *not* attempt this at home.

Key 39 Physically addictive drugs

OVERVIEW *Drugs that are physically addictive produce tolerance and withdrawal effects.*

The following survey of likely drugs of abuse reflects the "medical" approach to classifying drugs, with notes on their effects and their dangers. Note that the "legal" approach is somewhat different.

- **Medical classification** is based on the effects of the drug on the CNS. "Primary" effects are those that are intended, such as the painkilling effects of narcotics. "Secondary" effects or "side effects" are those that inadvertently accompany use of the drug, such as the euphoria and drowsiness associated with narcotics—which aren't strictly necessary in alleviating pain. From there, **tolerance** means that more and more of the drug is necessary to produce a given effect, and **withdrawal** means that the person suffers if the drug is suddenly discontinued.
- **Legal classification** instead focuses on the drug's potential for abuse. Here, in essence, any drug with a high potential for abuse is called a "narcotic."

Depressants have the basic effect of slowing down CNS functioning, also reducing heart rate and respiration, interfering with motor functioning, and so on, eventually producing sleep. Alcohol is the most popularly used and abused depressant drug. The category also includes sedative hypnotics (sleeping pills) such as the barbiturates, and "minor" tranquilizers such as the benzodiazepines. Depressants are usually taken orally, though abusers also sometimes inject barbiturates and benzodiazepines under the skin, which is called "skin popping."

- **Alcohol** (ethanol) is a physically addictive drug that produces tolerance and that can produce severe withdrawal effects ranging from irritability and inability to sleep, with mild abuse, to seizures and heart attacks and death in the case of sustained, long-term abuse. Alcohol abuse also tends to have physical effects throughout the body, including destruction of neurons in the CNS and damage to organs such as the liver. And it is quite possible to overdose on alcohol and die. Psychologically, alcohol may initially produce subjective feelings of an increase in arousal and energy level, perhaps through release of inhibitions and a sense of "partying," but its main effect is CNS depression. As measured by blood alcohol concentration, impairment of vision and motor coordination occurs at about .08%, which is a commonly used legal criterion for DUI (driving under the influence). However, people vary considerably in how drunk they are at .08%, depending in part upon their experience with alcohol and current tolerance level. Similarly, people vary in the rate at which they metabolize and eliminate alcohol from their bodies, which means that some people get noticeably drunk on a couple of beers or glasses of wine and other people seem little affected until they have consumed a lot more.

- **Barbiturates** such as Nembutal and Seconal, or in street language, "downers," were popularly prescribed as sleeping pills in the 1950s and 1960s but much less so today. Otherwise, barbiturates produce effects similar to those of alcohol and are physically addictive and potentially dangerous in the same ways. Barbiturates and alcohol also "potentiate" each other when taken together, meaning that the effects multiply and are therefore that much more dangerous in an immediate sense: In the blurred, confused, and nodding state produced by combining barbiturates and alcohol, it is easy to overdose accidentally.

- **Benzodiazepine tranquilizers** such as Valium, Librium, and Xanax, along with an assortment of other **minor tranquilizers**, tend more to reduce anxiety and produce feelings of calm and relaxed well-being, but also produce sleep when taken in sufficient quantity. The term "minor" is contrasted with the "major" tranquilizers used to treat much more serious problems, as discussed in Key 72. Benzodiazepines are also physically addictive in all respects, and like barbiturates, potentiate when taken with alcohol. Benzodiazepines, including an assortment of newer and less addictive derivatives, are still commonly prescribed.

Narcotics include **opiates** such as opium, codeine, morphine, and heroin, and synthetics such as methadone. Primarily used as painkillers, narcotics also tend to produce feelings of euphoria, plus drowsiness and eventual sleep and other effects similar to the depressants. Narcotics are also profoundly physically addictive, and with a very high risk of death from overdose. Withdrawal, in contrast, involves intense craving and pain and suffering throughout the body—attributable to the body having stopped producing its natural endorphins (Key 17). But withdrawal is often characterized as being no more dangerous than a bad case of the flu. Narcotics abuse is also linked to the transmission of diseases such as hepatitis and AIDS, when users inject the drugs intravenously and share paraphernalia and thus have blood contact. Otherwise, however, narcotics abuse actually tends to produce less bodily damage than abuse of alcohol.

- **Opium** is a dark, sticky substance obtained from opium poppies, which can be smoked in its raw form. **Codeine, morphine,** and **heroin** are derived from opium. Heroin is the most intense version, in terms of rapid onset and strong feelings of euphoria, and is therefore the most addictive. Heroin is available only illegally, as a whitish or brownish powder, and is usually injected intravenously for maximum effect. Death from overdose (typically involving respiratory failure) occurs in part because heroin has a relatively narrow **range of effect**: With respect to an abuser's current tolerance, the amount required to overdose is not that much greater than the amount required to "get off," meaning achieve the desired effect. Death from overdose also occurs because the concentration of the drug as sold on the streets can vary considerably. Heroin dealers tend to "cut" the drug with inert substances, to increase their profits and perhaps also to support their own habits. Heroin abusers, in turn, can easily overdose if they unknowingly inject an amount of heroin that's stronger than what they're accustomed to.
- **Methadone** is a synthetic narcotic used primarily for treatment of narcotics addiction, as a substitute. Methadone produces relatively little in the way of euphoria, but the pain and suffering associated with withdrawal from other narcotics is eliminated and the person can function. **Methadone maintenance programs** have been in existence since the 1950s. Such programs are controversial, however, because methadone is still an addictive drug and the abuser is still drug dependent.

Stimulants include caffeine, nicotine, amphetamines, and cocaine, all of which are physically addictive and any of which can be abused to the extent of physical damage to the CNS and organs throughout the body. Stimulants increase activity in the CNS, with accompanying feelings of heightened arousal and alertness and overall energy level, plus, at times, euphoria. Stimulants also tend to be appetite suppressants. Stimulant abuse increases the risk of heart disease in particular, and overdose can produce seizures and cardiac arrest. Withdrawal effects include irritability, difficulty in concentration, and drowsiness, accompanied by intense craving, but withdrawal does not tend to be life-threatening.

- **Amphetamines** are synthetic stimulants that were popularly prescribed in the 1950s and 1960s for weight control. Nowadays, the only true amphetamine widely available is illegally manufactured methamphetamine or "crystal meth," a powder that can be "snorted" nasally or injected in solution. Also available illegally is "ecstasy" or simply "X," which is an amphetamine derivative with distinctly euphoric effects. In general, medical usage was discontinued because amphetamines are physically addictive both in terms of tolerance and withdrawal effects, and sustained use tends to be highly damaging both within the CNS and throughout the body. Sustained use also interferes with concentration and especially memory. Plus, though amphetamines are highly effective appetite suppressants, the person tends to gain the weight back rapidly when the amphetamine is eventually discontinued.

- **Cocaine**, though primarily a stimulant with properties and effects similar to amphetamines, was once used medically as a local anesthetic and was even an ingredient in soft drinks. Cocaine is a natural substance derived from the leaves of the coca plant, and is distributed illegally both in highly refined powder and "rock" form. Powder cocaine is consumed nasally, and in solution can also be injected intravenously. The most rapid and intense effects, however, are obtained by smoking "crack" cocaine. Correspondingly, crack produces the most intense withdrawal effects and craving. Otherwise, the dangers associated with cocaine abuse depend in part on the means of ingestion, but also involve the presence of the drug in the body. And combining cocaine with depressants or narcotics, which is a popular form of abuse, can be extremely dangerous physically and psychologically because of the conflicting effects and the "roller-coaster ride" the person experiences.

As for **treatment** for the abuse of phsyically addictive drugs, an objective discussion is beyond the scope of this text. Treatment approaches vary considerably and are dictated by one's view of what causes drug abuse in the first place. Some take the view that there is a genetic predisposition to abuse drugs, which means that treatment includes whatever helps the person maintain abstinence for life. That's the view of volunteer organizations such as Alcoholics Anonymous, whose members help each other abstain. Others argue that drug abuse is learned and has present-tense causes (drugs *do* work, in the short run, and the ones that work the best are the most expensive), which implies that abusers of socially acceptable drugs such as alcohol might successfully return to moderate use. The argument is far from resolved. In either case, however, it is generally agreed that the first step in treatment is to "dry the person out," which mean getting the drug out of the person's system and typically getting the person temporarily out of the drug-abusing environment. From there, however, treatment in the form of psychotherapy might focus on anything from personal to family to social issues and problems, and might take many different forms (see Theme 13).

Key 40 Psychedelic drugs

OVERVIEW *Psychedelic drugs are hallucinogenic, and any tolerance or withdrawal effects they produce are minimal.*

Psychedelics, more properly called **hallucinogenics**, include mescaline, psilocybin, LSD, PCP, and in a lesser sense, marijuana. Hallucinogenics have in common effects such as perceptual distortions and hallucinations, heightened arousal, alertness, and euphoria, plus altered emotionality and consciousness that some describe in spiritual and metaphysical terms. Hallucinogens are not physically addictive, however, and the extent to which they cause physical damage is unknown. The primary dangers are instead cognitive and emotional. People don't always come back from hallucinogenic "trips," for one thing. And the experience is not always pleasant and stimulating—trips can be terrifying, sometimes with lasting psychological effects. And there is always the danger that a perceptually disoriented person will *do* something dangerous.

- **Mescaline** is a natural product of the peyote cactus and is used ritually (and legally) in some religions. The "buttons" of the cactus are chewed, the juice is swallowed, and as the nausea subsides, the experience begins. Mescaline can also be synthesized and is distributed illegally in pill form. The hallucinogenic effects of mescaline last perhaps four to six hours.
- **Psilocybin** occurs naturally in some mushrooms, which are chewed, and can also be synthesized. Effects and duration are very similar to those of mescaline.
- **LSD** (lysergic acid diethylamide) is a synthetic substance distributed in minute amounts typically on bits of blotter paper. Depending upon dosage, LSD tends to produce a much more intense and disorienting experience than mescaline or psilocybin, lasting 10 to 12 hours, and with distinctly stimulant-like effects.
- **PCP** (phencyclidene) is a synthetic originally developed for use as an anesthetic. Medical usage was discontinued, however, because of the hallucinogenic and other side effects. Illegally manufactured PCP powder, also known as "angel dust," can be ingested in any form, including smoking, and is often used as an adulterant in drugs such as cocaine or the other hallucinogenics. An unscrupulous drug dealer with a weak product, for example, might add PCP to improve the product's salability. That, in passing, is one of the greatest dangers of any illegal drug: You don't necessarily know

what you're getting, and you might even get poisoned. PCP effects tend to be profound, and depending upon dosage, can last horrifyingly for a couple of *days*.

Marijuana or cannabis, also known variously as "pot," "weed," or "herb," is a plant that was once widely cultivated for use in making rope (hence yet another name, "hemp"). The active agent is THC, tetrahydrocannabinol, which is psychoactively in a class of its own. THC can also be synthesized and is sometimes illegally distributed in pill form. Typically, marijuana is simply dried and smoked. Hashish or "hash," in turn, is a hard paste derived by cooking down marijuana leaves and flowers, and is also smoked. Regardless of form, however, effects include, at low dosages, relaxation and sedation similar to those of the depressants, especially the benzodiazepines. At high dosages, and also depending upon the "quality" of the marijuana, effects are somewhat like those of the hallucinogenics, including euphoria and mild perceptual distortion, but instead with drowsiness and sleep. Unlike the depressants, marijuana is not physically addictive and is not thought to cause physical damage, except for serious respiratory problems and diseases associated with smoking. Marijuana, in other words, is thought to be carcinogenic like tobacco.

Theme 8 CONDITIONING AND LEARNING

*L*earning is typically defined as a relatively permanent change in the potential for behavior as a result of experience. "Relatively permanent" corresponds to the assumption that underlying neural structures are somehow changed (Theme 3). "Potential" indicates that learning can often be covert at the time it occurs, perhaps only later producing an observable, overt change in behavior. And "experience" rules out changes attributable to simple maturation, as well as temporary changes attributable to motivational or emotional state.

Learning, then, is involved in virtually everything we know and do. *Conditioning,* in contrast, is derived from strict behaviorism and is based mainly on associations between observable stimuli and responses. Conditioning thus involves specific types of learning, although acknowledged pioneers of conditioning such as Ivan Pavlov, and later, B. F. Skinner, believed that *all* learning could be understood in terms of conditioning. Similarly, strict behaviorists tended to believe that the basic laws of learning were the same for all organisms, human or otherwise.

Theme 8 covers the basics of classical and operant conditioning, which can explain many instances of learning—but by no means all, as pointed out by the ethologists, the early cognitive psychologists, and later many others. Observational learning, which is sometimes cited as a third basic type of learning, is discussed instead in Key 81. And higher-level, more distinctly human learning that conditioning cannot explain well is the subject of Theme 9.

INDIVIDUAL KEYS IN THIS THEME

Key 41 Pavlov and classical conditioning

OVERVIEW *Classical conditioning involves the learning of associations between stimuli, in situations where responses are reflexive or habitual.*

Ivan **Pavlov**, around the beginning of the 20th century, was a Russian physiologist interested mainly in animal digestive processes. In one aspect of his research, dogs had special tubes surgically inserted into their throats to allow measurement of their salivation in response to being fed. And, as the story goes, Pavlov became puzzled by the observation that the dogs often salivated before the food was actually placed in their mouths, and even when lab assistants simply approached the dogs—with or without food. Pavlov dubbed this phenomenon "psychic secretions," an allusion to some kind of covert process. And from there, he and his colleagues set about discovering how and why they occurred, thereby launching a major line of research in psychology that is still active today.

In **classical conditioning**, the organism learns an association between two (or more) stimuli. In essence, the organism learns that one stimulus is often followed by a second one, based on temporal contiguity (Key 2). And whatever response is appropriate to the second stimulus becomes appropriate to the first as well. The first stimulus, in other words, becomes a "cue" for the second. For example, in Pavlov's lab, it appears that the stimulus features of the lab assistants—such as their white lab coats—had become associated with food stimuli. The lab coats cued the dogs that food might be on the way, thus eliciting salivation.

Classical conditioning experiments nowadays tend to be quite complex, but the **basic procedures and terms** can be illustrated by Pavlov's early experiments: Ring a bell, then immediately give the dog a bit of food; the dog salivates. Ring the bell again, feed the dog again, and so on. Eventually, the dog salivates in response to the bell alone. In technical terms, food is an unconditioned stimulus (UCS) that produces an unconditioned response (UCR) of salivation. The bell is a conditioned stimulus (CS), which eventually produces a conditioned response (CR) of salivation after repeated trials in which the bell and food are paired.

- **The CS is initially neutral** with respect to the CR. That is, with dogs, a bell elicits behaviors such as orienting the head and perking the ears, but it does not initially elicit salivation. Also note that *the CR and the UCR are not exactly the same*: A dog, for example, will never salivate as much to a bell as it will to food; nor will it begin salivating as quickly to the bell.
- **The acquisition phase** of a classical conditioning experiment consists of repeated trials in which the CS and UCS are paired and the CR gradually develops. The most efficient conditioning occurs if *the CS slightly precedes the UCS*, consistent with the idea that the CS comes to serve as a cue for the UCS. Conditioning will also occur, however, if the two stimuli are presented simultaneously.
- **The extinction phase** is when presentation of the UCS is discontinued. At first, the dog continues to salivate to the CS, demonstrating that classical conditioning has occurred. If the UCS is permanently discontinued, however, the dog gradually ceases to salivate and the CR is "extinguished." Except that subjects sometimes show **spontaneous recovery** of the CR: Extinguish a dog's salivation to a bell one day, then try the bell again the next day, and the dog may temporarily start salivating again.

Other often-cited phenomena in classical conditioning are as follows:
- **Generalization** occurs when small differences in the CS still produce the CR. Bells of a slightly different tone, for example, still produce salivation.
- **Discrimination** occurs when one CS produces the CR and a somewhat different CS does not. If the UCS is paired with a bell of one tone and not with a bell of a different tone, the dog eventually learns to salivate to the first bell and not to the second.
- **Second-order** or **higher-order** conditioning can be demonstrated by pairing a previously conditioned CS with a new CS: Having conditioned salivation to a bell, then pair a light with the bell alone, and the dog learns to salivate to the light alone. But the CR to the light will be weaker and will extinguish quicker.

Key 42 Skinner and operant conditioning

OVERVIEW *Operant conditioning involves the learning of associations between responses and consequences, in situations where behavior is voluntary.*

B. F. **Skinner** was a strict behaviorist who avoided all usage of terms such as "learning," "thinking," "being motivated," and anything else psychological that can't actually be seen (see also Key 4). In Skinner's view, such terms are often misleading and circular and therefore unscientific. For example, consider the classic, "Why does the chicken cross the road?" The answer, "Because it wants to get to the other side," can mislead us into thinking we understand the chicken when we actually don't. Instead, Skinner would argue that we need to look at the environmental influences on the behavior: Perhaps the chicken crosses the road to get food, or to get with other chickens, or whatever, all of which is at least potentially observable. In other words, the chicken is somehow being "reinforced" for crossing the road.

- **Reinforcement** occurs whenever a stimulus event such as a reward follows a behavior, maintaining that behavior and making it more likely to occur again. Reinforcement (and punishment) are discussed in detail in the next Key.

Skinner's **operant conditioning**, then, addressed relationships between observable stimuli and observable responses, and vice versa, without regard to what goes on in the subject's mind. And operant conditioning is primarily concerned with explanations that apply to all animals, including humans. Thus, at least in his early research, Skinner worked with rats and pigeons, whose behavior could be carefully controlled in experimental environments that came to be known as "Skinner boxes." In such an apparatus, operant behaviors can be established and systematically altered through meticulous attention to reinforcement and punishment contingencies—meaning the relationships between behavior and its consequences. Skinner believed that all behavior could be explained in such terms.

- **A Skinner box** is an experimental enclosure just adequate for the animal to be comfortable and move around a bit. Typically, console lights and a speaker provide stimuli for the animal to respond to, and manipulanda such as a bar for rats to press or a key for pigeons to peck allow for responses. Also provided are mechanical dispensers for food pellets or liquids, to which the animal gains access by performing the responses. Skinner boxes may also include steel rods as the floor, through which electric shocks can be administered as applicable. Finally, the box is connected to electronic equipment that automatically turns stimuli on and off, records responses, and administers payoffs, which means that operant conditioning experiments can run mostly unattended.

- **Operant behaviors** "operate" on the environment. In the real world, animals and humans perform operant behaviors continuously, in adapting to and controlling their environments. In a Skinner box, a rat's operant behavior of interest is pressing a bar, which can be directly measured and quantified in terms of when it occurs and especially the rate at which it occurs. Behaviors such as bar pressing do not come naturally for the rat, of course, so a preliminary step in an operant conditioning experiment is **shaping**: A naive rat gets a food pellet for approaching the bar, then perhaps for sniffing or touching the bar, and eventually only for a full bar press, at which point the electronic control equipment can take over. Another term used in conjunction with shaping is **successive approximations**, noting that the subject gets successively closer to the target behavior one small step at a time.

Key 43 Positive and negative reinforcement and punishment

OVERVIEW *Operant conditioning focuses on contingencies: When a behavior occurs, stimuli are either presented or taken away.*

A good place to start in understanding reinforcement and punishment is E. L. **Thorndike**'s "law of effect." Thorndike is perhaps best known for his work with cats in puzzle boxes back around the beginning of the 20th century: A hungry cat, for example, would be placed in an enclosure that includes a manipulandum such as a lever, which the cat can learn to press to open the door and escape and get to a food bowl. To Thorndike, an early behaviorist, the cat's eventual success was a result of simple trial and error, and occurred because of the "effects" the cat's behavior had—such as escape and access to food.

- **The law of effect** can be stated as follows: A behavior that leads to a satisfying state of affairs tends to be repeated; a behavior that leads to an unsatisfying state of affairs tends not to be repeated.

Note, of course, that "satisfying" is not really a behavioral term, but it is a bit more behavioral than talking about what the cat might "expect" or "want."

- **Trial-and-error learning** means essentially that the cat bumps around and explores randomly until it accidentally hits the lever— the solution. This was Thorndike's way around saying that the cat is "thinking" and "solving the problem," and it is true that some animal and human learning occurs this way.

In Skinner's terminology, the cat is **reinforced** for pressing the lever. And in the puzzle-box example, as it happens, both "positive" and "negative" reinforcement contingencies are in effect, which is sometimes the case in the real world as well. Both correspond to the first half of Thorndike's law of effect.

- **To avoid confusion**, note that when the terms **positive** and **negative** are used in the context of reinforcement (or punishment), the meaning is that a stimulus is "added" or "subtracted." That is, a stimulus is *presented* to the subject or *taken away* from the subject. The terms have nothing whatsoever to do with whether or not the stimulus is satisfying or pleasant—that's a separate issue. Also note that contingencies are defined in terms of what happens when the behavior *occurs,* not what happens when it doesn't occur (see Figure 8-1).

	Stimulus: Appetitive	Stimulus: Aversive
Present	Positive Reinforcement	Positive Punishment
Remove	Negative Punishment	Negative Reinforcement

Figure 8-1. Contingencies in operant conditioning. [Figure is from Baucum, D. (1999), Barron's *College Review Series: Psychology,* p. 115.]

- A **positive** reinforcement contingency occurs when an "appetitive" stimulus—something good—is presented to the subject as a consequence of the behavior, with the effect that behavior is maintained or becomes more likely in the future. The cat hits the lever and gets to the food bowl. A rat presses a bar and gets a food pellet. If you brush your teeth and therefore breathe good breath at other people, you get pleasant reactions. And on and on, in all cases with the result that the behavior is likely to continue, or occur again, as appropriate. Positive reinforcement is also called **reward training**.
- A **negative** reinforcement contingency occurs when an "aversive" stimulus—something bad—is taken away as a consequence of the behavior, and again the behavior is maintained or becomes more likely in the future. Cats tend to find confinement aversive, so the cat presses the lever and is negatively reinforced by getting out of the box. A rat in a Skinner box turns off a mild electric shock to its tootsies by pressing the bar. Brush your teeth, and you avoid unpleasant reactions from others. Negative reinforcement is also called **escape training** if the subject must first experience the aversive stimulus and then make it go away. It's called **active avoidance training** if the subject can avoid the aversive stimulus altogether, by performing the behavior in advance.

Punishment is not the opposite of reinforcement in terms of its effects, but the contingencies are exactly opposite. Both "positive" and "negative" punishment (noting that some authors do not make this distinction) correspond to the second half of Thorndike's law of effect.

- A **positive** punishment contingency occurs when an aversive stimulus—something bad—is presented to the subject as a consequence of the behavior, with the result that the behavior is suppressed or becomes less likely in the future. If a rat has previously learned to press a bar to get food, it might now instead be shocked for every bar press, with the result that bar pressing decreases. If your breath is bad, other people present you with unpleasant reactions. Such punishment is also called **passive avoidance training**.

- **A negative** punishment contingency occurs when an appetitive stimulus—something good—is taken away as a consequence of the behavior, again tending to suppress the behavior and make it less likely. Make food automatic for the trained rat, occurring regularly *unless* the rat presses the bar, and eventually the rat's bar pressing will decrease. If your breath is bad enough, other people punish you by removing themselves from your presence. This kind of punishment is also called **omission training**.

Otherwise, note the **Premack principle**, attributable to the work of David Premack in defining reinforcement and punishment more objectively and with less circularity. The problem actually goes back to Thorndike's use of words such as "satisfying" and "pleasant," which can't be directly observed. What is reinforcing, in other words, is subjective and in the eye of the beholder. Chocolate is a reward for some people and not others, so getting chocolate would be reinforcing for some but perhaps even punishing for others (especially someone on a diet). Skinner's terminology is an improvement, but it is still circular: How do we recognize reinforcement? It maintains the subject's behavior. Why is the subject's behavior maintained? Because it's reinforced. And again, except for common sense, we have no way of knowing what stimuli will work as reinforcers until we try them on an individual subject. Thus, Premack devised a way to get around this problem, at least in some situations, with the following definitions: Where "high" and "low" refer to what the subjects normally do on their own, which is readily observable, *reinforcement is when a high-rate behavior is made contingent upon a low-rate behavior*, and *punishment is when a low-rate behavior is made contingent upon a high-rate behavior*.

- **As an illustration of reinforcement**, suppose a teacher has a group of preschool children, some of whom spend their open periods reading storybooks and others of whom spend all their time playing with building toys. To even things out a bit, the first children could be required to build things for a while to gain access to storybooks, thus reinforcing them for building. And the second children could be required to read storybooks to gain access to the building toys, thus reinforcing them for reading.

- **Punishment** wouldn't be desirable in such a situation, but would occur if the first children were given toys whenever they tried to read, and the second children were given storybooks whenever they tried to play with building toys.

113

Key 44 Applications and interpretations of conditioning

OVERVIEW *Principles of classical and operant condition-ing govern much of what we do in an immediate sense and in the long run as well. Such principles have also been applied throughout society at large, especially in understanding and treating some problem behaviors and disorders.*

Examples of how classical and operant conditioning affect our lives are far too numerous and varied to discuss adequately, because condi-tioning affects us in a moment-to-moment sense and far beyond. Your dog or cat goes nuts at the whirr of a can opener or the rustle of a dry food sack, through classical conditioning. You acquired the skills necessary to ride a bicycle or drive a car a few steps at a time, oper-antly conditioned by your successes along the way. You read, in part, because you have been reinforced for reading—both in terms of how to read and what to read. You study, in part, to be reinforced by good grades. And you work, in part, to be paid. All of those things are cog-nitive too, of course, but they include identifiable elements of classi-cal and operant conditioning. The list is endless.

The selected examples in this Key therefore focus on often-cited phe-nomena and procedures that also serve as good illustrations of how conditioning works, with emphasis upon behavior modification.
  • **Behavior modification** is the application of learning and condi-tioning principles to problem behaviors and disorders, using tightly controlled procedures. Behavior modification is potentially effective with any organisms, animal or human, but nowadays is used more often with animals, very young children, and mentally retarded or otherwise disordered people at any age—in common is *difficulty in communicating*, making higher-level procedures either impractical or impossible. The advantage of behavior mod-ification, in other words, is that it doesn't necessarily require being able to talk with the subject. Behavior modification is also dis-cussed in Key 75.

Phobia (an anxiety disorder, Key 66) provides a good example on sev-eral counts. A phobia is an unreasoning, uncontrollable fear of an object or situation. And phobias can be acquired in various ways, including simply observing the behavior of others who have them.

But phobias can also result from conditioning, which works like this, noting that a complete explanation is also partly cognitive:

- **Phobias are acquired through classical conditioning** when a neutral object is associated with an object that really does cause fear or pain. As a simple example, suppose as a child you're startled by a large dog and it causes you to fall down and hurt yourself. Or it growls loudly at you and scares you. Or it even bites you. And suppose that such events happen several times, and with different dogs. You might well acquire a classically conditioned fear of dogs, where the dog is the CS, the contact with the ground or the growl or the bite comprise the UCS, and the fear backed up by pain provides for the UCR and the CR. Then you generalize your fear CR to dogs in general, regardless of what they do. You now have a phobia. Note in passing, however, that phobias and other aversions can involve a single, intense experience (Key 45), and can also be acquired through "observational learning" with no direct experience (Key 81).

- **Phobias are maintained through operant conditioning:** Having acquired the phobia, classical conditioning by itself predicts that the phobia should eventually extinguish on its own, given repeated experiences in which you encounter dogs that don't threaten or hurt you. Instead, however operant conditioning kicks in to maintain the phobia—perhaps for life—through **negative reinforcement**: Each time you see a dog, the fear sweeps over you, and you avoid the dog at all costs. Once you're away from the dog, the fear subsides. In effect, removing yourself means removing the aversive stimulus and reducing the fear, and thus your behavior of getting away from the dog is maintained and is likely to occur again and again. In other words, you don't stick around long enough to find out there might not be anything to be afraid of. Also note that phobic reactions can instead involve rage and attack. A person who is phobic for roaches, for example, might "take away the aversive stimulus" by drenching it with insect spray or angrily stomping it to mush.

- **Cognitively**, people also help drive themselves into a state of terror during phobic reactions, through subtly telling themselves about and perhaps visualizing the terrible things that could happen. But that's more the subject matter of Theme 13, which includes procedures that are used to eliminate phobias.

Treatment for enuresis (bed-wetting) is an example of classical conditioning at work. Here, the bed wetter's bed is equipped with a special mattress cover that detects urine electronically, in turn sounding a loud buzzer (UCS) that causes the child to wake up (UCR). The CS is actually the child's bladder distension—neutral in the sense that it isn't waking the child up when the treatment begins. Bladder distension, then, is paired with the buzzer, typically producing a CR of awakening after a few nights.

Children's temper tantrums often include a strong operant conditioning component, which works in several ways involving the dynamics between parent and child. Tantrums can occur anywhere and involve just about anything, but consider an example where a child consistently throws tantrums over toys and other goodies in department stores and grocery marts and the like, and the parent *occasionally* gives in:

- When the child drops to the floor and starts kicking and sobbing and screaming, "I want it!" the parent is placed under a strong **negative reinforcement** contingency: Buy the goody, and the shrieks from the child and the embarrassing stares of the onlookers will stop.

- The child, on the other hand, experiences **positive reinforcement**: Kick and scream, get the goody. And because the parent only occasionally gives in, a **partial reinforcement** contingency is also operating, which will make the behavior much harder to extinguish in the long run. When a behavior is only occasionally reinforced, the effect is that when reinforcement is discontinued, it takes the child longer to figure that out. Partial reinforcement also has the effect of **shaping** the child's tantrums into longer and louder and more desperate episodes, because longer and louder sometimes produce the goody when lesser measures don't.

Time-out procedures in schools and such are based on operant conditioning in the form of **omission training** (negative punishment). Likely dynamics of a child who becomes disruptive and unruly in class involve getting attention of any kind, whether it's laughs from the other children or scoldings from the teacher. The child is therefore removed for a while to an isolated area where attention doesn't happen—the social goodies, in other words, are taken away when the misbehavior occurs.

Otherwise, behavior modification has been applied to many other problem behaviors and disorders in everyday settings and in various kinds of institutions—sometimes successfully and sometimes not. One problem with humans is that they can come to resent the very fact of being controlled and render the procedures ineffective by consciously opposing them. In other words, the human—unlike the rat or the pigeon—might tell you to take your reinforcers and shove 'em.

Key 45 Ethological factors in conditioning and learning

OVERVIEW *Ethology emphasizes natural, built-in behaviors in conjunction with learning. Such behaviors sometimes conflict with the principles of classical and operant conditioning.*

Ethologists such as Konrad **Lorenz** studied many behaviors that are "species-specific," meaning behaviors that occur in some species but not others, thus indicating biological determinants. **Imprinting** (Key 25) is one example: The recently hatched gosling, during a critical period, permanently imprints on the first available moving object—such as its mother, or experimentally, perhaps Konrad Lorenz or some other moving object that's present at the time. Thus, the gosling normally "learns" who is its mother, but not according to the rules of conditioning. It isn't classical conditioning, because there's no UCS. And it isn't operant conditioning, because there's no reinforcer. It is instead a built-in behavior, an instinctive one, and the farther down the phylogenetic scale we get, the more we find that behavior is controlled by instincts. In other words, as we get farther away from humans, behavior gets less flexible and more directly attributable to biological processes.

- The term **instinct** has been abused extensively, especially in the early 20th century. Theorists developed a tendency to use "pseudo-explanations" of behavior in terms of instincts. As humans, for example, it might be said that we have "work" instincts, that we have "play" instincts, and on and on, which actually says nothing useful about the behaviors involved in work and play. Yet, hundreds of such instincts were once proposed in the attempt to explain everything we do.
- **The ethological approach to** instincts did much to correct the abuse. Scientifically, a behavior is an instinct only if (1) it occurs in all normal members of a species; (2) it has specific stimuli or "releasers" that elicit it; and (3) it involves a relatively fixed "action pattern," meaning that the behavior is the same every time it occurs. Few if any human behaviors meet such criteria.

Biologically determined behavior is where the paths of ethology and conditioning cross. For example, various researchers on conditioning and learning in animals have demonstrated **biological constraints** on learning that are attributable to instinctive behavior, one point being that the strict behaviorists' "universal laws" of learning are not as universal as once thought.

One category of biological constraints called "instinctual drift" was observed by Keller and Marian **Breland**, in training animals to perform complex series of tricks. For example, raccoons were trained to exchange tokens for food, which they readily learned to do. With continued practice, however, the raccoons developed a tendency to hold onto the tokens and "wash" them, as raccoons instinctively do with their food, which interfered with their ability to exchange the tokens. Similarly, in another act, it turned out to be impossible to get a chicken to stand still on a platform to get reinforcement. Instead, the more that food was associated with the platform, the more the chickens insisted on moving around and scratching, in accord with their instinctive behaviors in obtaining food. Thus, both with the raccoons and the chickens, operant conditioning was inadequate in overcoming biologically determined behavior.

A somewhat more systematic demonstration of biological constraints stems from the research of John **Garcia** on **conditioned taste aversions**, involving simpler, natural learning mechanisms instead of more complex instincts.

- **Garcia's early research** involved exposing rats to radiation sufficient to make them sick, and it happened that the radiation chambers included plastic water bottles from which the rats were free to drink. Soon, however, the rats quit drinking the water in the chambers even though they drank normally otherwise. That was because the rats had acquired an aversion for the "plastic" taste of the water by associating it with the radiation-induced sickness.

- **Subsequent research** by Garcia and many others indicated that animals can learn taste aversions (1) after a single trial, especially if the resultant sickness is severe; and (2) even when there is a long delay between the taste and the sickness—measurable in hours. Both of these points violate the principles of classical conditioning, which requires repeated trials and short delays between CS and UCS, thus implying the presence of natural learning mechanisms. Such mechanisms, it is argued, would be highly adaptive in avoiding poisoning in the natural environment and could easily have evolved—both in animals and in humans.

Key 46 Early cognitive approaches to learning

OVERVIEW *Even in the days when S-R behaviorism dominated the psychology of learning, there were theorists who argued that cognitive explanations were necessary as well.*

Edward **Tolman** provided a number of early demonstrations to the effect that S-R approaches to conditioning weren't adequate to explain all of learning, even for animals such as laboratory rats. As a rat learns its way through a maze, for example, Tolman proposed that the rat acquires a **cognitive map** of the maze, instead of the series of S-R associations that the strict behaviorists said were simply "stamped in" by reinforcement (as in Skinner's later view). Indirect support for the idea of cognitive maps was provided through experiments on **latent learning**, in which rats learned in the absence of any identifiable reinforcement.

- **Maze learning** with rats was a popular approach to research prior to Skinner's operant conditioning procedures. Mazes could be simple or complex, and the usual procedure was to place the rat at the beginning of the maze and measure the time the rat took to find its way to a "goal box" at the end, where it obtained reinforcement. Across repeated trials, the rat took progressively less time to get through, indicating learning. And in accord with the classic "learning curve" that applies to many behaviors, animal and human, the rats improved quickly at first and then more gradually as they approached the minimum time possible. Theorists such as **Hull** (Key 6) tried to explain that learning curve in terms of the gradual linking of S-R bonds throughout the maze, as a result of reinforcement at the end—specifically without any requirement that the animal "memorize" the maze or otherwise think about what was going on.

- **Latent learning** was demonstrated as follows: An experimental group was allowed to simply wander around and explore a maze in advance, which rats will readily do without being reinforced. A control group got no advance exploration. Later, when rats from both groups were reinforced for running the maze, the experimental group learned it significantly more quickly. So they had learned something about the maze in advance, something that was covert and "latent" in the sense that it couldn't be measured at the time.

That's the same as saying that only their *potential* for behavior changed during the advance phase, consistent with the definition of learning at the beginning of this Theme. And what they had learned, Tolman argued, was best described as a cognitive map of the maze, which they later used to find their way to reinforcement.

Another early proponent of looking at learning in terms of cognition instead of S-R associations was the Gestalt psychologist Wolfgang **Köhler**, who worked with chimpanzees and other primates. Köhler proposed that learning to solve problems often involves sudden **insight**—at least with higher animals—which in turn could not be explained in terms of the gradual development of S-R associations.

- **Typical experiments on insight learning** went like this: The chimp is in a cage, with a banana hanging from the ceiling out of reach. But on the floor of the cage are boxes, which if stacked will allow the chimp to climb up and get the banana. And what Kohler observed was that the chimp, after exhausting such possibilities as jumping, would seem to "study" the boxes and then suddenly stack them and climb up—indicating cognitive insight. Similar experiments required chimps to connect two sticks to reach a banana placed outside the cage, which the chimps again solved after apparently pondering the problem and suddenly achieving insight. Their behavior did not, in other words, seem to involve the random trial and error Thorndike would have expected, and neither did the solution come gradually, as predicted by S-R theory.

Theme 9 THOUGHT, MEMORY, AND LANGUAGE

Cognitive psychology cuts across many other disciplines, but the traditional or "core" topics of cognitive psychology are thought, memory, and language. Perception is also a cognitive process (Theme 4). And clearly intelligence is cognitive as well, though intelligence is more global and is usually discussed with emphasis on assessment (Theme 10).

Theory and research on thought, meaning covert, higher mental processes, has most often focused upon reasoning, concept formation, and problem solving—as deduced from overt behavior and self-reports. To that we might add *learning* to reason and solve problems, as in Piaget's cognitive-developmental theory (Key 28).

Memory is usually studied in terms of *information processing,* one goal being to distinguish different types of memory and their functions. Research on memory is strongly tied to overt behavior, but theories of memory also incorporate many hypothetical processes that cannot be directly observed.

Language, especially language development, has received a somewhat different emphasis. Aside from attempting to describe the functions and mechanisms of language use, theory and research have often dealt with an essentially nativist-empiricist argument (Key 2) as to how language is acquired.

Theme 9 begins with memory, which helps lay the groundwork for problem solving and language. And the perspective throughout, of course, is distinctly human.

INDIVIDUAL KEYS IN THIS THEME

Key 47 Stages and types of memory

OVERVIEW *From the information-processing perspective, sensory information enters, is acted upon, and is either dropped or retained for permanent storage.*

Three stages of information processing provide a basic framework for studying memory: encoding, storage, and retrieval. These are analogous to computer functions, and computers are sometimes used to simulate human memory processes (as well as other cognitive processes such as solving problems). Note, however, that not only do computers have a completely different physical basis from human brains, they also process information differently. Computer information processing is *sequential*, meaning that the information is acted upon one step at a time, from the beginning of a program to its end. The value of computers is that they can process extremely large amounts of information very rapidly and with perfect accuracy. Human information processing may or may not be sequential, depending upon the task, and it often involves shortcuts and approximations. We typically do not, for example, flawlessly remember every element of a visual image—we tend to remember only what's important, plus we often subtly alter memories to be consistent with what we know and understand. In contrast, when computer equipment scans a picture and stores it in memory, it accurately reproduces every single detail (limited only by the scanner's resolution capabilities).

- **Encoding** corresponds mainly to **perception**; raw sensory information is converted into information the CNS can process, analogous to the conversion of keyboard and other input into the binary data a computer can process. Also note the role of **attention** in human processing: Some information gets dropped at the sensory level, without being encoded; other information gets dropped at the perceptual level, depending upon what is or is not meaningful or useful at the moment. When you look up a number in a phone book, for example, you single out the number you want and barely notice the other numbers around it.
- **Storage** is the next step and can be either temporary or permanent. Some information is held only long enough to be acted upon, as when you look up a phone number and remember it just long enough to place a call. Other storage is permanent, as when you memorize a phone number you expect to use again. Analogously, a computer can temporarily store information in RAM (random access memory), meaning the memory that disappears when the

machine is turned off, or it can permanently store information on a hard disk.

- **Retrieval** applies mainly to permanently stored memories, as when you summon up a previously learned phone number—if you can. "Forgetting" can result from brain damage, but most often involves a simple failure to be able to retrieve information that is nonetheless still there. Computers, of course, forget only in cases of damage to the stored information, as when a hard disk crashes.

Three types of memory, in turn, mostly relate to the encoding and storage stages of information processing. These are sensory memory, short-term memory (STM), and long-term memory (LTM). Note that they're distinguished by *function*, and on the basis of considerable research; they should not be thought of as specific areas or structures of the nervous system.

Sensory memory (also called **sensory register**) involves retaining information long enough for it to be perceived and potentially processed further. Visual and auditory sensory memory have been the most extensively studied.

- **Visual sensory memory** or "iconic" memory works like the ongoing series of frames taken by a film or video camera. Images are updated on the order of milliseconds. As you visually scan a room, for example, you see a virtually continuous stream of visual input as each image is updated by the next.
- **Auditory sensory memory** or "acoustic" memory consists of brief echoes that can last up to a second or two, allowing more time for input to be picked up and processed further. That's functional when we contrast vision with audition: When sights get your attention, you can often continue to look at them; but discrete sounds occur and are gone.

Short-term memory (STM), which overlaps with what some call **working memory**, is temporary. STM involves consciousness, in the sense that it contains what you're thinking about right now as a result of attention and concentration. STM has limited capacity, meaning limited span, and information simply drops out after perhaps 15 to 20 seconds—unless it's rehearsed. Encoding tends to acoustic, as when you're thinking about names, numbers, words, and so on. Encoding can also be iconic, however, as when someone's face lingers in your mind. And the "work" performed by STM is often to process information further for permanent storage in LTM.

- **Rehearsal** is a broad term that can apply either to temporarily retaining information in STM or to processing it for permanent LTM storage. The simplest form of rehearsal is **repetition**, as when you say a phone number to yourself long enough to place a call. Information that is rehearsed long enough, however, tends to be transferred to LTM. One way to permanently associate people's names with their faces, for example, is to say the name over and over, both to yourself and conversationally—as salespersons often do with new customers. **Elaborative** rehearsal involves adding meaning, visualizing, organizing, or otherwise enhancing the information for storage in long-term memory. **Mnemonic devices** incorporate such processes, as discussed in the next Key.

Long-term memory (LTM) is permanent, barring some kind of physical damage to the cerebral cortex, in terms of constellations of neurons. LTM begins where STM ends, and lasts for life, although some researchers designate an "intermediate" memory up to about 30 minutes and assign LTM to periods longer than that. And the capacity of LTM is seemingly unlimited, noting the sheer number of memories that can accumulate during a person's lifetime. Where LTM is concerned, in other words, your brain never gets full. Encoding in LTM can be acoustic or iconic, as when you remember sounds (including words) or images, but semantic encoding is more the rule. And note, as mentioned earlier, that long-term memories often aren't accurate representations of the events that were experienced. Long-term memories tend to be altered and sometimes even grossly distorted, reflecting simple things such as what aspects of an event you were attending to or more complex things such as your attitudes and beliefs and what you *want* to experience and remember. Another way to think of that is in terms of **schemas** (Keys 28 and 77), whereby information is sometimes altered and becomes sketchy while being assimilated to prior knowledge. Similarly, in accommodation, a new memory can alter an older one.

- **Semantic encoding** involves assigning **meaning** to experiences in the process of remembering them. Such meaning can be emotional, can have to do with the importance of an experience, can involve how an experience fits in with other experiences, and so on. Semantic encoding, in other words, always "adds" information to what is being memorized. In turn, in language, **semantics** has to do with the meanings of the words and sentences we use in thought, speech, and writing (Key 50).

Key 48 Remembering and forgetting

OVERVIEW *Popular topics in memory include ways to improve memory and minimize forgetting, including situations and events that can affect each, sometimes dramatically, as in the case of amnesia. Forgetting and amnesia are discussed first.*

Various theories have been proposed for why we "forget." Sometimes, we forget because we didn't memorize in the first place, i.e., we weren't paying sufficient attention or whatever, and the memories simply didn't get stored. But, ruling that out, one early theory was that memories simply decay and fade away, which is much the same as the **leaky-bucket hypothesis**: Memories sort of drain out with the passage of time, like water through holes in the bottom of a bucket. A more general interpretation of forgetting, however, is provided by **interference theory**, which assumes that established memories are permanent and that forgetting is primarily a matter of not being able to retrieve them. A common analogy is that memories are like items stored in an overflowing closet: They're in there, whether you can find them or not. And a commonly cited example is the "tip-of-the-tongue" phenomenon.

- **Decay theory**, as it happens, applies best to STM. Information that is not rehearsed simply fades away in 15 to 20 seconds.
- Interference theory can apply to either STM or LTM. With regard to STM, suppose you're trying to remember a phone number and someone asks you to add a couple of numbers in your head; the numbers may well get jumbled in with each other. With regard to LTM, interference takes two basic forms: **Proactive** interference occurs when prior memory interferes with newer memory: Your high school French interferes with your college Spanish. **Retroactive** interference occurs when newer memory interferes with prior memory: Your college French interferes with your high school Spanish.
- **The tip-of-the-tongue phenomenon** is when you try to remember something you're sure you know, such as a familiar person's name, but it won't quite come—perhaps because something else is interfering with it at the moment. That's why if you simply let it pass for the moment, it will often come to you later.

Amnesia is a more substantial inability to remember, perhaps covering a significant period of one's life. Amnesia can be caused by physical trauma, such as a blow to the head or a stroke. Or amnesia can be caused by psychological trauma, typically of an emotional or stressful nature. The latter, in other words, is "psychogenic" in origin, and is classified as a dissociative disorder (Key 67; see also Key 58).

- **Amnesia attributable to physical trauma** can be **retrograde** or **anterograde**. Retrograde amnesia is loss of memory *after* the trauma, perhaps because of the shock to the person's CNS, and is usually reversible. Anterograde amnesia is loss of memory *before* the trauma, and is more often not reversible, indicating possible brain damage.

Mnemonic devices enhance LTM storage and retrieval by focusing and elaborating upon normal memory processes. Though mnemonic devices vary according to the type of information to be memorized, two popular aspects are (1) enhancement of visual imagery; and (2) addition of emotional content such as humor. The selected devices discussed below incorporate both of these elements. Note, however, that the amount of time you spend elaborating information through the use of mnemonic devices is often equivalent to what you would have spent using less striking methods such as organizing the information, giving yourself probing self-tests, and so on. Similarly, mnemonic devices often don't apply to the learning of complex subjects such as the material in textbooks.

- **The method of loci** is a classic—literally. As the story goes, the ancient Greek Simonides was at a large banquet, and had the good fortune to be called outside for a message just before the roof caved in and killed everyone else there. It became his task, then, to identify all the mangled bodies. And what he did was simply to look around the table and remember the people by the location at which they were sitting. Hence the term, "loci." To use the method of loci, first envision a place you're very familiar with and that has enough objects in it, perhaps your bedroom. To memorize a very long list—and in its exact order—mentally go around your room and visualize each list item in association with an object in the room. Also make the associations mildly humorous or bizarre. For example, in memorizing a grocery list, the first item might be bread, and the first object in your room might be a lamp. Thus, you might imagine the lamp with a loaf of bread in it instead of a light bulb. For the next pair, say, sandwich spread and an end table, imagine the end table with sandwich spread oozing all over the top. And so on, with the next item and object. Later, to recall the list of items, recall each room object first.

- **The peg-word method** can be used for tasks similar to the method of loci: lengthy lists, in order. First, however, you permanently learn pairings between numbers and rhyming items, which will then be paired with the list items you want to memorize. A standard sequence of pairings is "one-bun," "two-shoe," "three-tree," and so on. If your first list item is cola, imagine a bottle of cola in a bun. If the second and third items are chips and dip, imagine a shoe full of chips and then a tree being used to dip the dip. To recall the list, remember that number one involved a bun, number two a shoe, and so on.

- **The key-word method**, which can be helpful in learning the vocabulary of a second language, works like this: In Spanish, the word for money is *dinero,* which is pronounced in part like dinner. To make the association, imagine something silly like a having a plate of money for dinner. Later, the image brings *dinero* back to you. Note, however, that many second-language words can be difficult to associate with something visual, and also that the device is best when used only in the initial stages of learning a language—it slows you down when you actually try to converse with someone.

- Also note **chunking**, which is not actually a mnemonic device but is related in that it involves improving STM capacity. The span of STM is limited to about *seven* items. For example, a random and separate series of numbers such as 4, 8, 3, 9, 7, 5, 1 is about the limit you can have in STM at one time—if you think of them as individual numbers. But if you "chunk" them together into 48, 39, 75, and 1, you now have only four items and could add more. Thus, as a common example, we easily remember ten-digit phone numbers as only four distinct chunks: area code, local exchange, and the last four numbers as pairs.

- And the **SQ3R method** is not a mnemonic device either, but it can be very helpful in studying academic material. SQ3R is an acronym for **survey**, **question**, **read**, **recite**, and **review**. First you survey a chapter of the textbook just to see what's there, looking mostly at headings and such. Then you ask yourself questions about the headings. Next you start to read, a section at a time, answering your questions and adding new ones as necessary. Reciting, then, means momentarily closing your book after the section and reciting your questions and answers, making notes and checking back when memory fails. Finally, you review the chapter from your notes and try to do it entirely from memory.

Key 49 Problem solving and related processes

OVERVIEW *How we reason and solve problems can be described in terms of stages of information processing, in conjunction with the strategies we use.*

Reasoning underlies all logical thinking, including problem solving. Two basic types of reasoning are "inductive" and "deductive," both of which are also used extensively in **scientific method** (Key 7).

- **Inductive reasoning** involves drawing general conclusions on the basis of specific instances or cases. If, for example, every cat you encounter has whiskers, fur, four legs, and a tendency to purr, you might conclude that *all* cats have such features.

- **Deductive reasoning** involves working your way to the specific, having started with the general. If you encounter a purring animal with whiskers, fur, four legs, and other cat-like features, you might deduce that it's a cat.

Attempts to describe **how we solve problems** focus on identifiable stages, including representing the problem, generating potential solutions, and evaluating the final solution. Each of these stages are apparent in classic "logic" problems such as the following, which you must solve through asking only questions that can be answered by "yes" or "no": A person goes into a bar and asks for a drink of water, and the bartender instead pulls a gun. Why? Try it on your friends.

- **Representing the problem** or "sizing it up" is an important first step. In the logic problem, a good start is realizing that the main elements—the water and the gun—must be directly related to each other in some way. Another good start is to consider that water might have uses other than quenching thirst and that guns might have uses other than harming people; failure to consider all possible uses of objects and the like is called **functional fixedness**, which tends to interfere with problem solving. Also note that representing the problem includes deciding what strategies to use, as discussed later.

- **Generating potential solutions** can be simple or complex. In the logic problem, generating solutions means racking your brain for circumstances that might explain what happened. Was there a water shortage? No. Was the guy a weirdo? Was the bartender a weirdo? Maybe, but that's not it. Was there something unusual about the guy? Yes. Did the bartender want to hurt the guy? No....

- **Evaluating the final solution**, then, means checking to make sure your solution works. Here, evaluation is quick and simple when you suddenly realize what pulls the water and the gun together: The guy had the hiccups, and the bartender was trying to scare the guy to make them go away. The solution, in other words, fits perfectly (groan).

Strategies in problem solving include the following, noting that use of each depends in part upon the type of problem under consideration. Also note that some of the strategies overlap.

- **Trial and error** is sometimes the only means available, but it's time-consuming if there are many possible solutions. Trial and error means simply guessing at random, without much reasoning or thought.
- **Means-end analysis** applies to problems where there's an identifiable beginning and end. Getting from point A to point B in a city, for example, involves putting together a series of streets and moves that eventually take you to your destination.
- **Working backward** is another way to get from point A to point B. On a city map, for example, it might be easier to devise a route by starting with your destination and working back to find the best way to get there.
- **Use of algorithms** involves applying **rules** that guarantee a solution. Trial and error, for example, is an algorithmic approach: If you were to try all possible combinations to a lock, the correct one would eventually turn up. Mathematical formulas are also algorithms: To find the area of a rectangle, multiply the length times the width.
- **Use of heuristics** involves the many **rules of thumb** we apply that aren't necessarily foolproof, but that can simplify problems and sometimes produce solutions. If an appliance blows a fuse, first replace the fuse. Or suppose you're trying to figure out a "whodunit" murder mystery: Eliminate the most suspicious-looking characters and focus instead on the ones who seemingly have the best alibis.

Key 50 Structures and functions in language

OVERVIEW *Understanding the structure of language is a prerequisite to understanding how language works and where it comes from.*

Language is a characteristically human form of communication, which, in addition to helping make modern civilization possible through the continuous interchange of knowledge and ideas, is largely responsible for the existence of that civilization in the first place. Language—especially written language—is how knowledge has accumulated across generations and led us to where we are today, socially, culturally, and technologically. That easily distinguishes human language from the communicatory sounds and gestures of other animals, although other differences such as sheer complexity, the capability of conveying generalizations and abstractions, and the capability of distinguishing past, present, and future also set human language apart, as far as we know.

Linguistics is the study of language, with emphasis upon describing language structures and functions. Linguistic terminology in describing language is as follows, using English as the example.

- **Phonemes** are the smallest units of **sound** present in a language. Most languages use a relatively small set of the many possible phonemes that can be produced by the human vocal apparatus; English uses 45 or so. In turn, languages that have a written alphabet represent phonemes with characters and symbols. The English alphabet uses 26 letters to convey its 45 phonemes, noting that each vowel letter represents several phonemes, and also that letters are sometimes combined to represent phonemes, such as *th* in "the" and *ng* in "talking."

- **Morphemes** are the smallest units of **meaning** and consist of one or more phonemes. Morphemes often correspond directly to **words**, but words can also include two or more morphemes. The verb "sit" is a single morpheme, representing an action. "Sitting" contains two morphemes, where *ing* converts the verb to a gerund and makes it usable either as a verb complement or as a noun. "Sittings" then contains three morphemes, counting the plural morpheme *s*. Also note that there are implicit rules for combining phonemes to produce morphemes and words and the overall vocabulary of a language. English, for example, tends to disperse consonants with vowels rather than string out long series of consonants back-to-back.

- **Phrases and sentences** are the next levels of **meaning**. A phrase is a combination of two or more words, as in "the blue geese" (which contains four morphemes—count them). A sentence is a relatively complete statement or thought, containing phrases for **subject** and **predicate** that use nouns, adjectives, verbs, adverbs, and so on, plus "function" words such as prepositions (of, in, under, etc.) and connectives (and, or). Longer sentences also use **clauses**, which can stand alone or modify.

- **Syntax** is the set of implicit rules by which we combine morphemes, words, phrases, and clauses to produce sentences that are intelligible. Syntax is *not* written in stone; syntax changes across generations, just as other aspects of language do, and also varies among subdialects (differing subdialects of a language exist when their speakers can understand each other with only minor difficulty).

- **Semantics** is the overall set of rules for conveying **meaning**, at any level: morphemes, words, phrases, clauses, or sentences. Semantics too isn't written in stone, and meanings change across generations in accord with a natural process we might call the evolution of language. Word meanings can also differ markedly among subdialects.

- **Grammar**, then, is all of the above, and each language has its own distinct grammar.

Key 51 Early language development

OVERVIEW *How language develops, contrasting nativism and empiricism, heredity and environment, nature and nurture, and so on, has generated controversy throughout much of modern psychology. Nowadays, however, the reconciliation is that language results from heredity and environment in interaction.*

In the 1950s and 1960s especially, psycholinguists such as Noam **Chomsky** and behaviorists such as B. F. Skinner "squared off" on the issue of how human children acquire their native languages. Chomsky argued in favor of innate, built-in learning mechanisms, which he subsumed under the heading "language acquisition device" (LAD). Skinner, by contrast, argued that language development occurs entirely in accord with the principles of conditioning (classical and operant; Keys 41 and 42). Thus, the two approaches contrasted hereditary and environmental causes, and also cognitive versus behavioral explanations.

- **Psycholinguistics** is the study of language from perspectives such as how it develops, what causes it to develop, and what goes on mentally as we use it.

In controversies, the truth is often somewhere in between, and that's apparently the case with language development. The psycholinguistic view turns out to be predominant, but the role of conditioning is important as well. The following summary of early language development contrasts the two opposing views.

- **At birth**, the infant's vocalizations are limited to cries and whimpers and gurgles and such, which convey little information. Precursors of speech reception, however, are already in place: Neonatal perception is adequate to discriminate subtle differences in vowels and consonants, and neonates prefer to listen to human speech sounds (Key 27). Such observations favor Chomsky's view, that some sort of LAD is already present and active at birth.
- **Over the first several months:** Crying differentiates and becomes communicative, because of conditioning and reinforcement. For example, caregivers often learn to distinguish "hunger" versus "pain" versus "anger" cries. Infants can also develop "fake" cries, apparently just to get the caregiver's attention. And "cooing," a welcome sign that the infant is content for the moment, appears at about two months of age—at about the same

time that "smiling" becomes voluntary and meaningful. Note, however, that crying and cooing are *universals* in early development, meaning that they are displayed by all normal children everywhere. The presence of language universals favors the psycholinguistic view, that language mechanisms are built-in. Also remember that age ranges are only suggestive, meaning that normal children vary widely in the timing of their language development (Key 24).

- **By five or six months of age**, infants are "babbling" potentially all sounds possible with the human vocal apparatus—meaning sounds that are present in the native language they're hearing, plus many sounds that aren't and that therefore couldn't be learned. Babbling often involves repetitions of consonants and vowels, and appears playful, as if the infants are practicing using their speech apparatus. And babbling is universal as well, again favoring the psycholinguist's view. Notably, infants who are congenitally deaf babble like normal infants, strongly suggesting universal, built-in mechanisms.

- **From six to ten months or so**, babbling gradually becomes more articulate and narrows down to only the native speech sounds the infant is hearing from parents and caregivers—indicating conditioning and learning. Note, however, that parents typically don't teach or reinforce native language sounds; if anything, parents tend to imitate the infants' sounds instead, as in "baby talk." Thus, a more accurate view is that the infant is actively seeking to learn the native sounds, as opposed to being reinforced for learning them. Also note that deaf infants, if given special training, tend to "babble" with their hands and then narrow down to native language signs.

- **Toward the end of first year**, the infant has typically begun combining native phonemes into reasonable approximations of words, though the words don't necessarily make any sense or convey meaning. Infants in this age range do, however, understand many of the words they hear. And by about the end of the first year, the first true words appear.

- **Over the next year**, the child's vocabulary increases geometrically. At first, the child's utterances are **holophrastic**, meaning that the child uses one word at a time to convey whatever it is that the child wants to say. "Car!" for example, could mean the child wants a toy car, heard a car outside, or wants to go for a ride in a car. Gradually the utterances then become **telegraphic**, in that words such as nouns and verbs are combined but without connectives and modifiers and the like. Now the child says, "Want car!" which at least limits the range of possibilities as to what the child means. Telegraphic sentences at first involve two words, then three words, then more, with the function words and such appearing later.

- **From age two and on throughout childhood**, the child gradually fills in all the necessary words in sentences and learns nuances such as irregular verbs, plurals, negations, and so on—with vocabulary continuing to increase rapidly all the while. And as a final general note, it appears that **semantics** mostly follows the principles of conditioning and learning: Children learn what word stands for what, what word produces what, and so on. **Syntax**, on the other hand, is acquired more actively in the sense that children seek out how to say things effectively and accurately—as opposed to being taught to do so, at least in the years prior to grade school. Research indicates that parents and caregivers reinforce much more for content, meaning semantics, than for syntax and use of correct sentences. Yet, children acquire a thorough understanding of the rules of syntax anyway, and early on, long before they are taught how to "diagram" a sentence.

Theme 10 INTELLIGENCE AND ASSESSMENT

Some theorists propose that there's a single, general trait called *intelligence* that varies from one person to another, underlying and interacting with the gamut of cognitive abilities and functions. Others propose that there are several or even many intelligences, each of which is distinct and mostly independent from the rest, in which case individuals vary more in intellectual strengths and weaknesses than overall ability. Both views correspond at times with ways people use the term intelligence in an everyday sense.

But whatever the nature of intelligence is, it is not the same thing as intelligence quotient (IQ). IQ is a *measure* of intelligence, emphasizing *current* intellectual functioning. IQ tests do not measure intellectual "potential," whatever that may be. And though a few researchers have argued otherwise, IQ tests can't tell us the extent to which intelligence is determined by genetics and heredity versus learning and environment.

Still, IQ tests can be very useful when properly designed and properly administered. They are particularly helpful in identifying children who can benefit from special education and learning experiences designed to meet their needs, including mentally retarded children, children with learning disorders, and also gifted children.

Theme 10 begins with approaches to defining intelligence and measuring IQ, then covers how IQ tests are applied and what they tell us. The potentially profound effects of environment on intelligence are also considered.

INDIVIDUAL KEYS IN THIS THEME

Key 52 Defining intelligence

OVERVIEW *Intelligence refers to a broad range of cognitive abilities, but just what those abilities are and how they should be defined and measured remains a matter of debate.*

David **Wechsler**, originator of the Wechsler intelligence tests (Key 54), defined intelligence essentially as the ability to *act purposefully, think rationally*, and *deal effectively with the environment*. In Wechsler's view, intelligence is a general trait that underlies specific cognitive functions such as problem solving, creativity, and the various kinds of learning and memory, all of which is consistent with the earlier 20th century views of Charles Spearman and then Lewis Terman. Thus, a person's intelligence could be described simply as high, low, or anywhere in between, and a person who is smart in some ways would tend to be smart in other ways as well. When you casually refer to someone as being intelligent (or not), your statement reflects the view that it's a general trait.

- **Spearman**, the originator of **factor analysis** (a statistical technique for isolating variables), emphasized a single *g* or general factor of intelligence thought to underlie all cognitive abilities. In other words, an individual might be relatively better at one specific *s* ability than another, but all cognitive functioning would be strongly influenced by *g*, for better or for worse.
- **Terman**, a principal in the development of the early Stanford-Binet intelligence tests (Key 54), defined intelligence generally as *the ability to think abstractly*.

In contrast, L. L. Thurstone and more recently J. P. Guilford—also using factor analysis—argued in favor of *independent* intellectual abilities with essentially no general trait underlying them. In this view, an individual who is very smart in some ways could be quite unintelligent in others, with no necessary correspondence between cognitive abilities. If, for example, you characterize someone as good at academic stuff but lacking common sense, your belief reflects the view that there are different kinds of intelligence.

- **Thurstone** distinguished **seven primary mental abilities** that could vary independently: verbal comprehension, verbal fluency, numerical reasoning, abstract reasoning, spatial visualization, perceptual speed, and overall memory.
- **Guilford's structure of intellect** approach specified three major dimensions of intellectual functioning: **contents** (what we think

about), **operations** (how we go about thinking about it), and **products** (the results and conclusions we obtain). Viewed like a cube, with the dimensions subdivided according to the intellectual task, Guilford's approach yields 120 or more different kinds of intelligence.

Otherwise, in recent years, the information-processing approach of Robert **Sternberg** has been highly influential. Based ultimately on research on the stages people go through in solving problems, Sternberg's **triarchic theory** designates three kinds of intelligence: contextual, experiential, and componential, which are *not* entirely independent of each other. Thus, Sternberg's theory is somewhere in between those that favor a *g* factor and those that favor independent intelligences. And triarchic theory also includes more emphasis than the others on "social" and "practical" intelligence, meaning skills in interacting with others and getting by in the everyday world.

- **Contextual intelligence** has to do with adapting to (or changing) one's environment, i.e., functioning in the appropriate context.
- **Experiential intelligence** involves coping with new problems and situations and being creative, in the sense of taking advantage of one's experiences and knowledge and applying them effectively.
- **Componential intelligence** mainly involves analytical ability and mastery of steps and procedures used in solving problems. Here, the theory designates subprocesses such as **metacomponents** (planning strategies, thinking about what we're doing), **performance components** (the actual plans and procedures used), and **knowledge-acquisition components** (acquiring and retaining new information along the way).

Finally, research has yielded the *gf-gc* **theory of intelligence,** which traces to Cattell's work on the 16PF in the 1960s (see Key 61) and has attracted a sizable following. There is considerable support for the idea of two general intelligences rather than one.

- **Fluid general intelligence** *(gf)* primarily involves thinking, learning, and solving problems, with emphasis on acquiring new or novel ways of thinking and solving problems.
- **Crystallized general intelligence** *(gc)* refers to the knowledge that we acquire through fluid intelligence. This consists of ways of solving problems as well as the many facts and ways of understanding things that normally accumulate throughout the life span.

Key 53 Intelligence quotient (IQ) and assessment

OVERVIEW *Nowadays, IQ is assessed statistically, by comparing the individual's test performance to that of others in the same age range. In turn, the accuracy of an individual's IQ score depends upon the test's reliability, validity, and standardization.*

Intelligence testing dates to the beginning of the 20th century and the work of Simon **Binet** in France. With the goal of devising impartial tests to assess children's intellectual progress in school, Binet systematically developed sets of questions and problems to assess what children of different ages should know and be able to do, typically. An individual child's score on Binet's tests then yielded a "mental age" (MA), which could be compared informally to chronological age (CA) to determine where the child stood.

- **Mental age** was assumed to reflect an orderly process of intellectual growth common to all children. Thus, a child with MA about equal to CA was judged to be average overall, a child with MA higher than CA was ahead, and a child with MA lower than CA was behind or "retarded."

Then Lewis **Terman** of Stanford University adapted Binet's test items for use with American school children, producing the first Stanford-Binet intelligence test. That test included an assortment of items assessing mostly verbal and quantitative reasoning and memory, and it yielded an overall score called the intelligence quotient (IQ).

- To determine IQ, MA was divided by CA and then multiplied by 100 to get rid of the need for decimal places. That is, **IQ = MA/CA $\times$ 100**. Thus, an intellectually average child should score about 100, a child ahead over 100, and a child behind below 100. And the further ahead or behind the child was, the further away from 100 the child's score should be.

As the development and refinement of intelligence tests continued, however, the original IQ formula became problematic. Questions arose, for example, as to whether children's intellectual growth was all that orderly in the first place, meaning that summing it all up as MA might not be the best way to look at things. And when applied to adults, the concept of MA was even more troublesome, because intellectual growth becomes much less orderly in adulthood. Thus, the intelligence tests eventually developed by David **Wechsler** (Key 54) were instead scored on the basis of the normal distribution or "bell-shaped curve," yielding an approach called "deviation IQ."

- **The normal distribution** is derived from probability and describes many human physical and psychological characteristics reasonably well. Weight, for example, is normally distributed: The majority of people are fairly close to the average weight for their sex, and weights away from that average occur progressively less often—there are relatively few extremely light or extremely heavy people. Applying the normal distribution to IQ, for which the average is traditionally set at 100, it works out that about 68% of the population will have an overall IQ between 85 and 115, about 95% between 70 and 130, and 99.7% between 55 and 145.

- **Deviation IQ** refers to how the normal distribution is described statistically. **Standard deviation** is a measure of variability, meaning how dispersed or "spread out" a set of scores is, with respect to their average. On the Wechsler tests (Key 54), for example, the standard deviation is 15. Thus, using the scores for IQ noted above, about 68% of the population will be within plus-or-minus 1 standard deviation from average, 95% within plus-or-minus 2 standard deviations, and 99.7% within plus-or-minus 3 standard deviations.

Otherwise, it was also apparent early in the development of IQ tests that issues involving the **quality of tests** had to be addressed, including how well the tests measured whatever it was they measured, and how to create and administer tests to measure as well as they could. Such issues fall into three categories: reliability, validity, and standardization, each of which applies to all psychological tests, not just IQ tests.

- **Reliability** refers to how "consistent" a test is. If a person takes a test on two different occasions, for example, and if that person hasn't somehow changed in between, the person's test score should be pretty much the same. If not, the test is useless, the same way a flexible "rubber yardstick" would be useless for accurately measuring length. **Test-retest** reliability is a commonly used procedure: If participants take the test on two different occasions, are their scores consistent? Where possible, however, **split-half** reliability is more efficient: The participants take the test only once, and their performance, say, on odd-numbered items versus even-numbered items is compared for consistency. Both procedures are based on correlation (Key 10), and the higher the correlation coefficient, the better.

- **Validity** refers to "what" the test measures, which is assessed in various ways. **Face** validity is the simplest: Do the items on an IQ test look like they measure intelligence? If so, okay; face validity is an important consideration in whether people take a test seriously. **Content** validity is more particular: Noting that the specific items on an IQ test can only provide a small sample of all the cognitive behaviors that might be involved in intelligence, is the sample adequate? Is a bit of everything that's important in intelligence included? If so, okay. **Criterion** validity is more formal and is assessed by correlation: Do participants' scores on an IQ test correspond to their scores on some other measure of intelligence? Criterion validity is often assessed by comparing scores on the IQ test in question to those on some other, well-researched IQ test. Also, because IQ is strongly related to academic performance, criterion validity can involve correlating test scores with school grade-point averages. Finally, **construct** validity has to do with what the thing being measured actually is, which, as discussed in Key 52, has yet to be completely resolved where intelligence is concerned.

- **Standardization** refers both to the **procedures** used in administering tests and to the **norms** by which an individual's test score is evaluated. With regard to procedures, the test must be administered the same way every time, as to how questions and problems are presented, how much time is allowed, and so on down to the smallest detail. If not, an individual's test score means little. Norms, in turn, are obtained by giving the test to a large, representative sample of the population to get a handle on what test scores mean—what's average, what's high, what's low. Later, when the test is actually used, an individual's score is evaluated by comparing it to the normative sample (based on the normal distribution, as discussed earlier).

Key 54 IQ tests and what they measure

OVERVIEW *There are IQ tests designed to be administered to individuals versus IQ tests for groups, and there are IQ tests for all age ranges.*

Individual IQ tests, meaning those that are given one-on-one by a trained examiner, tend to be the most accurate and provide the best information about the person's intelligence. Individual IQ tests can also provide the examiner with informal observations on the test-taker's attitudes, motivation, emotional state, and the like. Clinical assessment (Key 62) often involves both personality tests and IQ tests, to provide thorough information about a person's current functioning. Three commonly used and individually administered child and adult IQ tests are emphasized in this Key, though there are many others currently in use.

There are also many **group tests,** such as the often-cited Army Alpha, which provide less information but have the advantage of being more efficient and cheaper to administer. And group-administered achievement tests should be noted here as well, because they assess a sort of "academic intelligence" and thus provide measures strongly related to IQ.

- **The Army Alpha** was developed in World War I but used primarily in World War II for screening the vast numbers of people being enlisted in the armed forces. A relatively unsophisticated test of general intelligence, the Army Alpha was used for decades, though now the armed forces concentrate instead on tests of vocational aptitude and the like.

- **Achievement tests** include the American College Test (ACT) and the Scholastic Assessment Test (SAT) for high schoolers, and then the Graduate Record Exam (GRE) and many others for college students applying to graduate school, though such tests clearly measure aspects of aptitude as well. They are oriented toward predicting success in higher education.

The **Stanford-Binet, Fifth Edition**, a popular *individual* IQ test, is the most recent version of the test that began with the work of Binet and Terman. The current version yields scores for overall, **General Intelligence *(g),*** plus scores in five primary subdivisions that are each further subdivided into nonverbal and verbal tasks.

- **Fluid reasoning** includes tracing puzzle matrixes and solving analogies.

- **Knowledge** includes recognizing what's wrong in "absurd" pictures and defining vocabulary items.
- **Quantitative reasoning** has both mathematical and verbal problems to solve.
- **Visual/spatial reasoning** has problems with patterns, positions, and directions of items to identify.
- **Working memory** primarily involves remembering patterns and sentences (also see Key 47).

The **Wechsler Intelligence Scale for Children, Fourth Edition (WISC-IV)** is derived from the Wechsler individual tests that first appeared in the 1940s. The test yields an overall **full-scale IQ score (g),** which is derived from four "indexes." The age range covered by the WISC is from 6 to 16 years and the test is commonly used throughout this range, though more often from age 7 or 8 years on. The following are the indexes and subtests.
- The **Verbal Comprehension Index** subtests are **Similarities** (understanding how things are alike), **Vocabulary** (giving word definitions), **Comprehension** (displaying social and practical knowledge), **Information** (displaying general knowledge about familiar things), and **Word Reasoning** (solving riddles and completing missing elements of paragraphs).
- The **Perceptual Reasoning Index** subtests are **Block Design** (using colored blocks to copy designs), **Picture Concepts** (identifying pictures that have something in common), **Matrix Reasoning** (selecting a picture that correctly completes a matrix of pictures), and **Picture Completion** (identifying what's missing in pictures).
- The **Working Memory Index** subtests are **Digit Span** (repeating strings of numbers), **Letter-Number Sequencing** (repeating a mixed sequence of letters and numbers, with the numbers in ascending order and the letters in alphabetical order), and **Arithmetic** (solving verbal math problems).
- The **Processing Speed Index** subtests are **Coding** (copying symbols that correspond to digits), **Symbol Search** (circling designated numbers and letters in an array), and **Cancellation** (marking designated pictures in an array).

The **Wechsler Adult Intelligence Scale, Third Edition (WAIS-III)** is the adult version of the Wechsler individual tests and is similar to the WISC-IV in cognitive abilities assessed—although with a different breakdown of the subtests. **Full-Scale IQ *(g)*** is derived from a **Verbal Scale IQ** score and a **Performance Scale IQ** score. Verbal IQ involves language-based and abstract cognitive skills; Performance IQ is oriented more toward spatial relations, perceptual skills, and speed of thinking. In turn, the Verbal and Performance Scales are subdivided into separately administered subtests. The test items are appreciably more difficult, of course, because the age range covered is from 16 years throughout older adulthood. The following are the scales and subtests of the WAIS-III.

- **Verbal** subtests are **Vocabulary, Information, Comprehension, Arithmetic, Similarities, Letter-Number Sequencing,** and **Digit Span,** with items of the same general types as those used in the WISC-III.

- **Performance** subtests are **Picture Completion, Block Design, Picture Arrangement** (putting pictures in a sequence that tells a coherent story), **Object Assembly** (assembling puzzles), **Matrix Reasoning, Symbol Search,** and **Digit Symbol** (WISC-like coding by a different name), with the same types of tasks—noting that two of the subtests do not appear on the WISC-IV.

Key 55 The extremes: Mental retardation and giftedness

OVERVIEW *Mental retardation constitutes the lower intellectual and behavioral extreme of the population. Giftedness constitutes the upper extreme.*

Mental retardation, as defined in the DSM-IV-TR (Key 65) and also by long-standing organizations that work and conduct research with mentally retarded people, is based on three criteria: (1) significantly subaverage intellectual functioning; (2) significant impairment of adaptive behavior; and (3) onset prior to 18 years of age. To be diagnosed as mentally retarded, a person must meet all three.

- **Intellectual functioning** can be assessed by IQ tests. Using the Wechsler tests, for example, on which the standard deviation (Key 53) is 15, mental retardation begins at an IQ of 70. (In contrast, the standard deviation of the Stanford-Binet tests is 16, which yields slightly different numbers.) As predicted by the normal distribution, then, mentally retarded people constitute just over 2% of the population.
- **Adaptive behavior** refers to self-help skills such as in eating and dressing and toileting, plus more generally being able to function in the everyday world. Impairment of adaptive behavior is assessed by checklists and scales designed for that purpose, filled out by caregivers, teachers, and others who know the person well enough.
- **Age 18 years** is traditionally the end of the "developmental period," and mental retardation is a developmental disorder. In other words, intellectual and behavioral impairment that first occurs during adulthood, because of brain injury or major mental disorder or whatever, isn't mental retardation.

Levels of mental retardation are based on the extent of intellectual and behavioral impairment. The levels are mild, moderate, severe, and profound, defined primarily by IQ, but with a strict requirement that impairment in adaptive behavior be consistent.

- **Mild mental retardation** is the IQ range from **70 to 55** (using Wechsler numbers), meaning two to three standard deviations below average. Characteristically, mildly mentally retarded people have the potential to learn basic cognitive and vocational skills and function somewhat independently in society. Hence the more-or-less parallel term, "educable." Also note that the IQ range from

70 to 85 is *not* mental retardation; it is instead called "borderline" intellectual functioning.

- **Moderate mental retardation** ranges from **55 to 40** on IQ, including people who typically learn only limited language usage and self-help behaviors, plus perhaps very simple vocational skills, and need a lot of help from others in daily living. "Trainable" is the older term that mostly applies here.

- **Severe mental retardation**, in the IQ range of **40 to 25**, and **profound mental retardation**, **IQ below 25**, are usually inferred from behavior instead of being based on IQ test scores as such. People in these ranges are often unresponsive to tests and perhaps to the examiners and others as well, with the barest minimum of abilities to learn and function. Such people are sometimes referred to as "custodial," noting that they usually require constant supervision and help to survive.

Causes of mental retardation can be complex and are for the most part irreversible, but are at least understood in many cases. A general distinction is sometimes made between mental retardation because of "organic" causes and that due to "psychosocial" causes, noting that these can also interact to reduce the person's level of functioning below what it might otherwise have been. In other words, if a person with known neurological defects is also neglected, that person will be even worse off.

- **Organic causes** include genetic abnormalities (Key 18), the effects of teratogens and other trauma during the prenatal period and the birth process (Key 26), and anything else that damages the nervous system during the developmental period—including sustained malnutrition and disease. Persons at the severe and profound levels usually have organic causes, with complications such as cerebral palsy and seizures; those at the higher levels more often don't.

- **Psychosocial causes** can be extremely debilitating as well, however. Serious intellectual and social deprivation, especially during the first years of life, can have irreversible effects as discussed in the next Key. Persons who experience such neglect typically function at the mild to moderate levels, however, and can also show marked improvement through special education and other enriched learning opportunities—the earlier, the better.

Otherwise, note that **learning disorders** (also called **learning disabilities**) have nothing to do with mental retardation. Learning disabilities instead involve *specific areas of deficiency*, such as in language or math skills, in a person who is at least normal in other basic cognitive abilities.

Giftedness is the happier extreme of intellectual functioning, also constituting just over 2% of the population. Giftedness is typically defined as IQ of **130 or higher**, though children who qualify for gifted programs must also have grades and teacher recommendations commensurate with their test scores. In other words, aside from high test scores, children (and adults) who truly qualify as "gifted" also display strong initiative, achievement motivation, creativity, and a variety of other cognitive abilities and behaviors necessary to excelling at academic work—and perhaps at life in general.

- **A classic longitudinal study of gifted children** was begun by Lewis **Terman** in the 1920s and continued into the 1970s, well into the adulthoods of children who were initially selected on the basis of high IQ. Generally, as compared to the general population, a much higher percentage of the children achieved advanced educational levels and professional careers, and were also more likely to be well adjusted in areas such as marriage and social life. The study was not without its problems and critics, however, noting that a disproportionately large percentage of the children came from "advantaged," higher-income homes, and might therefore have been more likely to pursue advanced education and professional careers on those grounds alone.

Key 56 Environmental effects on intelligence

OVERVIEW *Environment, as it relates to intelligence, includes the physical, psychological, and social world the child experiences all along the way.*

Though intelligence normally continues to develop throughout the life span, experiences during the early years are the most crucial and can have permanent effects. It is clear that infancy and the preschool period are when the foundations of intelligence are laid down. And though it may be that heredity and physiology set upper and lower limits on intelligence, as some have proposed, the range is normally broad, and environment goes a long way in determining where within that range the child's cognitive abilities will be.

- **Intelligence versus IQ:** Intelligence steadily increases through adulthood, as we continue to accumulate knowledge and skills—although it may show somewhat of a decline in later adulthood—especially where fluid intelligence (Key 52) is concerned. In contrast, IQ is a measure of intelligence designed to be stable across time. That's because IQ is test performance *relative to age,* so test performance is expected to remain stable. Even so, many studies have found that IQ can change, sometimes markedly, especially during childhood and later adulthood.

- **Heritability of intelligence** is studied by assessing correspondence (correlation, Key 10) between parents and children and between siblings—especially identical twins. Identical twins tend to show very high positive correlations for IQ, even in cases where the twins are adopted by different parents and reared apart. Lesser degrees of relationship show progressively lower correlations, though still positive and significant. And it has at times been found that adopted children correlate more highly for IQ with their biological parents than with their adoptive parents. So there does appear to be a significant genetic component to intelligence. However, correlation is not causation, and it is quite possible for high-IQ parents to have low-IQ children and vice versa. Chance, in conjunction with environment, determines the outcome—or better, the range of possible outcomes.

Environmental effects include **nutrition** and **health**, which are crucially important to intelligence. It is well documented that malnutrition and untreated diseases, if prolonged, can cause irreversible neural damage directly affecting cognitive functioning. Other important aspects of environment can be categorized in terms of the physical, social, and psychological world the child experiences, potentially affecting intelligence as well as personality and adjustment.

Early research focused on **stimulus effects** of the child's physical environment, noting, for example, that having a variety of toys and other objects to manipulate and play with is beneficial—as is, more generally, having a safe, comfortable, and predictable home environment relatively free of stress.

- **Stimulus effects** include sights, sounds, the feel of things, and so on, which can stimulate intellectual growth—given that the child is not bombarded and overwhelmed, and given that toys and such are age-appropriate. Perhaps more important, however, is *how* children play with and manipulate objects in their environment, which also involves what parents and other caregivers encourage them to do. Note that "disadvantaged" home environments aren't necessarily inadequate in that respect: Toys don't have to be expensive and elaborate to foster intellectual growth. However, it is unfortunately the case that disadvantaged, poverty-level homes are often chaotic and stressful, especially when there's only one parent to care for a number of children single-handedly. Similarly, disadvantaged homes are all too often characterized by malnutrition and poor health.

Social interactions in the child's environment have been studied in various ways, including studying children in "deprived" institutions such as orphanages and studying children (and caregivers) in their natural home environments.

- **Classic studies** of children in institutions were conducted by Wayne **Dennis** in the 1950s. These orphanages were also crowded and understaffed, so that infants were often left unattended in their cribs for extended periods of time. Consequently, they were retarded both in motor and intellectual development. Some of the children were adopted prior to age two years, however, and these showed rapid recovery of motor skills and improvement in intelligence up to within the normal range, all apparently as a result of the attention they began receiving in their adoptive homes. Importantly, however, note that in Dennis' studies and also those of Skeels, as well as in many similar studies, children who experience relative deprivation for the first couple of years of life rarely improve *beyond* an average level of intelligence. The implication is that recovery is only partial, and that irreversible damage occurs early.

- **Specific factors important in early interactions**, beyond attention and interaction, are suggested by Mary **Ainsworth's** research on caregiver-child interactions during the first year of life, with emphasis on **responsive caregiving**. In brief, responsive caregiving includes talking with and playing with the child, providing the child with learning opportunities, and encouraging the child to learn, in addition to attending to the child's physical needs. Infants who receive such caregiving become "securely" attached and in turn more confident, curious, and exploring, with obvious effects on intellectual development. And note again, as mentioned in the context of stimulus effects, that living in a disadvantaged home doesn't necessarily at all rule out responsive caregiving.

Finally, research on **Head Start** and other early intervention programs also indicates the long-range effects of environment on intelligence, here focusing on direct instruction and teaching. Head Start projects have typically included special, accelerated-learning day programs that disadvantaged and "at-risk" children enter at three to four years of age. Even at that age, the children are already behind, and accelerated programs are therefore necessary if the children are to catch up. Thus, other programs have attempted even earlier intervention, including during infancy, where child and mother attend the program daily. Still other programs have sent educators and trained peer mothers directly into the home very early in the child's life. In general, long-range research on such projects has indicated markedly better intellectual functioning for children who participate, as compared to children who don't.

- **Longitudinal research on Head Start programs** in particular has indicated many benefits for the children who participate. Though early studies indicated that initial gains in IQ tend to "wash out" by the second or third grade, long-range studies have found that participating children are more likely to have positive views about achievement and education, more likely to graduate from high school and become self-supporting, and less likely to become delinquent or otherwise come up against the criminal justice system.

Theme 11 PERSONALITY AND
ASSESSMENT

Personality consists of the relatively enduring thoughts, attitudes, emotions, and behavior tendencies that characterize the individual, thus making the individual's behavior somewhat predictable. Generally, theorists agree that many important aspects of personality begin forming in early childhood, perhaps influenced by innate temperament (Key 25). Theorists do not agree, however, on how permanent early personality characteristics are. Nor, for that matter, does everyone agree that personality even exists. Social psychology, for example, emphasizes the extent to which human behavior is predictable more by the situation the person is in, noting that people can behave quite differently in different social contexts (as discussed at various points in Theme 14). In that view, personality is more an illusion, perhaps a comforting one that makes the world seem safer to us. In other words, it may be that because we strongly prefer to believe in personality, we work at appearing consistent and predictable ourselves and we also look for it in others.

Theme 11 explores the viewpoints of theorists who very much believe in enduring personality characteristics. Freud's psychoanalytic theory comes first, followed by psychodynamic theories that arose with reference to his work. Next are humanistic theories that emphasize positive, uniquely human personality characteristics, and finally "trait" theories that are oriented more toward describing personality than explaining it. Personality assessment is also discussed in detail.

INDIVIDUAL KEYS IN THIS THEME

Key 57 Freud's psychoanalytic theory

OVERVIEW *Classic psychoanalytic theory was the first major theory of personality and treatment, and, with modifications, is still very much alive. The basics of the theory are presented here; psychoanalytic approaches to treatment are discussed in Key 73.*

Sigmund **Freud** developed his psychoanalytic theory of personality over a period of more than 40 years in the late 19th and early 20th centuries. And from the outset, the theory was not without its problems. Aside from its incorporation of cultural biases and especially the gender biases of the Victorian Europe of Freud's time, the theory was eventually roundly criticized for its heavy emphasis on inner, **unconscious processes** as the primary determinants of personality and behavior—especially sex. But Freud was not known for his tolerance of criticism, and as a result, the basics of his theory changed little over the years. Also note, importantly, that even though Freud's theory elaborates personality development primarily over the first five or six years of life, he rarely worked with children. Instead, he practiced psychoanalysis with adults and built his theory around their recollections of childhood. But, nonetheless, psychoanalytic theory remains the most influential theory of personality of all time.

There are two **developmental progressions** in psychoanalytic theory, i.e., two allied series through which personality develops beginning in infancy. The more basic progression involves id, ego, and superego, which are "systems," not actual entities or structures.

* **The id** is present at birth and is where all motivation originates, meaning that everything we do and everything we become is based on the influences of the id. The id is a small but busy part of the large, unconscious mind, and "forces" from within the id take the form of **instinctual wishes** that arise from built-in, biological needs. There are two categories of wishes, each subdivided: The **life instincts (Eros)** include basic forces in **daily functioning and survival** (hunger, thirst, etc.), plus, in a category all its own, **sex.** The **death instincts (Thanatos)** include **self-destructive** forces involved in self-defeating and masochistic behavior, plus, in its own category, **aggression.** Thus, all humans are driven by the basic instinctual wishes of the id, moment to moment and day to day, and all humans have strong pressures in particular for sex and aggression that permeate all functioning. And the id operates

according to the **pleasure principle**, seeking immediate gratification of its wishes—at any cost and with no regard for others.

- **The ego** develops next, gradually over the course of the first several years of life, as the child begins to develop capabilities for gratifying the id. The ego is essentially consciousness, and operates according to the **reality principle**: When an instinctual wish arises from the id, the ego is compelled to deal with it. And if the ego can't actually gratify the wish, it instead "fools" the id in various ways called **defense mechanisms** (discussed in the next Key), which also serve as ways of dealing with unpleasant or threatening memories and interactions with others. Defense, in other words, means "ego" defense.

- **The superego** is last to develop, as the preschool child begins to incorporate a sense of ethics and right and wrong in dealing with wishes from the id. The id is sometimes said to operate according to the **morality principle**, and its functions include both conscience, in an everyday sense, and "ego ideal," meaning a sort of preferred self-image that serves as the reference for moral judgments. The superego is also conscious and often intervenes in the machinations of the ego, designating some approaches to gratification as okay and others as reprehensible. When the ego doesn't go along, the result is guilt.

- **The dynamics of the three systems** go a long way in determining personality. The closest thing to a "healthy" person in psychoanalytic theory is one who has relatively good balance and harmony between the systems, so that the person functions with restraint but still gets things done. But a person can be born with a strong **libido**, meaning "life force," in which case wishes from the id will be intense and difficult to manage. Or a person can develop a weak ego and often be indecisive and ineffectual. Or a person can develop a weak superego with little in the way of moral constraints, or an overly dominant superego with a tendency to be guilt-ridden and excessively concerned with moral issues. And on and on.

The other developmental progression involves **psychosexual stages**. These are the oral, anal, phallic, latency, and genital stages, covering the age range from infancy to puberty. The stages are psychosexual because they involve the shifting of "erogenous zones" from one area of the body to another. Only the first three stages are emphasized in discussions of psychoanalytic theory, because that's where Freud did by far most of his work. In effect, he decided that all important aspects of personality are permanently laid down by about age six years, as a result of dynamics during the first three stages—especially "fixations." Also note that the personality dynamics given here as examples are highly simplified—Freud went to great lengths to consider all the nuances and interactions possible in psychosexual development.

- **Erogenous** apparently simply meant "pleasurable" originally, with regard to being stimulated. Somewhere along the way, however, it acquired the connotation of *sexually* pleasurable, noting that Freud's theory is sometimes called a theory of "infantile sexuality."
- **Fixation** occurs when something goes wrong during a stage, typically involving interactions between child and parents. The child's personality development becomes "arrested" with regard to the joys and pleasures of that stage, with permanent effects on personality.
- **The oral stage** is first, corresponding to infancy. The erogenous zone focuses in the lips and oral cavity, and the child receives the greatest pleasure from activities such as feeding and mouthing objects. In turn, how the infant is fed and otherwise orally stimulated can have lasting personality effects. Fixation in the oral stage can come about either from overfeeding or underfeeding, for example, producing an adult who still derives primary pleasure that way. People who spend a lot of their time talking, like college professors, might do it because they're fixated and **oral-corporative**. Smoking, drinking, and chewing gum are also said to be orally fixated habits.
- **The anal stage** kicks in during toddlerhood when the erogenous zone shifts to the anal region, and the child now derives great pleasure from activities associated with elimination. How the parents toilet-train the child—noting that toilet training often means that the child must delay gratification until the appropriate time—can have permanent effects on personality. Strict, punitive toilet training, for example, can produce a person who is **anal-retentive**, meaning picky and stingy, plus sort of emotionally "constipated" and unable to express feelings to others even when it's appropriate. Or, lax toilet training can produce a person who is **anal-expulsive**, meaning flighty and jabbery and unable to keep from expressing everything to others, sort of like having emotional "diarrhea."
- **The phallic stage** occurs when the erogenous zone shifts to the genitalia, where it stays for life, and the child from about age three years on derives primary pleasure from fondling and other genital stimulation. This is also the stage where two of the more curious of Freud's dynamics occur: the Oedipus and Electra conflicts. In each, the child's beginning genital sexuality leads to lustful desires toward the opposite-sex parent, though with somewhat different consequences. In the **Oedipus conflict**, the boy desires his mother,

and soon comes to fear being "found out" by his father and castrated for the desires—hence the term, **castration anxiety**. In the end, the boy "identifies" with the father and becomes as much like him as possible, on grounds that the father will therefore be less likely to castrate him. That's where superego comes from, especially the ego ideal. In the female version, the girl lustfully desires her father, especially his penis, because she doesn't have one. Hence the term, **penis envy**. But the girl only passively identifies with the mother as a way of symbolically possessing the father and his penis, because she lacks the driving force of castration anxiety that boys experience. In the end, without that terrible fear, girls don't develop superegos as strong as those of boys, in a sense turning out to be less "moral." How could Freud have come up such a non-egalitarian theory? Remember first that Western civilization as a whole was still extremely biased in Freud's time—American women couldn't even vote until the 1920s. Thus, the biases in his theory were quite consistent with those of society, and there was a general societal view that women were morally inferior (a view proferred by men, of course). And even in the 1960s and 1970s, researchers such as Kohlberg on moral development (Key 32) were still focusing on males and "finding" that females typically didn't achieve male standards.

Key 58 Defense mechanisms

OVERVIEW *Defense mechanisms are many and protect the ego, meaning consciousness, in various ways. In turn, they also affect behavior.*

The long list of **ego defense mechanisms** dates more to the work of others after Freud, especially his daughter, Anna. All involve some kind of cover-up or misdirection or other chicanery performed by the ego, in dealing with the id and the superego and people and situations in life. Defense mechanisms are not seen as unhealthy unless they become excessive and dominate a person's life. The following is a selected list of defense mechanisms that are often cited.

- **Repression** is the most basic. Wishes and other unacceptable thoughts and memories are automatically repressed into the unconscious, where "automatic" means that you aren't even aware of the act of repression. But the wishes and such still continue to exert pressure for gratification, and can also appear in disguised form in dreams (Key 37).
- **Denial** means refusing to accept reality, thereby avoiding having to deal with it. If you're seriously overweight, you might deny being even the least bit too heavy. Or you might ignore regular criticism from others and simply refuse to accept that it exists.
- **Rationalization** means talking yourself into believing that something desirable really isn't, or vice versa. If you don't get invited to a party, you might ease the pain by persuading yourself that you wouldn't have had a good time anyway. Or if you find yourself faced with food you intensely dislike, you might eat it anyway on grounds that it's good for you.
- **Projection** means placing the cause of your problems in someone else rather than accepting responsibility yourself. If you're angry, it's because that lousy person did something to make you angry. If you're attracted to porn, it's because those bad people made those movies to tempt you.
- **Reaction formation** also involves interactions with others, but here you behave in a manner opposite to your true feelings because your true feelings are unacceptable to you. If you strongly believe people should love their mothers, but you can't stand yours, you might be especially nice to your mother as a way of reconciling your negative feelings. Reaction formation is sometimes called **overcompensation**.

- **Displacement** is an emotionally based version of passing the buck. If your boss yells at you, you probably don't yell back because you might lose your job. So, instead, you go home and yell at your spouse, or kick your dog, or otherwise "get it out of your system" (also see **catharsis**, Key 81).
- **Sublimation** is socially acceptable displacement and is therefore one of the healthier of the defense mechanisms. Aggression, for example, might be rechanneled in competitive sports into achievement in job or profession, and so on.
- **Intellectualization** refers to becoming emotionally detached as a way of dealing with issues and situations that would otherwise be too difficult to handle. Paramedics, nurses, medical doctors, police, and others who often deal with human tragedy tend to intellectualize and approach the suffering instead from a "professional" perspective.

Key 59 Psychodynamic theories

OVERVIEW *One way or another, psychodynamic theories grew out of psychoanalytic theory, though often emphasizing quite different issues and processes in personality.*

Psychodynamic theories continue to develop and prosper, usually with emphasis on conscious, ego processes. The four views that follow are "classic" psychodynamic theories, sometimes also called **neo-Freudian**.

Carl **Jung's analytic psychology** was an early breakaway theory of personality that got Jung banished from Freud's inner circle. In contrast to the "personal" unconscious stressed by Freud, Jung placed much more emphasis on a somewhat mystical **collective unconscious** shared by all humans. Archetypes within the collective unconscious, such as "persona," "shadow," "anima," and "animus"—plus many more specific ones—guide each person's unique and individual personality. Also note that Jung originated the personality dimension of extraversion and introversion.

- **Archetypes** are universal *forms* we expect to encounter—and therefore seek—in our lives. We expect to find representations of powerful gods, leaders, mother, father, and many other "types," we live the ones that apply, and we also create them in art and literature.
- The **persona** or "mask" is the image presented to others, meaning the person you want other people to see. **Self**, in contrast, underlies persona and is who you really are, which can be quite different. Too much discrepancy between persona and self is a major cause of emotional problems.
- **Shadow** is the dark side of personality, analogous to Freud's idea of the id, wherein lie "animal" impulses such as selfishness and aggression. In the individuation process, getting in touch with your shadow lessens its power over your thoughts and behavior.
- **Animus** and **anima**, respectively "maleness" and "femaleness," reside in everyone to varying degrees. In other words, we all have male and female personality characteristics—also to be gotten in touch with and accepted. The concept is very similar to the more recent idea of **androgyny**, which is that well-adjusted people incorporate both traditionally "masculine" and "feminine" characteristics, regardless of their gender.
- **Extraversion** refers to a general personality tendency to be outgoing, gregarious, adventuresome, and so on. At the other extreme,

introversion refers to being shy, timid, quiet, and the like, with a tendency to be solitary. As with animus and anima, these traits reside in all of us to varying degrees.

Alfred **Adler's individual psychology** emphasized "striving for superiority" as a prime motivational force in the development of personality. Noting the very limited abilities of infants and young children, we're all born with **feelings of inferiority**, and much of the force behind development is "compensation" for that. Those who do not adequately compensate maintain an **inferiority complex**, perhaps for life, in which thinking is dominated by ideas of not being able to succeed and not being adequate as a human being.

- **Striving for superiority** means developing one's own individual talents, seeking self-perfection, and coping with adversities. It does *not* mean "being superior" or dominating people.
- **Compensation** refers to ways by which we overcome our individual inferiorities: The physically weak child perhaps excels intellectually, the child with poor eyesight develops a good ear for music. And in Adler's terminology, **overcompensation** means excessive striving to the point of fanaticism.

Erik **Erikson** was another early student of Freud, but one who did not argue with Freud's basic assumptions and who therefore remained personally and professionally close to Freud. Erikson's **psychosocial theory** is discussed in Key 29 because it's keenly developmental. Note that his approach is sometimes classified as **ego psychology** because of its emphasis upon conscious processes.

Karen **Horney** came along somewhat later, but is often classified as a neo-Freudian psychodynamic theorist because she directly took issue with much of Freud's theorizing. Most objectionable to Horney were Freud's arguments about castration anxiety and penis envy, plus, more specifically, the idea that women do not achieve the moral maturity of men because women lack penises. Any male-female differences in personality are instead a result of acculteration and stereotypes, not innate disposition or built-in conflicts. Otherwise, Horney's theorizing was oriented primarily toward her work with "neurotic" clients, emphasizing basic anxiety that must be overcome through learning to adjust to the social environment. Some children (and adults) display more basic anxiety and also basic hostility as a result of having neglectful, indifferent parents. This then manifests itself as "moving away from people," "moving toward people," or "moving against people," each of which constitutes maladjustment when taken to the extreme.

- **Neurotic** is an older term used to describe people who can function in the everyday world but who tend to be unnecessarily anxious and unhappy (see Key 63).
- **Basic anxiety** refers to feelings of helplessness and insecurity as a result of being small in a world full of adults, similar to Adler's idea.
- **Basic hostility** refers to anger and resentment toward parents (and later others), as a direct result of being neglected or dealt with harshly.
- **Moving away** means avoiding people as a way of coping with one's anxiety toward them.
- **Moving toward** means being overly compliant and self-effacing with people as a way of coping.
- **Moving against** means seeking control and power over people as a way of coping.

Key 60 Humanistic psychology

OVERVIEW *Humanistic psychology was in part a reaction to Freud's emphasis on the selfish, "animal" side of human nature, and instead emphasizes positive and uniquely human aspects of personality.*

Humanistic psychology, also known as the phenomenological approach, also continues to develop and change in contemporary psychology. The two theorists noted here, Rogers and Maslow, are regarded as the founders of humanistic psychology.

- The **phenomenological approach** emphasizes each individual's own, unique point of view, therefore making it necessary to understand people in their own terms.

Carl **Rogers**, like many other theorists, developed his **person-centered** theory of personality in practical terms, based on his work in psychotherapy. Many of his clients displayed conflicts between what Rogers called the **real self** and the **ideal self**, typically as a result of childhood experiences in which others imposed unrealistic standards upon them. Such standards are called "conditions of worth" and tend to be perfectionistic. That perspective led Rogers to the idea of "unconditional positive regard" as crucial in how the psychotherapist relates to the client or patient, an idea that is implicit in most psychotherapy. Otherwise, Rogers emphasized an **actualization** process as the moving force in personality development: What we do and what we become is motivated by inner desires to be all that we can.

- **Conditions of worth** are unrealistic demands and expectations imposed by parents and others upon children, with insistence that the conditions be met. For example, parents might insist that the child always be popular or always excel at school work, and deride the child as not even being worthwhile as a human being whenever the child doesn't meet their expectations. The child then develops an ideal self that includes such conditions, setting the stage for conflict and discrepancy with real self.
- **Unconditional positive regard** means universally accepting people as basically worthwhile and "good," which is fundamental to humanistic psychology. Even when a person's *behavior* is wholly unacceptable and needs to change, there is still a worthwhile *person* underneath—very much like Rousseau's idea (Key 2). Thus, parents should love the child regardless and not make that love contingent upon the child meeting their expectations, even when

the child's behavior warrants change. Similarly, the therapist must "accept" the client regardless, quite apart from the client's problems or behaviors (see also Key 74).

Abraham **Maslow's** work was oriented more toward a comprehensive theory of **motivation** underlying personality development and life in general, and thus he is best known for his **hierarchy of needs**. Beyond our basic physiological needs, Maslow proposed that there are progressively higher levels of needs just as important to being human and becoming all that we can be. Working up the hierarchy, there are safety needs, belongingness needs, esteem needs, and the needs related to self-actualization. Normally, lower-level needs must be met before the person can grow and fulfill the higher, more characteristically human needs. That is, a person who is chronically preoccupied simply with getting enough to eat is not likely to be concerned with self-actualization. And in addition to those placed directly in the hierarchy, Maslow also proposed **cognitive** needs and **aesthetic** needs that relate to things like esteem and self-actualization; people need to think and contemplate and solve problems, and they need to appreciate works of art and the like.

- **Physiological needs** are basic to survival, such as those involving hunger and thirst and the other homeostatic drives discussed in Theme 6.
- **Safety needs** are also necessary to survival, including having adequate shelter and avoiding threat and pain and the like.
- **Belongingness needs** have to do with the many varieties of human social interaction, including personal love, family relationships, and society in general.
- **Esteem needs** involve positive self-image, mastery, achievement, and legitimate respect from others.
- **Self-actualization** involves knowing and understanding, plus aesthetics and appreciation of order and beauty, with emphasis upon developing one's own unique talents and potential and growing toward self-fulfillment. Maslow conducted extensive studies of famous people he judged to be "self-actualizers," and found that they consistently displayed characteristics such as being realistic, objective, spontaneous, creative, and accepting of self and others, plus highly concerned with humanity and the quality of life.

Key 61 Trait theories

OVERVIEW *Trait theories agree that personality is relatively stable, but differ as to the number and the types of traits that describe the individual adequately.*

A **trait** is a personality characteristic, attribute, or behavioral tendency that can vary along a *dimension*, say, from low to high. And by definition, traits are relatively stable and consistent across the situations they apply to. From there, however, theories differ in how traits should be described and classified, and to an appreciable extent, what traits are viewed as the most basic.

Gordon **Allport** was among the first to describe personality in terms of measurable traits, within a view that traits are "building blocks" of personality that guide and otherwise determine behavior from one situation to the next. After narrowing the many thousands of English adjectives that relate to personality traits down to about 4,500, Allport then classified traits in two different ways: (1) common versus personal, with reference to how generally they apply to *people*; and (2) cardinal versus central versus secondary, with reference to how generally they apply to the *individual* across situations.

- **Common traits** are those that apply to people in general and which therefore can be used to compare one person to another. A trait such as "trustworthiness" potentially applies to everyone, and one person can generally be more trustworthy than another.
- **Personal traits** are unique qualities that are more specific to the individual. Two people might both be highly trustworthy, and yet differ in how their trustworthiness interacts with other traits: One person might view being "honest" as an important part of being trustworthy, another person not.
- **Cardinal traits** are those that are evident in an individual's behavior across all relevant situations. Trustworthiness is cardinal in a person who is absolutely trustworthy, no matter what's at stake and regardless of the situation or context. Thus, cardinal traits—meaning individuals with cardinal traits—are relatively rare.
- **Central traits** affect a broad variety of situations but not necessarily all. A person who is mostly trustworthy, with only occasional lapses, has a central trait of trustworthiness. Approaches to assessing and describing personality (Key 62) tend to use central traits, meaning that it's understood that an individual who scores high or low on a given trait won't necessarily behave that way all the time.

- **Secondary traits** involve specific situations. A person might be highly trustworthy in business relationships and yet not especially trustworthy otherwise, such as in relationships involving friendship and romance.

Raymond **Cattell's** approach was oriented more toward *what* traits work in accurately describing individuals. Cattell began with Allport's list and reduced it further to about 200 traits, to which he then applied factor analysis to determine which traits tended to cluster together and which tended to vary independently, on the basis of extensive data derived from rating scale and questionnaires. That eventually yielded 16 "source" traits Cattell believed could describe and differentiate people reasonably well, giving rise to the 16 PF Questionnaire.

- **Source traits** are those at the "core" of personality, corresponding to Allport's central and perhaps cardinal traits. Examples are intelligence, dominance/submissiveness, and sensitivity toward others. Source traits underlie and determine **surface traits**, which refer to a person's overt behaviors.
- **The 16 PF Questionnaire** is a popular personality test often used in identifying the kinds of interests people have and the kinds of vocational pursuits that might be best for them. Examples of kinds of things assessed on the test are intelligence, ego strength, practicalness, guilt-proneness, and self-sufficiency, noting that the actual names of the dimensions are based on Cattell's relatively idiosyncratic terminology and therefore differ somewhat.

Finally, **The Big Five** is a more recent approach based on five central or core personality traits. Derived from factor-analytic research using a number of different personality tests, the dimensions are **extraversion, emotional stability, agreeableness, openness**, and **conscientiousness**. The first two refer to traits as discussed above; the others have meanings essentially the same as in everyday usage.

Key 62 Personality assessment

OVERVIEW *Personality assessment is based on various kinds of information about the person, ranging from relatively informal interviews to standardized personality tests.*

Personality assessment is sometimes done in the context of job hiring and promotions, but it's much more often *clinical*, meaning oriented toward identifying problems with self and others, behavioral and mental disorders, and so on. As such, assessment typically includes an in-depth interview to obtain a social history and determine current mental status, and then a "battery" of tests that address different aspects of current functioning and personality traits. Finally, the various kinds of information about the person are considered as a whole, yielding, when warranted, diagnosis and recommendations for treatment.

- **Interviews** can be "structured," with a specific list of questions that are asked in order, or interviews can be more casual and flowing. The latter is typical of clinical interviews, with the goal of putting the person being examined as much at ease as possible.
- **Social history** means background information that might be relevant to current functioning, information involving family, childhood development, schooling, vocation, and so on, with emphasis on prior problems.
- **Mental status exams** address specific issues such as the extent to which the person is "oriented" and aware of what's going on, experiencing memory problems or other cognitive difficulties, having problems with eating, sleeping, or other bodily functions, feeling anxious or depressed, and especially the extent to which the person is currently capable of self-control—or, in contrast, potentially dangerous to self or others.
- **Test batteries** are determined by the examiner, based on professional preferences, but typically include preliminary tests for neurological problems, an intelligence test (Key 54), and one or more personality tests as warranted.

Otherwise, reliability, validity, and standardization are important issues in personality assessment (see intelligence testing for reference, Key 53). And in general, research over the years indicates that the different aspects of personality assessment taken alone don't fare especially well. But, taken as whole, personality assessment fares much better, which is the basic reason for obtaining as much information as possible about the person during clinical assessment.

Popular personality tests include the Minnesota Multiphasic Personality Inventory (MMPI), the Rorschach inkblot test, the Thematic Apperception Test (TAT), and the 16 PF Questionnaire noted in Key 61. Brief notes are as follows:

- **The MMPI-2** is an **objective** test on which the person being examined responds to true-false statements about preferences, physical and psychological conditions, and so on. "Objective" means only that the test can be scored mechanically or by computer—interpreting the results of an MMPI can be quite subjective. Originally developed in the 1940s, and revised in the 1980s to update the language of the test, the MMPI produces a personality "profile" that can be compared to thousands of profiles known to correspond to various types of problems and disorders. The true-false items are statements, along the lines of "I occasionally feel funny all over," "I hear things other people don't," "My head hurts a lot of the time," "My sex life is over," "I think shoplifting is okay," "I like chocolate," and on and on. Some items are obvious with regard to what's normal, others aren't obvious at all—thus making it harder for someone to "fake" being normal or being disordered.

- **The Rorschach** is a **projective** test on which the person responds open-endedly to a set of ambiguous inkblots derived in the 1920s. "Projective" means that the person's thoughts and feelings and problems are reflected in the person's perceptions of the inkblots. Some of the inkblots are in black and white, some are in color. All are complex, in the sense that many different objects and situations can readily be "seen" with only a minimum of imagination. The various scoring systems include whether a response is "popular," meaning that normal people regularly see it, but then go into much subtler and more sophisticated analyses involving what determines the response (shape, shading, etc.) and what the content of the response is (human versus animal versus other, for example).

- **The TAT** is also a **projective** test, on which the person tells stories about ambiguous illustrations of people and things. The TAT is not standardized, except for the assessment of achievement motivation (Key 30). Clinicians tend to use the TAT primarily as an interactional tool, noting that people can sometimes reveal things in story form that they otherwise would be unwilling or unable to discuss.

Theme 12 ABNORMAL
PSYCHOLOGY

A bnormal behavior is easy to define and identify, at least when it's severe and frequent. The person often says and does things that are unusual and maladaptive. And such behaviors can take a wide variety of forms, but they tend to occur in patterns and have common themes, which makes it possible to view abnormal behavior in terms of *disorders.*

In many disorders, the person is also miserable and incapable of functioning effectively—at least at times—and with a tendency to disturb and disrupt the lives of others as well. Seriously disordered people can also be thoroughly unpredictable and can sometimes be dangerous to self or others, though often without intention and without fully realizing what they're doing, but clearly warranting treatment as well as temporary restraint and other intervention.

Theme 12 begins with a discussion of approaches to defining and understanding psychological abnormality, which is necessarily followed by a discussion of theoretical viewpoints on what causes it. Classifying disorders is discussed next, after which specific disorders not covered in other Themes are presented in detail.

INDIVIDUAL KEYS IN THIS THEME

Key 63 Defining abnormal behavior

OVERVIEW *Approaches to defining abnormality vary, but center around the effects on the person's life and that of others. In turn, possible causes depend upon theoretical viewpoints.*

There are few behaviors that can be universally defined as abnormal—culture and society are always involved, and what's abnormal in one culture may be quite normal in another. In most human cultures, for example, people wear clothing to conceal themselves in public. But in some, people don't. In most cultures, it's considered abnormal to hear and see things other people can't. But in some, it's considered acceptable, perhaps even inspired. And, similarly, cultures vary considerably with regard to the kinds of fears, the emotionality, and the basic personality traits their people "normally" display. Thus, abnormal behavior is usually relative to the norms of the culture the person belongs to.

- **Norms**, in this context, are rules and guidelines for behavior in everyday life, with emphasis on what's appropriate and acceptable and what's not. Norms can be general or specific, meaning that they can relate to the overall conduct and progress of one's life or that they can apply to very particular things one should or shouldn't do. Norms can also be unwritten and implicit or precisely spelled out and enforced. Norms that are enforced by criminal penalties are called laws.

In turn, discussions of abnormal behavior vary from author to author. Typically noted, however, are the following general points: Behavior is abnormal if it is sufficiently unusual, bizarre, maladaptive, or troublesome to self or others, and from there, if it is sufficiently frequent or severe. Truly abnormal behavior also tends to elicit treatment or other kinds of intervention.

- **Unusual behaviors and bizarre behaviors** come in a wide variety and can be overt or covert. For example, cultures tend to have very specific norms regarding nudity, bathing, eliminating, and engaging in sexual behavior, plus an array of things that have to do with other people's rights and property. Violating such norms can be both abnormal and criminal. There are also many subtler norms for how you comport yourself in public, and behaviors such as grimacing, howling, flapping your arms, speaking in unknown tongues, and a great many others might be considered bizarre and therefore abnormal, even though essentially harmless. And there are many covert behaviors that tend to be considered abnormal as well, such as seeing and hearing things that aren't there, believing that people are conspiring against you (assuming they're not), believing you're someone you're not, believing you have diseases you don't, being afraid of things that are harmless, having emotional responses and moods that are inappropriate or exaggerated, and on and on, including having difficulty in perceiving and thinking and reasoning and feeling in the first place.

- **Maladaptive behaviors** are sometimes unusual or bizarre and sometimes not, with emphasis instead on the effects on daily existence. Adapting to your world means functioning, surviving, contributing to family and society, and so on. Disordered people are often dysfunctional, varying in degree from not being able to get things done efficiently to not being able to get things done at all. A somewhat dated distinction here is **neurotic** (Key 59) versus **psychotic**: By definition, neurotic people manage to function in everyday settings such as home and work, in spite of problems with excess anxiety, fears, mood swings, difficulties in thinking and reasoning, and so on. Psychotic people's problems are much more severe—from time to time, at least, they cannot function in everyday settings.

- **Behaviors that are troublesome to self or others** can include most of the above, but here with emphasis more on the *quality* of a person's life. Though with some notable exceptions, disordered people tend to be unhappy, upset, nervous, distracted, incapacitated, or otherwise miserable much of the time. In turn, people in misery are at risk of harming themselves, perhaps even to the extent of suicide. And though often unintentionally, disordered people can make other people thoroughly miserable as well. In the extreme, they can pose a threat to others, ranging from occasional abuse and harm to homicide.

- **Frequency and severity** refer to observations that everyone from time to time feels anxious or depressed, everyone has eccentricities, everyone is capable of doing things other people don't understand and might call bizarre, everyone is at least mildly capable of seeing or hearing things that aren't there, and so on. With respect to each of the above categories, behavior must be *sufficiently* frequent, extreme, or severe if it is to be deemed abnormal.

Key 64 Explaining abnormal behavior

OVERVIEW *Your view of what causes abnormal behavior often depends upon your perspective on psychology in general.*

With regard to possible **causes of abnormal behavior**, perspectives vary according to the theoretical approach. Explanations of abnormal behavior can reflect most of the general theoretical approaches to psychology discussed throughout this text, and such explanations can differ considerably. Applied to abnormal behavior, general perspectives can be grouped as medical/biological, psychodynamic, behavioral, and cognitive—perspectives that often complement each other.

- **Medical/biological** explanations tend to be based on a "disease" model, the essence of which is that abnormal behavior is caused by something physical and *within* the person. That something can be genetic, in the form of a **predisposition** that makes a person more vulnerable to the development of psychological abnormality, and many forms of abnormality do show a significant pattern of inheritance from parents to children. Or that something can be acquired along the way, as a result of viruses, drugs, and other teratogens (Key 26), plus direct trauma to the brain. Either way, however, abnormality involves some kind of CNS malfunctioning, perhaps at the level of neurotransmitters. An example often cited is schizophrenia (Key 69). Schizophrenia runs in families at a relatively high rate and therefore might involve genetic predisposition, which in turn is thought to produce an excess of the neurotransmitter **dopamine** in certain areas of the brain. And drugs (Key 72) that are the most effective in alleviating the symptoms of schizophrenia also reduce or block dopamine, which strengthens the case further. Similar reasoning applies to severe depression (Key 68) and a deficiency in the neurotransmitter **serotonin**, which is involved in emotional and physiological arousal.
- **Psychodynamic** explanations also place the cause within the person, but more in terms of frustrated wishes and desires, guilts, faulty early childhood interactions, and in general inner conflict—whether conscious or otherwise. A common example here is multiple personality (Key 67), which from this perspective is thought to involve early psychological trauma in the form of abuse by parents: The child develops additional personalities as a way of coping with the physical and emotional pain and perhaps removing it from consciousness.

173

- **Behavioral** explanations place more emphasis on conditioning and learning experiences and motivation. That is, even though learning and motivation are clearly "within" the person, abnormal behavior is viewed more in terms of its overt consequences, such as how it is reinforced and maintained. And in strict behavioral approaches, the abnormal behavior *is* the problem, meaning that if the behavior can be eliminated, the problem is solved. Phobias (and other anxiety disorders, Key 66) are typically cited here. And as discussed in Key 44, one way of understanding what *maintains* phobias is that person gets a payoff for avoiding the object or situation: The person avoids fear and anxiety. Thus, in a sense, the current avoidance is both the problem and the cause, regardless of where it ultimately came from.

- **Cognitive** approaches emphasize perceiving, thinking, reasoning, and the like as causes in themselves. In this view, mistaken assumptions and reasoning about self, about others, and about the nature of life in general are primary in abnormal behavior. An example here is depression (Key 68). Many of the symptoms of depression are cognitive, taking the form of assumptions and chronic self-statements about being worthless, helpless, hopeless, and so on, which in a real sense "cause" the person to become depressed—or at least *more* depressed—quite apart from possible genetic predispositions and such. And the cognitive view is highly consistent with theories of emotion, which stress both cognitive and physiological factors in all emotionality (Key 34).

Key 65 Classifying abnormal behavior

OVERVIEW *The most widely used classification scheme for mental and behavioral abnormality is primarily psychiatric, though with input from psychologists and other mental health professionals.*

In **classifying abnormal behavior**, the American Psychiatric Association's *Diagnostic and Statistical Manual of Mental Disorders, Fourth Edition–Text Revision* (DSM-IV-TR) is the standard reference for psychiatrists, psychologists, and other mental health professionals alike. Not everyone agrees with the idea that everything is "mental"—some distinctly prefer the term "behavioral," at least for some disorders. And not everyone agrees with the criteria for every disorder. But virtually everyone uses the DSM-IV-TR. That's in part simply because there needs to be a common reference and guide, but also in part because of money: For many people, mental health treatment (like other forms of health care) is unaffordable without reimbursements from insurance companies or other outside sources, and such reimbursements require DSM-IV-TR diagnoses. In general, however, the DSM-IV-TR uses widely accepted language and criteria regarding abnormality, and it also includes informative notes on etiology and prevalence of the various disorders. It does not make recommendations about treatment.

- **Etiology** refers to factors that cause or at least contribute to disorders.
- **Prevalence** deals with the statistical occurrence of disorders. Some disorders are relatively common, others are rare.

With that in mind, the **general classifications of mental disorders** are as follows. Note that the basic strategy of the DSM-IV-TR is to classify disorders based on what abnormal behaviors are *primary*, because some abnormal behaviors occur to varying degrees in many different disorders.

- **Disorders usually first diagnosed in infancy, childhood, or adolescence** include mental retardation (Key 55), learning disorders, attention deficit disorder, with or without hyperactivity (Key 72), autism, and an array of other developmental problems in conduct, communication, eating, and eliminating (such as enuresis, Key 44).
- **Delirium, dementia, and amnestic and other cognitive disorders** occur in other disorders, but are classified here when they are primary and attributable to a known *medical* condition such as Alzheimer's disease.

- **Substance-related disorders** include intentional use and abuse of psychoactive substances (Keys 39 and 40), and also side effects of medications and of inadvertent ingestion of toxic substances.
- **Schizophrenia and other psychotic disorders** involve a variety of severely abnormal and often bizarre behaviors, with emphasis on basic disturbances of thought that pervasively disrupt functioning (Key 69).
- **Mood disorders** involve primary disturbances of emotionality and emotional states that disrupt functioning, as in major depression and bipolar (formerly manic-depressive) disorder (Key 68).
- **Anxiety disorders** include panic attacks, generalized anxiety, and an array of phobias. Anxiety disorders in general are discussed in Key 66; phobias are also discussed in Key 44.
- **Somatoform disorders** include hypochondriasis, chronic pains, and other physical problems thought to be psychological—not medical—in origin.
- **Dissociative disorders** include amnesia, problems with identity and self, and "multiple personality" (Key 67).
- **Sexual and gender identity disorders** include sexual dysfunctions and sexual deviations that are sufficiently severe to interfere the person's life.
- **Eating disorders** include anorexia nervosa and bulimia nervosa (Key 31).
- **Sleep disorders** basically involve problems with getting a good night's sleep, including insomnia, nightmares, and sleep terrors, but also narcolepsy (Key 37).
- **Impulse-control disorders not elsewhere classified** include kleptomania, pyromania, pathological gambling, and others, where the defining characteristic is lack of self-control in specific situations.
- **Adjustment disorders** involve disturbances in emotionality and functioning in reaction to known stressors (Key 35).
- **Personality disorders** involve long-standing, well-ingrained personality traits and behaviors that tend to be maladaptive, self-defeating, and troublesome as much to other people as to self (Key 70).

Key 66 Anxiety disorders

OVERVIEW *Anxiety disorders are characterized by excessive apprehension and fearfulness, and often include related physical symptoms.*

Anxiety is an emotional state characterized by sympathetic nervous system arousal such as increased heart rate, increased levels of hormones like epinephrine, and other effects associated with "fight or flight" in response to perceived threat (Key 14). More cognitively, anxiety involves apprehension, fear, horror, and perhaps terror and a sense of panic. Anxiety is *normal* if the situation warrants it. It's normal, for example, to be anxious when you're immediately at risk of being bitten by a poisonous snake or falling off a ten-story building. Anxiety is *abnormal* when it's extreme and inconsistent with the situation.

In **anxiety disorders**, anxiety tends to be uncontrollable and thoroughly out of proportion, with the effect of impairing a person's behavior and overall functioning. In some cases anxiety is triggered by very specific situations; in others the situation is harder to identify and is unpredictable. But either way, the person becomes extremely anxious and perhaps even goes into panic. The following are included:

- **Specific phobias** involve identifiable objects or situations that produce intense anxiety. Phobias can involve just about anything in the environment that has an element of danger or risk, common examples being phobias for objects such as dogs, snakes, spiders, stinging insects, rats, and roaches, and phobias for situations such as being up high or being confined or being alone in the dark. People with specific (and other) phobias generally avoid the objects or situations whenever possible. And when inadvertently confronted, the person overreacts and tries to get away, or in some cases attacks the object relentlessly (see also Key 44).

- **Social phobia** is a special case involving intense anxiety about being in groups, especially when having to perform in some way, such as giving a speech. The person dreads the situation, anxiety builds as it approaches, and then the person either avoids it at the last minute or reluctantly suffers through it. A typical scenario is that the person *expects* to forget what to say or do, to appear stupid or incompetent, and to be mortally embarrassed. And the irony is that the anxiety itself directly interferes with memory and concentration, making messing up the performance all the more likely.

- **Agoraphobia** is another special case, involving anxiety about being in open places, being in anonymous crowds, and generally being in situations where help might not be available if needed—perhaps to the extent that the person avoids even leaving home. Agoraphobia is often associated with **panic attacks**, which are extremely intense physical reactions that can include hyperventilation to the point of passing out. Thus, the person might fear having a panic attack in a crowd or in an open place, with effects ranging from being embarrassed to being seriously injured by falling. People who have agoraphobia with panic attacks often fare better in their feared situations if accompanied by a friend, i.e., someone who can help if necessary.
- **Generalized anxiety disorder** is characterized by frequent and chronic anxiety, in the form of uncontrollable worrying and restlessness, and sleep problems, and other physical disturbances without identifiable situations that produce it.
- **Obsessive-compulsive disorder**: **Obsessions** are uncontrollable, exaggerated thoughts and worries associated with anxiety. Examples are not being able to keep from worrying about becoming contaminated by touching someone, worrying about being safe and secure at home, worrying about having everything tidy and orderly, and worrying about losing control and doing something hurtful or harmful. **Compulsions** are repetitive and often ritualistic behaviors typically performed because of obsessions. Obsession about contamination might lead to washing and scrubbing to the point of pain and skin damage, obsession about being secure at home might produce checking of doors and windows over and over throughout the night, obsession about tidiness might lead to constant and excessive housecleaning, and obsession about losing control might yield all kinds of "distracting" behaviors that temporarily suppress the thoughts. In general, obsessions and compulsions tend to go together, but either can occur without the other as well.

Key 67 Dissociative disorders

OVERVIEW *Dissociative disorders, one way or another, involve a "split" within cognitive functions or within personality and the sense of self.*

Dissociation refers to a splitting or separating of functions that normally are interrelated. Hypnosis, for example, is sometimes described as a dissociative state, noting that the person's contact with external reality is diminished and also that memories can be separated from the emotional responses that normally accompany them (Key 38). In hypnosis, however, the dissociation is relatively mild and temporary; in **dissociative disorders**, the dissociation tends to be severe and enduring, to the point of seriously interfering with the person's life. Types include dissociative amnesia, depersonalization disorder, and dissociative identity (multiple personality) disorder.

- **Dissociative amnesia** involves extensive memory loss that can be global, or that can be specific only to certain kinds of memories, such as those involving stressful or traumatic events. It differs from anterograde and retrograde amnesia (Key 48) in that no physical trauma is involved; it is instead "psychogenic" in origin.

- **Depersonalization disorder** refers to a kind of separation of mind and body, as if the person is "outside looking in" and not in voluntary control of thoughts and actions—like watching a movie. Note that anyone can have a depersonalization experience, just as anyone can become anxious or depressed. It becomes a disorder if it's frequent or severe.

- **Dissociative identity disorder**, formerly and still more popularly called **multiple personality disorder**, involves a splitting into two or more personalities. The personalities have different names, and each personality tends to come and go according to the situation the person is in. In some cases, one personality may have little or no awareness of another; in other cases, the personalities struggle for dominance and are openly in conflict with each other. Relatedly, characteristics of each personality tend to be quite different, say, one being quiet and shy, another being boisterous and aggressive. Various degrees of amnesia also tend to be present, sometimes involving only one personality, other times involving them all. Otherwise, note that dissociative identity disorder has nothing whatsoever to do with schizophrenia (Key 69), in spite of public misconceptions to the contrary.

Key 68 Mood disorders

OVERVIEW *Mood disorders primarily involve distur-*
bances of emotionality and emotional state, to the extent
that the person's general functioning is seriously disrupted.

Mood refers to a person's overall, global emotional state that potentially
underlies all aspects of functioning. Thus, a person might generally
be in a "good" or a "bad" mood, or more clinically, in an "elated" or
a "depressed" mood. In contrast, the term **affect** refers to momentary
changes in emotionality as a function of the situation. Laughing at a
joke or being sad when told about something tragic are affective
responses.

In **mood disorders**, the person's mood goes to an extreme and the person may show little in the way of appropriate affective responses. The
frequency and severity of the emotional disruption is primary in classifying the various degrees of mood disorder, in conjunction with the
kinds of emotional disruption the person experiences. The more
severe mood disorders are major depressive disorder and bipolar disorder.
- **Major depressive disorder** is characterized by severe and sustained bouts of depression, during which the person feels "helpless
  and hopeless," worthless, guilt-ridden, sad, and generally very
  down. On the outside, the person tends to appear lethargic and
  lacking of enough energy even to take care of basic bodily functioning; on the inside, the person is typically in a state of emotional turmoil and suffering. Loss of interest in life and loss of a
  sense of pleasure in anything are also typical, as are related physical problems such as loss of appetite, loss of sexual desire, and
  inability to sleep. And in major depression, as well as in less
  severe forms of depression, suicide is always a possibility as a
  result of the misery the person is experiencing. Also note that
  although suicide attempts can occur at any point in the depression
  cycle, they are most likely when the person is beginning to come
  out of it. Going into the depths of the cycle, the person is less able
  or perhaps unable to make an attempt; coming out, the memories
  of the misery are still intense and fresh, prompting action.
- **Bipolar disorder**, formerly called **manic-depressive disorder**,
  involves cyclic variations in emotional state between depression
  as described above and "manic" episodes. Manic episodes are
  characterized by elated or perhaps highly irritated mood, during

which the person's activity level increases markedly and the person's needs for rest and sleep decrease. In the elated version, the person tends to be grandiose, euphoric, and intensely enthusiastic—all with poor concentration and judgment. In the irritated version, the person's manic feelings instead produce feelings of misery. Behaviors such as talking incessantly and dramatically are typical in either, and the person experiences racing thoughts and flights of ideas. Bipolar disorder is further subdivided into "bipolar I," in which manic episodes occur more often, and "bipolar II," in which depressive episodes occur more often. Also note that it is possible to have manic episodes without having alternating cycles of depression, but that's extremely rare.

Key 69 Schizophrenia

OVERVIEW *Schizophrenia primarily involves distur-bances in perception and thought, with corresponding loss of the ability to function.*

The term **schizophrenia** traces to Greek terms for "split" and for "mental functions." However, in contrast with dissociative disorders (Key 67), in schizophrenia the splitting or separating is much more basic and involves moment-to-moment perceiving and thinking with corresponding effects on speech and other behavior. During a schizophrenic episode, the person's basic cognitive processes are severely disrupted with regard to being able to think and talk coherently and being able to reason and comprehend. In a different sense, there also tends to be a split between the inner person and the external world, meaning that the person's ability to distinguish thought and fantasy from reality is impaired. Two forms such impairment can take are hallucinations and delusions. And, typically, schizophrenia also involves disturbances of emotional affect and extreme social withdrawal.

- **Speech disorders** include what is sometimes called "word salad," in which the person talks in loosely flowing sentences that make no sense even though they may be grammatically correct—the words and phrases don't relate to each other in a way that can be understood. Another form is use of **neologisms**, meaning made-up or combined words that can't be understood. A third form is **echolalia**, in which the person simply repeats others' words meaninglessly.
- **Hallucinations** are perceptions that have little or no basis in reality, but which nonetheless seem real. Auditory hallucinations are the most common in schizophrenia, often taking the form of hearing voices that convey instructions about what to think, feel, and do. Visual hallucinations occur to a lesser extent, as in seeing imaginary people and creatures, as do hallucinations involving having rotting or missing body parts.
- **Delusions** are beliefs that have little or no basis in reality, and that can be quite elaborate. Delusions of **persecution**, for example, involve believing that others are conspiring against you or plotting to destroy you. Delusions of **influence** involve believing that others are somehow directly controlling your thoughts. Delusions of **grandeur** involve believing that you're someone important and powerful, such as some famous person or a god.

- **Disturbances of affect** include **flattened** affect, in which the person shows little or no emotional responsiveness, and **inappropriate** affect, in which the person's emotional responses don't match the situation. An example of the latter is being amused by something most people would find sad or even tragic.
- **Social withdrawal** means feeling (and being) emotionally detached and isolated from others. Relatedly, schizophrenic episodes often include deterioration of adaptive behaviors such as bathing, dressing, and toileting.

Paranoid schizophrenia, by far the most common type, is characterized by auditory hallucinations and related persecutory delusions with a theme of conspiracy. Though perhaps at times incoherent and otherwise disordered as discussed above, the central theme is that the person displays anger, resentment, and avoidance of others out of a conviction that others are enemies.

Catatonic schizophrenia is a less common type that takes various forms, each involving primary disruption of motor activity and behavior. In one form, the person displays complete immobility, including **catalepsy** or "waxy flexibility" in which the person remains indefinitely in poses and postures after, say, being placed that way by others. Another form involves excessive, repetitive activity that has no identifiable purpose. And in either form the person tends to display mutism and relatively complete lack of responsiveness to others.

Key 70 Personality disorders

OVERVIEW *Personality disorders involve long-standing and typically maladaptive traits in people who are otherwise essentially normal.*

With the view that personality is relatively stable and enduring (Theme 11), **personality disorders** apply to people who have traits that cause their behavior to be maladaptive, self-defeating, and often troublesome to others. Personality disorders generally don't involve excessive anxiety, fluctuations of mood, disruptions of thought processes, and so on, which sets them apart from the other disorders. People with personality disorders, in other words, don't tend to be in personal distress and also don't tend to perceive a need to change. Yet, in various ways, their behavior often interferes with personal and social accomplishment and puts them at odds with culture and society. Selected types are narcissistic personality disorder and antisocial personality disorder.

- **Narcissistic personality disorder** involves a firm set of beliefs and attitudes about superiority, uniqueness, and being "special," and in particular the idea that other people should recognize the same and defer. A narcissistic personality, in other words, leads to the person seeking and expecting constant attention and admiration from others—often at others' expense. And the person typically doesn't have much empathy for others and their feelings and rights, within a basic justification of self as more important than others—a theme that's present in most personality disorders.

- **Antisocial personality disorder** is defined primarily in terms of manipulativeness, exploitativeness, and a self-centered lack of concern for others and for the consequences of one's actions. Historically also called **psychopathic** or **sociopathic** personality, the person's lifestyle is characterized by lying, cheating, stealing, and otherwise disregarding the rights of others, with no indications of remorse or regret except perhaps over getting caught or being punished. Aggressiveness and attitudes such as "Everyone's out to help themselves" and "There's a sucker born every minute" are also typical.

Theme 13 APPROACHES TO TREATMENT

A pproaches to treating mental and behavioral disorders vary according to perspectives on what causes them (Key 64), and, in turn, perspectives on human behavior in general. Etiology and treatment, in other words, go hand in hand, which has given rise to the many different approaches and techniques in what is generally called "psychotherapy."

Nowadays, in keeping with the *eclectic* view that characterizes modern psychology (Key 6), psychotherapists tend to use treatment approaches that have the best chance with the various disorders, based on research. Although there are few if any "cures" where mental and behavioral disorders are concerned, psychotherapy and other forms of treatment can nonetheless be highly effective.

Theme 13 begins with notes on treatment of psychological abnormality throughout the ages, and then outlines the general approaches to individual treatment practiced today. Notes on the kinds of disorders for which the various psychotherapies have been shown to be the most effective are included. Also note that there are "family" and "group" therapies (not discussed) that incorporate elements of the individual approaches.

INDIVIDUAL KEYS IN THIS THEME

Key 71 A brief history of treatment

OVERVIEW *One's view of the nature of abnormality determines how one goes about treating it.*

The idea that abnormal behavior is caused by evil spirits and "demons" goes back a very long way, into human prehistory. Fossils several hundred thousand years old show evidence of **trephining**, which involved boring holes in the skull in an apparent attempt to let the demons out. With similar intent, religious rituals in the form of **exorcism** have been employed throughout historical times and presumably before, and cultures have at times added beatings, floggings, and an array of more ingenious torments in attempting to persuade the demons to leave. The history of "treatment" for mental and behavioral disorders, in other words, is not a happy story. People with relatively milder disorders were on their own, and people with more serious disorders were subjected to everything from torture to being put away in asylums and worse, if it was decided that the demons had turned them into "witches."

- Nor were the early **asylums** happy places, contrary to what the term might imply. Asylums were basically prisons in which people were chained and neglected and offered little in the way of treatment except perhaps as noted above. The term **bedlam** evolved from the name of one such institution in 16th century London, with reference to the chaos and horror within.

Things began to change with the work of Philippe **Pinel** in an asylum in 18th century Paris, marking the beginnings of modern "mental institutions." At first as an experiment, and later as institutional policy, the patients' chains were removed and they were afforded humanitarian kindness and attention and concern in addition to much better physical treatment. And some of the patients even improved to the point of being able to return to life in the outside world.

Although conditions in mental institutions steadily became better from there, effective approaches to treatment still had a long way to go. It was more the rule that people who were placed in such institutions stayed there—consistent with conceptualizations of psychological abnormality as untreatable and permanent, along with a common public misconception that disordered people (including mentally retarded people) are inherently undesirable and dangerous and must be removed from society. The applicable term is **warehousing**, in the sense that people were simply stored away in institutions and left there.

Though such views still surface at times, things have changed considerably in the latter part of the 20th century. Our understanding of psychological abnormality has steadily improved, as a result of the efforts of researchers and practitioners from each of the various perspectives on abnormal behavior—along with their many colleagues throughout psychology, medicine, and related fields. In turn, the stigmatization associated with having a diagnosable mental disorder has declined, and more people in need of treatment now seek it out. And more **outpatient treatment** has gradually become available, both for milder disorders and for more serious ones, along with more public and private funding for that treatment. At the same time, outpatient treatment for people with serious disorders has become more feasible because of the availability of more effective psychiatric medications. And in the United States, for example, court rulings in the 1970s underscored a **right to treatment** in addition to rights involving humane care: While in an institution, a person must receive timely and effective treatment, and in the end, must be released. That, in turn, contributed to a general movement toward **deinstitutionalization** and treatment within the community, which has its own problems, but which almost has to be better than the warehousing that once was the norm.

Nowadays, **community mental health** augments institutional treatment, and in both settings the "team approach" prevails: For milder and more serious disorders alike, treatment plans are determined and maintained by teams of mental health professionals, including psychiatrists, clinical psychologists, social workers, psychiatric nurses, and allied professionals. Although treatment and treatment settings still have a long way to go, a disordered individual's prospects are now a lot more favorable.

Key 72 Medical/psychiatric treatment
approaches

OVERVIEW *Medical and psychiatric approaches emphasize chemotherapy and other physiological interventions.*

Within the view that mental and behavioral disorders have underlying
physiological causes that are primary, it follows that psychiatry and
other branches of medicine emphasize physiological approaches to
treatment—though psychiatrists are trained in psychological
approaches as well, such as the therapies discussed in the Keys that
follow. And, consistent with the team approach, treatment often
involves a combination of treatments tailored to the individual's
needs. But medical interventions are a psychiatric mainstay and provide the focus here. Typically cited are chemotherapy, electroconvulsive therapy (ECT), and prefrontal lobotomy. Surgery to remove brain
tumors or to eliminate seizures also falls in this category. **Behavioral
medicine** does too, though it's perhaps better thought of as an inter-
disciplinary approach that applies medical, psychological, and social
research to understanding and treating disorders—physical as well as
mental. Also note that behavioral medicine often incorporates techniques and procedures used in the behavior therapies (Key 75).

Psychopharmacological intervention means administering psychoactive medications (also called **psychotrophic** medications), and an
important distinction is whether the medications are administered on
a temporary, "as needed" basis, or on an extended, "maintenance"
basis. Medications usually given only temporarily include sleeping
pills, minor tranquilizers such as the benzodiazepines, and most stimulants, which are discussed in Keys 39 and 40 because they also happen to be popular drugs of abuse. In general, such medications tend to
be used for anxiety disorders, sleep disorders, and the like, where warranted and in conjunction with ongoing psychotherapy. Maintenance
medications, in contrast, do not tend to be drugs of abuse—they don't
produce the sort of "high" drug users seek—and they are used with
more severe disorders. Maintenance medications typically cited are
the major tranquilizers, the antidepressants, and special cases such as
lithium carbonate and methylphenidate hydrochloride (Ritalin).

- **Major tranquilizers**, also called **antipsychotics** and **neurolep-
  tics**, began being prescribed widely in the 1950s primarily as a
  treatment for schizophrenia. Early versions were Thorazine and

Mellaril; later came Haldol and an array of others. Such medications generally block or inhibit dopamine transfer at neural synapses (see Key 64), with psychological effects that include calming the person, alleviating hallucinations and delusions to a significant extent, and generally making the person more functional. A major problem, however, is that they also tend to have a variety of undesirable side effects, ranging from somatic complaints such as dryness of mouth and digestive problems to a severe and irreversible disorder known as **tardive dyskinesia**, which includes uncontrollable muscular movements of the face and mouth that resemble intense grimacing.

- **Antidepressants** constitute a broad category that includes Sinequan and Triavil, plus the newer Paxil, Prozac, and Zoloft, which are used in the treatment of moderate to severe depression. The former are "tricyclics" that increase and prolong the effects of the neurotransmitters serotonin (Key 64) and norepinephrine (noradrenaline). The latter are "selective serotonin re-uptake inhibitors" that affect only serotonin, but in each case with stimulant-like effects that tend to counteract depression. Side effects, unfortunately, include a broad range of somatic complaints and problems.

- **Lithium carbonate**, classified as an **antimanic** medication, is not strictly psychoactive but can be highly effective with bipolar disorder. For reasons that still aren't understood, lithium tends to reduce both the frequency and severity of manic episodes, and to a lesser extent, depressive episodes—with little in the way of side effects.

- **Methylphenidate hydrochloride (Ritalin)** is a medication frequently prescribed for attention deficit disorders in children, especially when hyperactivity is also present. Such children display extreme inattentiveness, impulsiveness, and inability to sit still and stay on task, and are thus very difficult to control and teach—even though they otherwise seem normal. Paradoxically, even though Ritalin is a CNS stimulant, it tends to have effects such as calming the child and greatly improving the child's attention and concentration. Common side effects, however, include tenseness, nervousness, insomnia, and various others associated with stimulant use in general (Key 39), making Ritalin especially controversial because it's used even with very young children—and possibly overused, simply to make very active but otherwise normal children more "controllable." Increasingly, Ritalin is also being used illegally by students to study for exams and the like, even though in this context it is indeed a dangerous drug.

Electroconvulsive treatment or therapy (ECT) was used more in the days before the major tranquilizers and the antidepressants in treating a wide range of mental disorders, but is still used in cases of severe depression, typically as a preliminary approach, and accompanied by medication and other treatment. ECT consists of sending a high-voltage, low-current charge briefly through the brain, with global effects that still aren't well understood. A positive effect, however, is that severely depressed people sometimes come out of their depression enough to respond to other treatments. Negative side effects include memory loss, presumably through damage to association areas in the CNS. And some severely depressed people don't respond at all.

Prefrontal lobotomy is a major brain lesion (Key 17), performed through relatively minor surgery, in which the frontal lobe is permanently severed from the rest of the brain—neural tissue doesn't heal. Historically, meaning prior to the 1950s and prior to the widespread use of major tranquilizers, the procedure was used with uncontrollable and combative patients who posed a serious threat to self or others. The logic of the procedure is to eliminate frontal association areas that either intensify or complicate the patient's thinking and emotionality, and the effects are usually profound: The person becomes thoroughly passive and calm. But such patients tend to be calm to the point of also being intellectually and emotionally unresponsive—permanently, in most cases. And, in some cases, patients become even more uncontrollable than they were before surgery.

Key 73 Psychodynamic and insight therapies

OVERVIEW *Psychodynamic approaches focus on revealing inner conflicts and providing insight into them.*

Classical psychoanalysis as developed by Sigmund **Freud** is still regarded as a basic framework for the more contemporary psychodynamic approaches to therapy, though with some important differences as discussed later in this Key. Freud's psychoanalytic approach was designed for treating "neurosis" in patients who were fairly intelligent and motivated for change, which is still the case with psychodynamic therapies. They apply to a broad range of disorders in which the person's basic thinking and reasoning processes are intact, plus cases where the person isn't exactly disordered but is chronically preoccupied and unhappy and not getting everything out of life because of inner conflicts—conscious or otherwise. But psychodynamic therapies aren't, for example, appropriate with schizophrenia. Few if any psychotherapies are.

- **Neurosis** is an older term that includes what we now call anxiety disorders, somatoform disorders, and some dissociative disorders (see also Keys 59 and 63).

Freud's view was that neurotic disorders are caused by unconscious conflicts, often attributable to fixations and other events of early childhood, especially those one way or another involving sexuality (Key 32). Thus, classical psychoanalysis was oriented toward bringing such matters into consciousness. The logic was that fixations, unacceptable desires, guilts, and other "causes" of neurosis were problematic *because* they were dark and unconscious, and that they would cease to be problematic when brought into the light of day. The goal of psychoanalysis, then, was (and is) for the patient to attain **insight**, which means understanding the origins and nature of conflicts and knowing them for what they are.

Throughout his lengthy career as theorist and practitioner, Freud used various **techniques** for delving into the unconscious:

- **Hypnosis and age regression** (Key 38) were oriented toward identifying the sources of conflicts in early childhood. And throughout most of his adult life, Freud used self-hypnosis and age regression to better understand himself and to aid in developing his psychoanalytic theory, which was based a lot on himself.

- **Dream analysis** meant getting underneath the manifest content of dreams to the latent, unconscious meaning of them (Key 37). Then, as now, people interpreted their own idiosyncratic dreams rather having the therapist do it for them and risk misinterpretation. Freud did believe, however, that there were a few "universal" dreams that had the same meaning for everyone. An example is the dream of "flying," which Freud thought represented repressed desires to open up sexually to others.
- **Free association** meant that the patient was encouraged to relax, drift, and say whatever came to mind, with only occasional and subtle direction by the therapist in the form of suggestions and emphasis. Freud's logic here was that unconscious material exerted constant pressure and would sooner or later turn up in what the patient said. Jung (Key 59) later developed a somewhat more efficient version of free association in which the patient responds to a list of words designed to elicit emotional content.
- **Interpretations** by the therapist tended to come in the later stages of psychoanalysis, when the therapist was fairly sure what the underlying problems were. Comments and statements by the patient would be directly interpreted in terms of their presumed underlying meaning.

Freud also made a number of observations about **processes** that occur during psychoanalysis and that can augment its effectiveness:

- **Resistance** was characteristic of most patients, in Freud's view. The patient shows a pattern of avoiding certain kinds of topics, even when encouraged to talk about them, thus indicating underlying conflicts. Similarly, down the line, if a patient has difficulty accepting an interpretation, Freud would view it as additional evidence that the interpretation was correct.
- **Transference** stems from Freud's belief that childhood experiences with parents are crucial. The patient might unconsciously come to view the therapist as a father figure or mother figure, and behave accordingly, also providing evidence as to the nature of underlying conflicts dating to childhood.
- **Catharsis** refers to the patient's tendency at times to become highly emotional and "vent" feelings by crying or perhaps displaying anger and verbal aggression. In Freud's view, catharsis was to be encouraged (within limits), on grounds that it eased underlying pressures and could help in attaining insight (but see Key 81).

Classical psychoanalysis, then, tended to be a lengthy and expensive undertaking requiring patient-therapist sessions several times per week for many years—especially because of free association. And many theorists and therapists in years since have believed that Freud placed too much emphasis on the unconscious anyway (as in Key 59). Thus, **modern psychodynamic therapies** still use many of Freud's techniques and processes but attempt to address problems more directly and speed things up. The following differences from classical psychoanalysis are typical, noting, however that modern psychodynamic approaches are diverse and vary considerably both in techniques and in the kinds of issues they address.

- **Sessions are conducted face-to-face**. Freud preferred having the patient lie on a couch, thus ruling out much in the way of eye contact and personal interaction. Nowadays, patient and therapist face each other directly and personal interaction is encouraged.
- **Time limits** on the long-term duration of therapy are often set in advance, with sessions held only once per week.
- **Current conflicts** and also values and outlook on life in general are stressed as opposed to early childhood experiences. Even though early experiences may be important, what's happening here and now tends to get much more emphasis.
- **Conscious conflicts** and **ego analysis** are emphasized. Patients are encouraged to consider their conscious thoughts and desires and work on them directly, with the goal of *deliberately* changing both personality characteristics and overt behaviors. Relatedly, the therapist tends to offer interpretations freely and doesn't necessarily view a patient's rejection of them as resistance.

Key 74 Humanistic therapies

OVERVIEW *Humanistic therapies emphasize increased awareness and understanding of self, integration of personality, and an overall goal of personal growth.*

The **person-centered** or **client-centered psychotherapy** of Carl **Rogers** is the origin of humanistic psychotherapies and is based directly on his phenomenological approach to personality (Key 60). As with psychodynamic therapies, it applies where the person is intelligent, articulate, and motivated for change, but lacking awareness as to what to do. Humanistic therapies in general also apply to a broad range of disorders in which thinking and reasoning are intact, and especially to people who have somewhat more ambiguous life problems such as low self-esteem, basic unhappiness, and lack of a sense of fulfillment or purpose in life, including perhaps being "stalled" with regard to personal growth. Also note that person-centered therapy was designed with a premise that *clients must figure it out for themselves*, with the therapist functioning as a nonjudgmental companion and at most as a guide. Hence the term "nondirective."

- Being **nonjudgmental** is implicit in **unconditional positive regard**. Rogers strongly believed that each person is unique, that each person should be responsible for the conduct and direction of his or her own life, and especially that one person should not impose beliefs and values on another.

- The **nondirective** approach is similar to the free association used by Freud, in that the content of sessions is open-ended and determined mostly by the client. And it can be similarly time-consuming and expensive. Humanistic therapies nowadays tend to be much more directive and to the point, as was Rogers in his last years as a practitioner.

From there, Rogers employed various techniques to keep the therapeutic process going and make it optimally beneficial for the client with a minimum of influence and input by the therapist. In addition to the above, important elements of the person-centered approach are active listening, genuineness, and empathic understanding.

- **Active listening** is a set of techniques that help maintain the conversational flow and keep it focused. From time to time, for example, the therapist slightly restates what the client says, perhaps posing it as a question, but without adding or implying anything in the way of interpretation.

- **Genuineness** refers to the therapist being open and also expressing feelings toward the client where appropriate—negative feelings as well as positive ones. For example, if the therapist becomes irritated by what the client is expressing, the therapist acknowledges it openly instead of trying to hide it.
- **Empathic understanding** means seeing and feeling things from the client's own point of view, consistent with the phenomenological approach.

Existential psychotherapy, such as the **Gestalt therapy** of Fritz **Perls**, is consistent with the humanistic orientation toward self-exploration, self-awareness, and personal growth, and it applies to essentially the same clients. But it's even more focused on the present tense, as opposed to the ultimate causes of problems, and there is considerable emphasis on getting inner conflicts and contradictions out in the open and facing them—as in psychodynamic approaches. Gestalt techniques differ from most other approaches, however, in emphasizing role-playing and especially outright confrontation.

- **Gestalt** here has nothing to do with Gestalt psychology as discussed in earlier Themes, except that is expresses a comparable idea: Consider the whole person instead of the parts, and work toward the person "becoming " whole.
- **Role-playing** is a technique used from time to time in many approaches to psychotherapy: The client takes someone else's role and acts it out, which can provide insight into another's behavior as well as one's own. In Gestalt therapy, the role-playing can also be more abstract and the client acts out feelings, thoughts, and portions of personality. Sometimes the therapist plays roles as well, including the role of the client.
- **Confrontation** stands in marked constrast to most other therapies. The typical Gestalt therapist, for example, isn't hesitant to become highly animated and to interpret and even attack the client's statements, perhaps getting right in the client's face about absurdities and contradictions.

Key 75 Behavior therapies

OVERVIEW *Behavior therapies focus on the problem behavior itself, with little or no emphasis on underlying thoughts, feelings, or personality characteristics.*

Behavior therapies logically follow from the behavioral approach to understanding disorders (Key 64). Strict behaviorists tend to take a disparaging view of "inner" processes as unfit for scientific endeavor in the first place, further arguing that the abnormal behavior *is* the problem and that the best ways to treat it are classical and operant conditioning (Theme 8). Somewhat less strict behaviorists acknowledge that underlying thoughts and feelings and such can be important too, and use procedures such as "observational learning," but still focus on the behavior itself. In general, the behavioral approach has been applied broadly in abnormal psychology, including treatments for anxiety disorders, substance abuse, enuresis, and a variety of other highly specific problem behaviors, and even psychotic disorders such as schizophrenia—the latter with regard to adaptive behaviors.

- **Observational learning** is sometimes cited as a third basic type of learning where classical and operant conditioning are the first two. The basic approach is still thoroughly behavioral: Learning can readily occur when the participant simply observes another person or "model" receive reinforcement or punishment, and beyond that, even when the model experiences no consequences at all (see Key 81). Less behavioral is the underlying process called **imitation**, which is presumed to be inherent and intrinsically motivated in many species and especially humans.

Systematic desensitization is a primarily behavioral treatment based on the work of Joseph **Wolpe** in the 1950s, applicable to phobias and other disorders that involve anxiety and avoidance, and incorporating elements both of classical and operant conditioning. Procedures vary, but typically the phobic person first learns and practices a relaxation technique for reducing muscle tension and anxiety. Then the therapist and the client devise a "hierarchy," progressing gradually from mild and nonthreatening instances involving the phobia to intensely threatening ones. Therapy begins with the mild instances and goes forward, and as the client becomes anxious, the therapist pauses and instructs the client to relax. Many phobias can be eliminated in a matter of weeks, not months or years. And in the behaviorist view, once the phobic behavior no longer occurs, the problem is gone.

- **Relaxation techniques** typically involve attending to muscle groups one at a time, starting perhaps in the feet, working up through the legs, and eventually through the entire body until the person is completely relaxed. Such techniques are also used in hypnosis (Key 38).
- A **desensitization hierarchy** can involve phobic objects or situations. For example, if a person is phobic for bees and other stinging insects, the first item in the hierarchy might be as simple as the word "bee" printed on a card. Next might come a card with a very simple outline drawing of a bee, then cards with bees drawn in progressively more detail, then color drawings, then photographs, and so on. Down the line, the goal might be having a live bee present. And at the point where the person can consistently be exposed to bees without becoming anxious, the phobia has been eliminated.

Behavior modification, based on operant conditioning, has been applied broadly to everything from specific problem behaviors to more complex and severe mental disorders. As noted in Key 44, a major advantage of behavior modification is that it doesn't necessarily require being able to communicate with the client, unlike other approaches to therapy. That can be a disadvantage too, of course, if the person doing the modifying is perceived as coldly scientific and if the person whose behavior is being modified isn't entirely willing, each of which has sometimes been the case in the history of behavior modification. Apart from such issues, however, treatments based on behavior modification are generally very effective in eliminating undesirable behaviors as well as fostering desirable ones. Examples often cited in this context are biofeedback and token economies. Bear in mind, however, that behavior modification can be applied to just about any behavior, given that the behavior can be objectively defined and measured, and given that it's possible to exert control over reinforcement contingencies.

Biofeedback can be used in treating specific problems with blood pressure, heart rate, and muscular tension, and more generally in treating the effects of stress and emotional tension. The basic procedure is that the client is hooked up to electronic equipment that monitors the behavior in question and provides ongoing visual or auditory feedback. While watching or listening, the client then concentrates on changing the behavior, such as lowering blood pressure or heart rate. And in general, the treatment is highly effective—except that people typically don't learn to alter the behavior when not hooked up to the equipment.
- **Applied to emotional tension**, a popular procedure is to use an EEG and have the client attempt to produce alpha waves associated with being in a relaxed, peaceful state (Key 37).

Token economies were once used on a widespread basis in institutions for the mentally disordered (and those for the mentally retarded), and were intended to be therapeutic as well as to help in managing patients in a positive, nonaversive way. In a typical token economy, an extensive set of physically and socially adaptive behaviors was specified, including everything from behaviors involved in keeping oneself and one's area neat and clean to behaviors having to do with interacting appropriately with others. For each instance of performing such behaviors, patients received tokens (more often tally marks on a list) that could later be exchanged for treats and privileges. And when conducted fairly and consistently, and combined with basic requirements that the staff be friendly and attentive toward the patients and concerned about their needs, token economies fared well. And patients responded well.

- **Problems** were that a large, dispersed institutional staff won't always be consistent and impartial in giving tokens. Plus, it was apparently sometimes the case that the token economy "took over" and was viewed by staff as more important than other considerations such as being friendly and attentive and concerned. But more basically, there were ethical issues that were difficult to resolve. For example, in order for the tokens to be meaningful, they had to buy things that otherwise weren't available. That meant that the patients who didn't (or couldn't) cooperate had to do without the treats and privileges, which was hard to defend on humanitarian grounds. Similarly, it was argued that token economies exerted undue influence and control over the patients, especially with regard to the necessarily strict definitions of what was "desirable" and what was not.

Key 76 Cognitive therapies

OVERVIEW *Cognitive therapies focus on the thinking that underlies abnormal behavior.*

In **cognitive psychotherapy**, the emphasis is on perceptions, thoughts, beliefs, and attitudes that underlie mental and behavioral abnormality, consistent with the cognitive approach to explaining disorders in the first place. Cognitive approaches generally apply to the same kinds of disorders as psychodynamic and humanistic approaches, including people who aren't exactly disordered but are unhappy and poorly adjusted and so on, along with people who have problems such as lacking assertiveness and not being able to make decisions. And cognitive approaches especially require fairly intelligent and verbal clients who can think extensively about their own thinking. "Cognitive-behavior" therapies, in turn, also apply to out-of-control behaviors such as substance abuse, overeating, and more generally bad habits. Like humanistic psychotherapies, cognitive therapy is very much oriented toward the here and now. But it can instead be extremely interpretative and confrontational. Examples include cognitive restructuring, rational-emotive therapy, and self-control/self-regulation therapy.

- **Cognitive-behavior therapy** is best thought of as a subcategory of cognitive therapy, a possible distinction being that more emphasis is placed on having the client *do* things differently as well as well as think about them differently. But all cognitive therapies emphasize that to an extent, the purpose being that the client experience consequences in life that reinforce changes in thinking.

Cognitive restructuring, as developed by Aaron **Beck**, is a good starting point in understanding how cognitive therapy works—especially as applied to depression. In Beck's view, of primary importance are attitudes toward self and the negative "self-talk" depressed people regularly engage in. In depression, for example, people engage in an endless stream of negative self-statements regarding being helpless and powerless, being hopeless that things will ever change, being worthless, being guilty and unpardonable, and on and on (Key 68). Such self-talk, in Beck's view, has four characteristics: The person tends to (1) selectively perceive the world as harmful and ignore evidence to the contrary; (2) overgeneralize; (3) magnify events all out of proportion; and (4) think about things in absolute terms. A major part of psychotherapy, then, consists of enabling the client to identify negative self-talk and challenge it, and in turn put changes in thinking into practice in daily living.

- **Self-talk** tends to be automatic, extremely rapid, and often not entirely conscious. The idea is that when we think about ourselves and about situations involving others, we often do so in the form of statements that reflect our general observations and beliefs about life. For example, if you strongly believe that people are basically rotten and untrustworthy, little reminders to that effect will frequently show up in your thinking. In cognitive therapy, the client first learns to slow down and identify such thoughts, then to change them where warranted.

The **rational-emotive behavior therapy** practiced by Albert **Ellis** is similar to Beck's cognitive restructuring and works from the same basic assumptions, but Ellis goes further in specifying how thoughts influence emotions and behavior with his "ABCDE" theory and also gives a more specific list of the kinds of irrational beliefs people sometimes hold onto dearly. Another difference is that rational-emotive behavior therapy tends to be based much more on debate and confrontation, at times even to the point of the therapist labeling the client's thinking as ridiculous and absurd, but while nonetheless maintaining rapport. As in cognitive restructuring, however, the client basically learns to slow down automatic thinking and identify and challenge irrational self-statements and beliefs.

- **ABCDE** refers to an event (A); the client's mistaken appraisal of it (B); the client's emotional responses and other behavior (C); the client's eventual ability to challenge and dispute the mistaken beliefs inherent in the B-phase appraisal (D); and the new emotional responses after therapy (E). For example, prior to therapy, the person might be rejected by a potential lover (A), decide that the rejection is evidence of being completely unlovable and worthless (B), and become anxious or depressed and avoid future romantic efforts (C). The goal of therapy, then, is to establish a D process, in which the person argues with the tendency to overreact and overgeneralize, resulting in the E phase, when the client has succeeded in making changes. One instance of rejection doesn't logically imply being unlovable or worthless, and the client learns to challenge such thoughts whenever they occur, thereby eliminating the undesirable emotional responses and behavior and substituting desirable ones.

- **Irrational beliefs** Ellis frequently encountered in developing his approach include that it is a dire necessity to be loved or approved by everyone, that you must be thoroughly competent in all respects to be a worthwhile human being, that it is awful and catastrophic when things don't go your way, that it is easier to avoid difficulties than to face them, that there is a right and perfect solution to every problem, and many others.

Self-control/self-regulation therapies take a variety of forms and are classified by some authors as behavior therapies instead, but they usually involve what the client thinks about as well as what the client does. General characteristics are (1) that the therapist and the client identify target behaviors to be changed and define them clearly; (2) that a method by which the client charts or otherwise monitors the behavior is devised and put into effect; and (3) that the client does everything possible to make the target behavior less likely to occur.

- **Identifying target behaviors**: As in operant conditioning, there's no room for equivocation as to what does or doesn't constitute an instance of the behavior. In dieting and weight loss, for example, eating specific kinds and amounts of foods would be okay, others not.

- **Charting** takes the form of an hourly or daily record of the target behavior, as appropriate. In dieting, a record of calories (or other nutritional measures) would be kept, perhaps in addition to amounts of foods consumed—with no cheating. Similarly, as the bottom line, a daily weight record would be kept as well.

- **Making the behavior less likely to occur** includes things like avoiding situations in which it's more likely, making recreational and pleasurable activities contingent upon progress, substituting incompatible activities, and regularly thinking about things that make the behavior less desirable. In dieting, respectively, the client would avoid loitering in the kitchen and wouldn't have tempting treats in there in the first place, would perhaps go a movie at the end of the week only if criterion weight loss is met, might do things like jogging and exercising whenever the urge for a treat arises, and might try imagining all sorts of horrors and undesirable consequences whenever the urge to overeat occurs. Note in particular that there's no mention of "will power" as the way to get behavior under control. Will power is involved in staying on track, but every effort is made to minimize it. Dieters who believe that they "should" be able to resist temptation, say, by having forbidden treats around and refusing to eat them, invariably set themselves up for failure—and disappointment and frustration as well.

Theme 14 SOCIAL PSYCHOLOGY

Social psychology is an area of psychology broad enough to constitute a discipline in its own right. Defined generally as the study of how people influence and are influenced by others, social psychology differs from disciplines such as sociology in its greater emphasis upon the individual. And traditionally placed last in surveys of psychology, it includes theory and research on human interactions relevant to many other areas, especially areas within developmental psychology and clinical psychology. Humans are, in essence, social animals. And who we are and what we do is strongly affected by our experiences with other people all along the way. That includes, with emphasis here, how we are affected by the social situations we find ourselves in. In contrast with the trait approaches discussed in Theme 11, much of social psychology is disinclined to view people in terms of stable personality characteristics—although a large body of theory and research is based on relatively stable beliefs and attitudes and the like. And it is also acknowledged that whether personality meaningfully exists or not, people often behave as if it does.

Theme 14 begins with discussions of beliefs, attitudes, and other basic elements and processes in social psychological theory. The remainder of the Theme then presents selected topics social psychologists have often addressed, including methods of persuasion, what's involved in conforming and complying, what determines aggression toward others, and what happens to people in groups.

INDIVIDUAL KEYS IN THIS THEME

Key 77 Beliefs, attitudes, and schemas

OVERVIEW *The "building blocks" of social psychological theory are cognitive.*

Beliefs are ideas we hold to be true about people and things, and which influence our behavior, whether they're accurate or otherwise. Often taking the form of propositions and assumptions, beliefs are acquired through our own experiences as well as through what others tell and teach us. Beliefs can vary from general to specific. For example, the idea that all people are basically good (or bad) is a very general belief; the same idea about a certain group of people is much more specific. Beliefs also vary in the intensity with which they are held. Some beliefs are held strongly and are hard to change, others less so.

Attitudes incorporate beliefs and add an **evaluative** component. Attitudes, in other words, tend to have emotionality associated with them, as when we "like" or "dislike" someone or something. As with beliefs, attitudes can range from general to specific and can vary considerably in intensity. Social psychological theory and research have often addressed issues such as where attitudes come from in the first place and in turn the extent to which they influence our behavior, plus how attitudes can be changed (see especially Key 79).

- **Where attitudes come from** can be understood in terms of classical conditioning, operant conditioning, observational learning, or higher cognitive processes—the common theme being that something pleasant or unpleasant is involved. Consider phobias as an example (Keys 44 and 66), because, in addition to anxiety and avoidance, they incorporate intense dislike of the object or situation—an intense attitude. Phobias and the negative attitudes that underlie them can be learned and maintained in any of the preceding ways. Similarly, positive or favorable attitudes toward people and things can be learned where pleasant occurrences are involved. Advertisers, for example, often associate pleasant situations and outcomes with name-brand products, the goal being to foster favorable attitudes and make you more likely to buy their product.

- **Attitudes influence behavior**, but don't necessarily determine it, which means that we don't always behave in accord with what we believe and feel. A classic study by Richard **LaPiere** in the 1930s on American prejudice toward people of Chinese origin is often cited here. A Chinese couple visited hotels and restaurants and was refused service only once. Later, however, over 90% of the ho and restaurants that replied to a questionnaire indicated that the establishments would *not* serve Chinese people. Thus, though the study was not without methodological problems, the indication was that prejudiced attitudes don't always produce actual prejudiced behavior. More generally, research has often found that the *situation* strongly influences whether behavior corresponds to attitudes, ethics, personality traits, and the like. Behaving in accord with a trait such as honesty, for example, sometimes depends on just how much is at stake and the chances of getting caught.

Schemas are cognitive or "mental" representations comprised of knowledge, beliefs, and attitudes. Similar to the way Piaget used the term (Key 28), schemas are how we organize knowledge and understanding, and the new situations we encounter can either be assimilated or cause us to accommodate. In social psychology, the schemas of interest often involve overgeneralizations and other kinds of errors in how we understand and feel about people, at times to the point of stereotyping. **Schematic processing**, for example, refers to evaluating other people "automatically," wherein we assimilate them to our existing schemas for that supposed type of person and perhaps behave accordingly. Schematic processing is more likely to occur in situations where we don't have much time or much reason to think about the person in question as an individual.

- A **stereotype** is an interrelated set of beliefs and attitudes that is evoked, say, when encountering a person with certain features or characteristics. Stereotypes can involve general categories of people based on race, ethnicity, religion, gender, and so on, in turn based on physical characteristics and appearance, speech accent, mode of dress, or you-name-it. **Stereotyping**, then, is when you ascribe certain abilities or traits to the individual standing before you based on such a schema and its associated characteristics. **Bias** and **prejudice** involve intensely negative beliefs and attitudes associated with stereotypes, noting that stereotypes can just as often be erroneously positive. And **discrimination** is when you actually do something to a person as a result of stereotypes. One basic way stereotypes are formed is by overgeneralizing from a few experiences or even a single intense experience with people of some type. Stereotypes can also come about through what our significant others tell and teach us, and especially how we see them behave toward other people.

Key 78 Impressions and attributions

OVERVIEW *Two traditional areas of study pertaining to how we perceive ourselves and others are impression formation and attribution.*

Impressions involve attitudes toward a person, as when we have a favorable or unfavorable impression of the person, and necessarily include any personality traits we ascribe. **Impression formation**, in turn, has long been an area of study in social psychology, within the more general areas of **person perception** and **social perception**. Research on how we perceive others and form impressions of them has focused on the kinds of information we receive and the order in which we receive the information.

- **Kinds of information** include physical features, nonverbal behavior, and verbal behavior. Generally, we give the most credence to what we can see. A favorable first impression, for example, is more likely when the person is attractive, self-composed, and articulate—even before we know much else. Note that stereotypes, as discussed in Key 77, are often involved in forming impressions. There are many, often subtle stereotypes based on physical features and behavior that can creep into our thinking, examples being notions that attractive people are more sensitive and kind, that muscular people are less intelligent, that macho women and effeminate men are likely to be homosexual, and on and on, especially where race, ethnicity, gender, and age are concerned.

- **Order of information** refers to what we see and hear first. First impressions can indeed be lasting ones, which is referred to as the **primacy effect**. Classic research by Solomon **Asch**, for example, found that participants' overall impressions of a supposed person were strongly influenced by what they heard first, based on a list of adjectives such as intelligent, warm, and cautious. Also noteworthy was that the participants could and would form impressions on the basis of such limited and sketchy information, in turn being able to write lengthy descriptions of the hypothetical person.

Attributions are the inferences we make about *why* people do things, which we do all the time, and which is directly related to the impressions we form. Attributions, in other words, involve assessing people's behavior and inferring reasons and causes for it, including, in some situations, our own behavior. Attributions are classified as being stable or unstable, in interaction with internal or external.

- **Stable versus unstable** refers to whether potential causes of behavior are relatively enduring or instead variable and changeable.
- **Internal versus external** refers to whether the attributed causes are "within" the person or "outside" of the person.
- **In interaction**, the two dimensions produce a table of potential causes for someone's behavior, as follows. Internal-stable attributions include personality traits, intellectual capabilities, and enduring motives. Internal-unstable includes mood, effort, and such as that. External-stable includes relatively enduring environmental factors that help or hinder, such as the difficulty level of the things we attempt to do. External-unstable includes environmental factors that vary, such as luck and opportunity.

Selected phenomena in how we make attributions include the fundamental attribution error, the discounting principle, the social desirability effect, the actor-observer effect, and gender biases. **Correspondent-inference theory**, an early approach to understanding attribution, incorporates most of these phenomena.

- **The fundamental attribution error** is to pay too little attention to other possible causes and attribute a person's behavior to internal-stable ones, consistent with earlier notes that people prefer to believe in stable personality traits. For example, if you think this book is a good one (hopefully), and knowing nothing about the author, your first reaction might be to attribute the book's quality mainly to the author knowing a lot about psychology.
- **The discounting principle** is that your attributional tendencies change when other possible causes get your attention. If you're told that the author of this book had to work really hard at writing it, you might make more of an internal-unstable attribution. Or if you find out that the author had access to many excellent reference works, you might make an external-stable attribution. And if you find out about the author's good fortune in having excellent editors and reviewers, you might go with external-unstable.
- **The social desirability effect** has to do with whether a behavior is generally viewed as socially negative or positive: Information that is negative tends to be believed and weighted more heavily. If the author tells you that this book was written entirely out of greed and self-interest, you might find that easier to believe than if the author swears it was because of a genuine desire to inform and educate. The latter, in other words, could be the result of a greedy author trying to cover up and appear more socially desirable.
- **The actor-observer effect** is that we tend to attribute others' behavior more to internal causes and our own behavior more to external ones, especially in situations involving disappointment

and failure. If *you* write a book like this one and it's lousy, the author might be inclined to attribute that to your lack of knowledge about the subject matter. If *this* book is lousy and the author is forced to admit it, the author might instead attribute it to difficulties in the subject matter that couldn't be overcome.

- **Gender biases** in attributions are less likely nowadays than they were a few years back, as is gender stereotyping in general. Classic research, however, found consistent differences in the attributions both men and women make with regard to success. Consistent with that, if this book turns out to be a success and you're told the author is male, your attributions might involve stable things like knowledge and understanding. But if you're told the author is female, you might instead attribute it to unstable things such as trying hard or being given lots of help.

Another classic theory of attribution is the **covariation** or "cube" model proposed by Harold **Kelley**. Given three interacting dimensions called consistency, consensus, and distinctiveness, each of which can vary from low to high, various predictions are possible as to the kinds of attributions that will be made—particularly with regard to internal versus external ones.

- **Consistency** refers to how much a person's behavior varies across comparable situations. High consistency means that the person behaves much the same way, say, always being reliable and satisfying obligations. Low consistency means that behavior varies considerably from one situation to the next.

- **Consensus** refers to what other people do. High consensus, for example, would be when most people behave reliably in a given type of situation. Low consensus applies when the person's behavior stands out from the rest.

- **Distinctiveness** refers to how comparable the situations are with regard to the behavior they elicit from people. High distinctiveness applies when one situation stands out from the rest, and low distinctiveness applies when situations are highly comparable.

- **Predictions** are that high consistency, low consensus, and low distinctiveness lead to internal attributions. In contrast, high consistency, high consensus, and high distinctiveness lead to external attributions. Think about it.

Key 79 Persuasion and attitude change

OVERVIEW *Changes in beliefs and attitudes can be accomplished directly through persuasive appeals, but also indirectly by changing behavior.*

Persuasive appeals are attempts to produce attitude change and therefore behavior change down the line. The term applies to situations such as persuading people to like your ideas and vote for you, to like a consumer product and buy it, and so on. **Fear appeals** are a special case when frightening, perhaps terrible consequences are used in an attempt to persuade people to drive safely, to quit bad habits, and the like. In addition to Hovland's considerations, fear appeals must avoid overwhelming the audience and must provide the audience with a workable means to accomplish the behavior change in question.

A general model of persuasion and attitude change was developed by Carl **Hovland** and colleagues in the 1940s. The model specifies four categories of considerations in persuasive appeals that determine their effectiveness: characteristics of the communicator, the message, the channel, and the audience.

- **Communicator characteristics** include attractiveness, status, reputation, and anything else that makes the person delivering the message seem more *credible*—whether the characteristics are relevant or not. Television commercials, for example, often use stars and other famous people to pitch their products, whether or not the stars have any relevant expertise or knowledge regarding the product.
- **Message characteristics** include obvious things such as whether the message is logical and understandable, plus subtler things like repetition and whether to present only one side of an argument or both sides. Repetition, within limits, helps get the message across: Again consider television commercials, which tend to repeat a product name and image several times, and which also tend to be aired repeatedly. As for arguments, political speakers sometimes present their opponents' views as well to refute them, depending upon the audience, as discussed below.
- **Channel characteristics** have to do with the medium through which the message is conveyed. Attractive and personable communicators fare better face-to-face and on television; less attractive ones fare better on radio and in written media. The complexity of the message is also a consideration: More complex messages

and arguments fare better in written media that allow the audience more time to contemplate and reflect.

- **Audience characteristics** involve whether or not the recipients of the message are relatively intelligent or informed about the topic. Two-sided arguments and complex arguments are more effective with a more intelligent audience that's informed about opposing views. One-sided arguments are better with a less intelligent audience, especially if the propositions are also relatively simple.

Another classic is the **cognitive-dissonance theory** of Leon **Festinger** from the 1950s. Given that we generally strive to reconcile differences and especially conflicts between our attitudes, and similarly between our attitudes and our behavior, cognitive-dissonance theory notes that attitudes can be changed by changing behavior first. This is essentially the reverse of Hovland's approach, for example, which is based on the idea that attitude change comes first. The **classic experiment** to demonstrate cognitive dissonance went like this: A participant is first required to perform a boring and monotonous task. Then the participant is asked to help the experimenter persuade another participant (actually a confederate) that the task is instead interesting and fun—basically, the participant is asked to lie. Some participants, then, are paid a very small amount for lying, others are paid a good bit more. And in the end, the participants who were paid a very small amount rate the boring task much more favorably, indicating attitude change.

- **Confederates** are often used in social psychological experiments. Confederates pretend to be participants, to influence the actual participants' behavior or simply to make the experiment possible in the first place.

- **Cognitive-dissonance is demonstrated** in that the participants who were paid a lot for lying had plenty of justification for it and had no reason to change their attitudes. Participants who weren't paid much had little justification, so they instead persuaded themselves that they weren't really lying at all, that the boring task actually was interesting and fun. Note the similarity here to rationalization (Key 58).

- **Note** that other explanations are also possible. Daryl **Bem's self-perception theory**, for example, argues that such participants' "self-attributions" account for any attitude change: Those who are paid a large amount attribute their behavior to external causes and go no further, whereas those who are paid very little must account for their behavior internally and change their attitudes.

Key 80 Conformity, compliance, and obedience

OVERVIEW *Conforming means changing your attitudes and behaviors to match those of others; complying means behaving in accord with the wishes of others; obeying means doing what others tell you to do, whether you like it or not.*

Conformity has long been a topic for theory and research in social psychology, and concerns why and under what circumstances we seek to be consistent with significant others. Classic experiments by **Asch** are representative: Put a participant in a room with a group of the experimenter's confederates, and have the confederates make erroneous judgments to see if the actual participant will do the same—which the participant often will. Factors in conformity that are indicated by such research, and that presumably apply to larger issues in conforming to social norms and fashions in everyday life, include the extent to which the reference group agrees, how big the group is, and how similar the group is to you.

- **Judgments** can be as simple as whether the lengths of lines projected on a wall are the same or different, as in Asch's original research.
- **Group agreement** makes it more likely you'll conform. If "everyone" is wearing a certain style of clothing, for example, do you really want to be the only one who dresses differently?
- **Group size** interacts with group agreement: The bigger the group of people who are all doing the same thing, the more likely you are to conform.
- **Similarity to you** simply notes that "everyone" is a relative term. It could mean people on a national level or people in one region, all the way down to the people you hang out with, meaning people you care about and identify with. On the other hand, if you perceive a reference group as distinctly different from you, say, in terms of interests or perhaps gender or ethnicity, you're much less likely to conform.

Compliance involves directly influencing behavior with little or no concern for underlying beliefs and attitudes. Complying, in other words, simply means going along with what someone else wants, likely examples being when someone wants to sell you something or wants you to donate to a charity. Best known are the foot-in-the-door technique, the door-in-the-face technique, the that's-not-all technique, and low-balling.

- The **foot-in-the-door technique** means asking for a little at first, thus getting you started, and later asking for considerably more. In the context of charitable donations, you might be asked to sign a token pledge and later be asked for substantially more money or time, once you're "committed."
- The **door-in-the-face technique** instead involves someone asking you for a lot at first and then accepting less, sort of as a compromise. Thus, you might be asked to make a very large donation to a charity, and when you refuse, the person settles for less and you find yourself donating. Such a technique (and others) is based on the **norm of reciprocity**, which is that when someone gives us something, we feel obligated to give in return. Here, when the person offers to settle for less, you want to concede something in return, perhaps without even realizing what you're doing.
- The **that's-not-all technique** applies better to occasions when someone's trying to sell you something. Before you even have time to refuse the initial price of a new car you're interested in, for example, the salesperson offers to throw in accessories and other stuff "for free." You reciprocate by accepting the initial price, which of course initially included the price of the goodies and more.
- **Low-balling** instead means offering a lot at first and then backing off. Here, at the outset, the salesperson offers to include lots of extras with your new car. But once you agree on a price, the salesperson gradually cuts back on grounds that the goodies aren't available right now, the boss wouldn't approve the deal, and so on.

Obedience differs from compliance mainly in degree: Rather than simply going along, you do what you're told, regardless of what you think and how you feel about it. Now-classic research of Stanley **Milgram** and colleagues, mostly in the 1960s, went like this: A participant is seated before a display panel that has switches corresponding to levels of electric shock. Designated as the "teacher," and with an officious experimenter supervising, the participant reads words into a microphone to a supposed "learner" participant in another room. Each time the learner makes a mistake in recalling the words, the teacher is to deliver progressively higher levels of shock to the learner, who is of course a confederate, and no electric shocks are actually given. But the learner acts out a script that includes mild complaints about the shocks at first, then cries of pain, and eventually no response at all. And the question is how far the teacher will go.

- **Milgram's findings** were that about two-thirds of the participants went all the way to the highest levels of shock marked "XXX," in spite of the learner having mentioned in advance having a heart condition. They had to be urged and even commanded by the experimenter to continue, and they disliked it to the point of stalling and becoming extremely anxious and upset, but they did it. The participants obeyed, and many of them remained upset and concerned about their behavior even after they were debriefed and told the true nature of the experiment.
- **Important variables in obedience** based on subsequent research of the same kind are many. Often cited are (1) allowing the participant to see the learner through a window; (2) having the learner in the same room; and (3) having a second experimenter present who disagrees about continuing. In each case, not nearly as many participants go to the highest levels of shock.
- **Also note** that such research is often cited in discussions of **ethics** in psychological research (Key 12). It can be argued that it violates the principle of voluntary participation and also risks lasting psychological harm. At the same time, of course, it can also be argued that such research is justified in shedding light on how otherwise normal people can obey superiors and commit atrocities such as those commanded by the Nazis toward the Jews and others in the 1930s and 1940s—which was Milgram's purpose in the first place. Ethical issues, in other words, can be hard to resolve.

Key 81 Aggression and observational learning

OVERVIEW *Aggression may or may not have origins in our biological make-up, but it is strongly influenced by social learning either way. Observational learning, in turn, influences aggression as well as many other human behaviors.*

Aggression is defined generally as behavior intended to injure or harm another, in which the intent is the main consideration. Harming someone entirely by accident is not aggression, though it can at times appear to be. True aggression can take many forms, ranging from verbal insults or threats to serious physical harm. Also note that a distinction is sometimes made between "instrumental" aggression and "hostile" aggression, with respect to the *kinds* of intentions involved, though both can be involved in a given instance. And finally, note that aggression is a distinctly *social* behavior, which is why social psychologists have been interested in studying it.
  • **Instrumental aggression** involves wanting something someone else has and inflicting harm in the process of getting it. Anything from a child threatening or pushing another child down to get a toy, to a mugger using a weapon on someone while committing a robbery, and up to a nation invading another nation to gain territory is an example. More acceptable "aggressive" behaviors such as being intensely competitive, doing whatever it takes to make sales and wrap up deals, and so on, would also fit here to the extent that harm is inflicted along the way.
  • **Hostile aggression** means inflicting harm *for its own sake*. Threatening or striking someone you don't like are examples. Rape is usually classified here also, in that rape often includes hostility toward women in addition to whatever sexual motives might be involved. Child abuse and spouse abuse often qualify here as well, whether verbal or physical.

Where aggression ultimately comes from is still a matter of debate. Freud, for example, believed that aggression is biologically determined (Key 57), yielding impulses that are always in need of control and that must be "vented" from time to time. His basic reasoning was that aggression has been with us throughout the ages, in forms ranging from individual conflicts up to war, and it therefore must be a part of being human. Similar arguments have been proposed by the ethologists and others, at least with regard to a biological basis for aggression, perhaps related to our being "territorial" animals. Aggression is both a means of gaining territory and defending it.

- **Venting** aggression, from the psychoanalytic point of view, is necessary because aggression exerts constant pressure to be expressed. Releasing that pressure is possible through socially acceptable outlets such as contact sports. Or aggression can be vented through **catharsis** (Key 73), meaning "getting it out of your system" suddenly and explosively, though again, in socially acceptable ways and against socially acceptable objects.
- The evidence for **territoriality** in humans is not conclusive either. The argument is similar to Freud's on aggression: Humans have always had territory, so territoriality must be built in. The problem, both with territoriality and aggression, is that *some* cultures and peoples throughout history and beyond didn't display much of either.

The social learning view is that aggression is primarily learned, or at least thoroughly modifiable by learning, beginning in early childhood. That is, regardless of where aggression ultimately comes from, the perspective is that the extent to which aggression is expressed depends entirely on the environment and learning experiences all along the way. And there is considerable research support for such a view, some of which is discussed below. Note in general that children have ample opportunities to learn aggressive behaviors in school settings, in and around the neighborhood, and at home from aggressive family members, plus from watching characters in television programs and movies. Observational learning is a likely means, though other forms of learning and conditioning can be involved as well. Also note that "prosocial" behavior can be learned the same way.

- **Observational learning** experiments involve having a participant attend to the behavior of a model. The participant is then given the opportunity to imitate the behavior, which children will readily do, especially if they like and respect the model, if they identify with the model, if they see the model get favorable consequences for the behavior, and so on. In the real world, parents and teachers and peers serve as models, along with television and movie characters, from which the child learns a lot about how to behave in general. Here, in particular, the child learns a lot from models about how to deal with conflicts and how to go about getting things he or she wants.
- **Televised violence**, which necessarily includes aggression, tends to be less explicit nowadays than in years past. But it's still there. And the Saturday cartoons children watch are still among the most

violent programs, at least verbally and implicitly. There is extensive research indicating that children become more aggressive by watching violence on television and in movies, enough, as it happens, that the point is rarely even argued any more. What is sometimes argued about instead is that most such programs also involve having the "bad guy" get it in the end, which is intended to discourage violence. Also, in the United States in particular, it is argued that there's a constitutional right to freedom of speech and expression, which is not an easy issue to resolve.

- **Prosocial behavior** is largely the opposite of aggressive behavior, at least with regard to getting what you want and resolving conflicts. Behaviors such as sharing and taking turns, cooperating, helping others, and generally being concerned for the rights and feelings of others are prosocial, as in popular children's educational programs that have been around for years. A lot of research indicates that such programs are effective in promoting prosocial behavior and reducing aggressive behavior.

Classic research by Albert **Bandura** illustrates various points noted above with regard to children learning aggression and expressing it. In one version of the research, young children first observed an adult model playing with a "Bobo" doll. The model punched and hit and kicked and otherwise mistreated the doll, which of course kept smiling and bouncing back up for more. At the end of the sequence, however, the children saw different outcomes: One experimental group saw the model praised and otherwise reinforced for doing such a thorough job of beating up Bobo, a second group saw the model punished for the same, and a third group saw the model receive no consequences. Later, all the children were individually given the chance to play with Bobo themselves.

- **Initial findings** were that the children who saw the model reinforced were much more aggressive than the children in the other two groups. Plus, they imitated many of the model's specific behaviors regarding how to go about beating up Bobo. On each count, consider the implications for encouraging a child to vent aggressive impulses, as discussed earlier.
- **Additional findings** were even more interesting. Later still, all the children were offered *incentives* for beating up Bobo in the ways they had seen the model do it, and the group differences disappeared. That is, even the children who saw the model punished imitated the model at a high and accurate rate. And the clear implication is that seeing the "bad guy" get it in the end still teaches aggression, which can then readily be expressed in other circumstances.

Key 82 Group dynamics and group behavior

OVERVIEW *When people get together in groups, their behavior often changes—sometimes for the better, sometimes otherwise.*

Groups form on the basis of factors such as proximity, similarity, and common interests, plus to accomplish specific tasks, as in what committees try to do. Groups can range in size from a few people to a nation, or even larger; social psychologists tend to be more concerned with the smaller groups, leaving the larger ones to sociologists and others. Selected topics that pertain to the kinds of groups social psychologists study are social facilitation, bystander intervention, and diffusion of responsibility. Related topics are also discussed.

- **Group formation** is an area of study within itself. **Proximity** is one basis upon which groups form: People who live close to each other or work together may develop group allegiance simply because they interact with each other a lot. **Similarity** refers to people forming groups on the basis of things like ethnicity, race, and gender, plus philosophical, religious, and political beliefs. **Common interests** obviously overlap with similarity, but focus more on the kinds of things people *do*, such as anything from recreational activities to helping others in the sense of social action. And, of course, **ad hoc groups** form temporarily to get specific things done.

Social facilitation focuses on an individual functioning in a group context, including simply having an audience. Many researchers have found that behaviors can be facilitated by the presence of others, meaning that the person can jump higher, run or ride or drive faster, play a musical instrument better, and on and on. A popular theory proposed by Robert **Zajonc** in the 1960s states that such facilitation is a result of increased arousal that occurs when others are watching, where arousal refers to tension, excitement, and the like. Similarly, the individual becomes more motivated cognitively to perform well, make the best impression on others, and in general, succeed. If arousal and motivation become too high, however, the effect is instead "social impairment." Both social facilitation and social impairment are highly consistent with the optimum level of arousal curve and the Yerkes-Dodson law (Key 33), in that increased arousal improves performance only up to a point, and it depends as well on the kind of task.

- **Social impairment** means that an individual doesn't perform as well around others as when alone, which is more likely when the behavior or task is relatively unfamiliar or complex. If you're highly accomplished at playing an instrument, for example, you should play your best before an audience. But if you're still "just learning," you'll probably play better with no audience. Otherwise, note the similarity of social impairment to social phobia (Key 66).

Bystander intervention developed into an area of study in social psychology after several widely publicized events in the 1960s in which passers-by and observers didn't help a person in distress. Initiated by the work of Bibb **Latanè** and John **Darley**, central questions involve what it is about the situation and the person in distress that determines whether a bystander will help. As it turns out, relevant variables include individual differences in bystanders, perceived characteristics of the person in distress, perceived costs of helping the person, and especially the extent to which other bystanders are present. Such variables interact to determine whether a bystander will intervene.

- **Individual bystanders** may or may not be oriented toward helping people in general—people can vary considerably in how altruistic they are. And some people might help in one situation but not another: A person who is phobic for blood, for example, is less likely to help an injured person who is bleeding profusely. Also note that generally feeling "anonymous," as some people do as a result of living in large cities, doesn't help. People who feel like they "belong" are more likely to help a person, especially if the person also belongs.
- **Characteristics of the person** relate mainly to whether the bystander perceives the person as needing and deserving help. As an example of the latter, a bystander would be less likely to help a person perceived as being unconscious from passing out drunk than a person perceived as being unconscious from having a concussion or a heart attack.
- **Perceived costs** involve what it takes to help a person in distress. Though we often hear about cases to the contrary, bystanders are less likely to help if there's a serious risk to life or limb: It takes a hero—and a physically competent one—to intervene directly in a mugging or to run into a burning building to save someone. Costs, however, also apply to what the bystander might have to live with emotionally and socially after *not* intervening. In other words, bystander intervention is often a trade-off between the costs of helping and those of not helping.

- **The number of other bystanders** is important. Research has generally found that the more people who are present, the less likely it is that a given bystander will help the person in distress. One explanation is "diffusion of responsibility," discussed next.

Diffusion of responsibility is a very general phenomenon that happens in group situations from small to large, and the larger the group, the more likely it is to occur. If you're the only person involved in a situation, it's your responsibility and yours alone. The more other people there are, the less responsibility accrues to you. In addition to the specific case of bystander intervention, diffusion of responsibility applies to what happens in group decision making and other task-oriented situations, such as those involving committees, juries, and the like, plus situations involving mob violence. Related phenomena are "social loafing," "deindividuation," "groupthink," and "group polarization," which are distinguished mainly by the situations and behaviors to which they apply.

- **Social loafing** is similar to what happens when a bystander doesn't intervene: The individual feels less responsibility and correspondingly does less. In the context of decision making, the larger the group, the less likely it is that a given individual will participate—a notable exception, of course, being the individual we think of as a "leader" and who flourishes in group situations. But in college classes, for example, the larger the class, the less likely it is that individuals will be motivated to ask questions and otherwise participate. Similarly, the larger the constituency, the less likely it is that each individual will perceive a need to vote.

- **Deindividuation** is usually discussed in the context of mob violence, riots, and the like—situations involving relatively larger groups and often accompanied by noise, crowding, and hysteria. Here, in part through diffusion of responsibility, the individual gets completely lost in the crowd and typically becomes highly aroused and even frenzied. And also having temporarily lost a sense of personal identity and personal restraint, the otherwise normal individual engages in acts ranging from vandalism to theft to murder. Afterward, the individual goes back to normal, though often not without feelings of guilt and fears of someday being identified.

- **Groupthink** applies more to task-oriented groups, and focuses on the way individual attitudes can yield to a group position. In essence, given pressures to conform, individual members seek unanimity and consensus and the group takes on a life of its own. The beliefs and attitudes of individual members may or may not change, but the individuals consistently behave in accord with those of the group. Such a process is more likely when a group is highly cohesive, when it has opponent groups and outside pressures, and when it is endowed with power. An often-cited example is what happened in the Nixon presidential administration leading up to Watergate.

- **Group polarization** overlaps with groupthink, but focuses more on the decisions groups make and the behavior groups opt for, which tend to be more extreme than what its individual members would want to take responsibility for. The basic rationale is that when a group makes a decision, the group takes responsibility, and individuals tend to be off the hook for consequences. Thus, a group can be more extreme and also more willing to take risks than most or even any of the individuals who make up the group. A jury, for example, can readily sentence a defendant to death, even when no individual on the jury would be willing to make such a pronouncement alone. Or a committee, in business and legislative contexts, can decide to allocate much more money than any of its members would be willing to if they had to take personal responsibility for it.

GLOSSARY

association A mental link between stimulus events, thoughts, memories, and so on.

attachment The emotional bond between children and their caregivers, either direction.

attitude A relatively enduring idea about people and things that also has an emotional component (compare **belief**).

autonomic nervous system The part of the peripheral nervous system that relays information to and from internal organs.

behavior Anything the organism does, whether overt or covert.

behavioral neuroscience The study of relationships between behavior and processes in the brain.

belief A relatively enduring idea about people and things (compare **attitude**).

catharsis In psychoanalytic theory, a venting of emotions thought to relieve underlying pressures.

central nervous system (CNS) The spinal cord and all of the structures of the brain.

cerebral cortex The grayish, convoluted, outer layer of the brain involved in all higher mental functions.

chromosome A long, threadlike cluster of genes; in normal human cells (except gametes) there are 46 chromosomes that exist in 23 pairs.

classical conditioning Learning based on associations between stimuli.

cognition Any aspect of thinking.

cognitive neuroscience The study of relationships between behavior and processes in the brain, with an emphasis on what constitutes "mind."

conception The point at which ovum and sperm unite, marking the beginning of an individual's life.

confounding A situation in which two or more causes are likely and can't be separated.

congenital Present at birth, whether because of genetics, the prenatal environment, or both.

contingency In operant conditioning, the relationship between a behavior and its consequences.

conscious mind Current thinking and awareness.

correlation A statistical procedure in which two or more variables are compared to see how they correspond.

covert Internal and not objectively observable or measurable, involving for example what organisms think and feel (compare **overt**).

critical period A developmental range during which a behavior must be acquired or it won't be acquired at all (compare **sensitive period**).

cross-sectional research A procedure in which the researcher studies two groups of participants at the same time, such as participants of different ages or developmental periods.

crystallized general intelligence (*gc*) Refers to the knowledge that we accumulate, such as ways of solving problems as well as the many facts and ways of understanding things that normally accumulate throughout the life span.

debriefing A procedure in which participants are told afterward what an experiment was all about and are given the opportunity to ask questions and express concerns.

delusion A belief that has little or no basis in reality.

deoxyribonucleic acid (DNA) Chemical molecules in genes.

dissociation In the context of hypnosis, a state in which awareness is separated from reality or in which thoughts and feelings are separated from each other; in the context of mental disorders, a condition in which aspects of personality and memory are separated from each other.

drive A psychological state arising from a need.

eclectic Oriented toward taking what's accurate and what works in diverse points of view.

electroencephalograph (EEG) Electronic equipment used to monitor global brain activity via electrodes attached to the skull.

emotion A state of physiological arousal accompanied by the cognitive interpretation of it.

empirical Potentially observable by anyone.

endorphin A neurotransmitter that functions as a painkiller.

environment Usually applied to the determination of traits and characteristics by experience, meaning anything that happens to an organism from conception on.

event-related potentials (ERPs) Tiny fluctuations in brain electrical activity (see **quantitative electroencephalography**).

experiment Any procedure in which the researcher systematically arranges conditions and exposes subjects to them to assess what happens.

external validity Refers to the extent to which the results can be extended beyond the particulars of a study to the real world.

factor analysis A correlational procedure to compare variables and determine the extent to which they interrelate and overlap.

fluid general intelligence (*gf*) The kind of general intelligence that primarily involves thinking, learning, and solving problems, with emphasis on acquiring new or novel ways of thinking.

functional magnetic resonance imaging (fMRI) A technique that assesses and localizes minute magnetic changes during brain activity.

gamete A reproductive cell (sperm or ovum) that contains 23 chromosomes in humans.

gene A unit of structure in the nucleus of a cell that's involved in physical or psychological development and functioning.

genotype The biochemical make-up of an organism's genes.

***gf-gc* theory of intelligence** The theory that there are two forms of intelligence: **fluid general intelligence** (*gf*) and **crystallized general intelligence** (*gc*).

habit A highly repetitive behavior.

hallucination A percept that has little or no basis in reality.

hedonism The pursuit of pleasure and the avoidance of pain.

heredity Genetic determination of traits and characteristics (compare **heritability**).

heritability The extent to which a trait is determined by genetics and passed along from parents to children; often assessed by correlation (compare **heredity**).

homeostasis Any of a variety of processes that occur to keep the organism within functional and viable limits.

hormone A biochemical that affects the operation of cells and organs, or acts like a neurotransmitter.

hypothalamus An area in the central core of the brain that's primarily involved with homeostatic functions.

hypothesis Anything from a hunch to a calculated guess about what will happen, what causes what, and so on.

inferiority complex Adler's term for people who see themselves as inferior to others across the board.

information processing An approach to understanding thinking and memory in terms of sequential operations.

informed consent An ethical consideration in research, meaning that participants know what they're going to be exposed to and participate voluntarily.

instinct A built-in, relatively complex behavior that occurs in specific situations and involves learning (compare **reflex**).

intelligence quotient (IQ) Originally, a number based on the ratio of test performance (mental age) to chronological age; nowadays, a number based on how a person's test performance compares with that of others in the same age range.

internal validity Refers to how well the study was conducted, and in an experiment, the extent to which conclusive statements about cause-and-effect relationships can be made.

introspection Looking inside yourself and describing what you're thinking or feeling.

lesion A cut or severation, whether small or large.

longitudinal research A procedure in which the researcher studies one group of participants and how they change as they develop.

long-term memory (LTM) Permanent memory that accumulates for life.

magnetic resonance imaging (MRI) A technique involving radio waves that provides structural information about the body and brain.

motive A cognitive state arising from needs, drives, or other sources, in which the organism seeks satisfaction.

need A physiological state of depletion that gives rise to drives or motives.

nerve A bundle of sensory-motor neurons.

neuron The basic unit of the nervous system, meaning a specialized cell that receives, relays, or processes information.

neurotic An older term for mental and behavioral conditions that interfere with a person's life but that generally don't make the person dysfunctional (compare **psychotic**).

neurotransmitter A biochemical that operates at the synapses between neurons.

norm In the context of development, an age at which a behavior tends to occur; in the context of psychological testing, the basis for interpreting an individual's performance; in the context of abnormal or social psychology, a behavior that is deemed acceptable and appropriate by society.

observational learning Learning based on observing what others do and what consequences they experience.

operant conditioning Learning based directly on consequences.

overt Objectively observable or measurable, whether external to the organism or internal (compare **covert**).

parasympathetic nervous system The part of the autonomic nervous system that returns the organism to normal following stress, emergency, and situations involving homeostasis.

participant In psychological research, the preferred term for humans (compare **subject**).

percept A specific instance of perceiving something.

peripheral nervous system The sensory and motor tracts that relay information to and from the central nervous system.

phenomenology Essentially, the idea that each individual is different and must be understood from his or her own unique point of view.

phenotype A physical or psychological characteristic an individual displays, as a result of the interaction of genetics and environment.

population Theoretically all of a designated type of subject (compare **sample**).

positron emission tomography (PET) A technique involving blood sugars tagged with radioactive isotopes, which provides ongoing images of brain activity.

preconscious mind Long-term memory that can be accessed when we want to or need to.

psychoactive Affecting cognitive and emotional functioning; usually applied to drugs that interact in various ways with neurotransmitters.

psychoanalytic Of or pertaining to Freud's classic theory and similar versions that followed it.

psychodynamic Of or pertaining to theories that grew out of Freud's theory but differ substantially from it.

psychomotor Involving movement and the cognitive activity that directs it.

psychotic A term still used for mental and behavioral conditions that make a person thoroughly dysfunctional and potentially dangerous to self or others (compare **neurotic**).

punishment Learning in which a behavior is suppressed or becomes less likely because of unfavorable consequences (compare **reinforcement**).

quantitative electroencephalography (QEEG) A computerized approach that uses a skull cap fitted with electrodes to assess brain electrical activity (see **event-related potentials**).

quasi-experiment A procedure that looks like an experiment, except that the researcher takes conditions as they naturally occur and has little or no control over what happens.

rapid eye movement (REM) Movements of the eye muscles that tend to occur during dreaming.

reflex A built-in, relatively simple behavior that is only minimally under voluntary control (compare **instinct**).

reinforcement Learning in which a behavior is strengthened or becomes more likely because of favorable consequences (compare **punishment**).

reliability In the context of psychological testing, the extent to which a test yields similar results on different occasions.

replication A very general procedure in which hypotheses and theories are tested with different subjects and settings to see if the theories hold up.

response Any specific behavior the organism is capable of performing.

sample A group of subjects selected for research (compare **population**).

schema A cognitive structure (meaning mental structure) that provides the basis for perception and knowledge.

sensitive period A developmental range during which a behavior can be acquired the most efficiently, noting that the behavior can be acquired at other times as well (compare **critical period**).

short-term memory (STM) Temporary memory, with a span of 15 to 20 seconds barring rehearsal.

significant other Anyone important to you who potentially affects who you are and what you do.

somatic nervous system The part of the peripheral nervous system that relays information to and from the external world.

standardization In the context of psychological testing, applies both to the procedures used to administer the test and to the procedures used to establish a basis for interpreting what test scores mean.

stereotype An erroneous belief or attitude involving traits and characteristics thought to apply to all members of some designated group.

stimulus Any sensory event the organism is capable of detecting, whether simple or complex.

subconscious mind Cognitive functioning we normally aren't aware of, but which can be accessed when we want to or need to (compare **unconscious mind**).

subject Any living organism—except humans—that is the focus of study and research (compare **participant**).

sympathetic nervous system The part of the autonomic nervous system that initially reacts to stress, emergency, and situations involving homeostasis.

synapse A junction between neurons, in the form of a gap across which neurotransmitters pass.

temperament Global personality characteristics more or less present at birth.

theory An organized set of predictions and relationships in understanding behavior.

trait An enduring aspect of an individual's physical or psychological make-up.

unconscious mind Cognitive functioning to which we normally have no access and aren't aware of (compare **subconscious mind**).

validity In the context of psychological testing, the extent to which a test measures what it's supposed to measure.

variable Anything measurable that can differ along a dimension, such as from low to high.

INDEX

Projection, 158
Prosocial behavior, 217
Proximity, 50
Psilocybin, 103
Psychedelic drugs, 103–104
Psychiatric treatments, 189–191
Psychoactive substances, 38
Psychoanalysis, 6, 192–194
Psychoanalytic theory, 154–157
Psychodynamic theories, 6, 160–162
Psychodynamic therapies, 192–194
Psycholinguistics, 133
Psychology, 2, 4–5. *See also specific psychology*
Psychosexual stages, 155–156
Psychosocial theory, 74–76, 161
Psychotherapy, 185, 195–196, 200
Psychotropic medications, 189–190
Punishment, 112–113

Quantitative electroencephalography, 39–40
Quasi-experiments, 17

Random sampling, 22
Rational-emotive behavior therapy, 201–202
Rationalization, 158
Reaction formation, 158
Reasoning, 129
Reflexes, 33, 67
Reliability, 141
REM sleep, 94–95
Replication, 23
Repression, 158
Research
    animal, 24
    ethical considerations, 24–26
    experimental, 12–13
    field, 21–22
    on groups, 2
    laboratory, 21–22
Response, 7
Retina, 48
Retrograde amnesia, 127
Rods, 48–49
Rogers, Carl, 8, 163–164, 195
Rousseau, Jean Jacques, 5, 63

Sampling, 22
Schachter-Singer theory, 87
Schemas, 206
Schizophrenia, 173, 176, 182–183

Secondary motives, 79
Selective attention, 91–92
Self-actualization, 164
Self-control, 202
Self-perception theory, 211
Self-regulation, 202
Semantic encoding, 125
Semantics, 132, 135
Semicircular canals, 57
Sensation, 44, 56–57
Sensory adaptation, 46
Sensory deprivation, 85
Sensory memory, 124
Sensory receptor neurons, 31
Sensory thresholds, 45–46
Sensory-neural loss, 54
Sexual disorders, 176
Sexual motives, 83–84
Short-term memory, 124–125
Signal detection theory, 46
Skinner, B. F., 7, 109–110
Sleep, 93–96
Sleep disorders, 96, 176
Smell sense, 56
Social desirability effect, 208
Social facilitation, 218–219
Social impairment, 219
Social loafing, 220
Social phobia, 177
Social psychology, 203
Somatic nervous system, 31
Somatoform disorders, 176
Somatosensory cortex, 37
Sound waves, 53
Spearman, Charles, 139
Spinal cord, 33
S-R behaviorists, 7
Stages, of life span, 59–61
Standard deviation, 141
Standardization, 142
Stanford-Binet, 143–144
Statistical analysis, 15
Stereotype, 206
Stereotyping, 206
Sternberg, Robert, 139
Stimulants, 101–102
Stimulation motives, 85
Stimulus, 7
Stress, 88–89
Structuralism, 5
Subjects, 2, 22
Sublimation, 159
Substance-related disorders, 176